Sons
of the
Wind

Sons of the Wind

The Search for Identity in
Spanish American Indian Literature

Braulio Muñoz

RUTGERS UNIVERSITY PRESS
New Brunswick, New Jersey

The author gratefully acknowledges permission to reprint material from the following works:

Andrés Bello: Obras Completas Volumen I, Poesía. Copyright © 1952 by the Comisión Editora de las Obras Completas de Andrés Bello, Ministerio de Educación, Caracas. Reprinted with permission of the Comisión Editora de las Obras Completas de Andrés Bello.

Aztec Thought and Culture: A Study of the Ancient Nahuatl Mind by Miguel León-Portilla, translated by Jack Emory Davis. Copyright © 1963 by the University of Oklahoma Press. Reprinted with permission of the University of Oklahoma Press.

The Broken Spears: The Aztec Account of the Conquest of Mexico edited by Miguel León-Portilla. Copyright © 1962 by The Beacon Press. Originally published in Spanish under the title *Visión de Los Vencidos*; copyright © 1959 by Universidad Nacional Autonoma de Mexico. Reprinted with permission of Beacon Press.

César Vallejo: The Complete Posthumous Poetry, translated by Clayton Eshleman and José Rubia Barcia. Copyright © 1978 by the University of California Press, Los Angeles. Reprinted with permission of Clayton Eshleman.

Major Trends in Mexican Philosophy by Mario de la Cueva, edited and translated by A. Robert Caponigri. Copyright © 1966 by the University of Notre Dame Press. Reprinted with permission of the University of Notre Dame Press.

Todas las sangres by José María Arguedas. Copyright © 1964 by Editorial Losada, Buenos Aires. Reprinted with permission of Editorial Losada.

Library of Congress Cataloging in Publication Data

Muñoz, Braulio, 1946–
  Sons of the wind.

  Bibliography: p.
  Includes index.
  1. Spanish American fiction—20th century—History and Criticism. 2. Indians in literature. 3. Indians—Cultural assimilation. 4. Indians, Treatment of—Latin America. I. Title.
PQ7082.N7M8   863'.009'98   81–15403
ISBN 0–8135–0973–4   AACR2
ISBN 0–8135–0972–6 (pbk.)

To my mother
María Dominga Terrones Warniz

The people heard in the night the voice of a weeping woman, who sobbed and sighed and drowned herself in her tears. This woman cried: "O my sons, we are lost . . . !" "O my sons, where can I hide you . . . ?"

The sixth omen announcing
the coming of the white man to America
—*Visión de los Vencidos*

Contents

Contents

Preface

During the last half century, Spanish America has experienced dramatic changes ranging from radical communist revolution in Cuba to radical counterrevolution in Chile. Yet these and similar social upheavals can only be considered minor events when compared to what must be the single most important sociocultural development in Spanish America since its inception, namely, the almost total sublation of cultural pluralism. After centuries of experimentation and expectation, Spanish Americans can now truly claim to have one all-embracing culture. The regionalisms still extant in dress, diet, or language are almost negligible in view of the overwhelming cultural homogeneity in the region. The cultural unity of Spanish America, sought through different and often contradictory means, has finally come to rest on the shoulders of the mestizo, the New Man of Spanish America.

This work explores the issues surrounding the long search for, and the reality of, cultural unity in Spanish America. It is an effort to take inventory of what has been won and what has been lost in the process of realizing the hegemony of the mestizo and his culture. Since the first days of conquest, and with increasing intensity, Spanish Americans have searched for a cultural identity. This search for identity has been accompanied by the dream of sociocultural unity for Spanish America; and both the search for identity and the Dream of unity have been highly detrimental to those who have stood in their way. Within this general framework, my work is particularly concerned with the fate of the Indian caught up in the long process of Spanish America's cultural definition.

The task is clearly ambitious, but it is tempered by the knowledge that this work cannot exhaust all the issues it treats. My goal is not to settle old issues but to open new ones for further reflection and research. Still, there are points that have to be brought to the reader's attention to avoid possible misinterpretations of either the intentions or scope of this work. I shall discuss these points briefly here.

First, this work interprets key issues related to Spanish American cultural development from the point of view of those who have suffered and lost the most in the process, namely, the Indian people. In this sense, my work may be considered polemical. However, as will be abundantly clear in the text itself, precisely because it takes the Indian's point of view seriously, the polemics here do not follow traditional lines; that is, *Sons of the Wind* is neither a Marxist attack on liberalism nor a liberal attack on Marxism. In fact, there are occasions when the theories of both Marxists and liberals are questioned in view of their eagerness to destroy Indian culture.

Second, a work of this nature risks being found wanting by specialists in various disciplines, and there is little that can be done to remedy this situation given the work's intention and scope. However, some clarification of this work's relation to disciplines that it most directly draws on— literary criticism, the social sciences in general, and the sociology of literature in particular—may be useful.

As I see it, two main objections might be raised by literary critics. Objections could be made to using literature as a social indicator to shed light on nonliterary issues. To this criticism I can only reply that taking literature as a social indicator is standard practice among sociologists. A more pertinent objection might be how the texts themselves are treated, that is, that I have not done justice to their literary aspect. This objection is acknowledged as correct insofar as it is not my intention to conduct comprehensive analyses of all or even some of the texts used. This is not a treatise in literary criticism nor, for that matter, in the sociology of literature; it is a work that may properly be viewed as part of the sociology of culture. Literary texts are used here to

illuminate broader issues, and in this context a partial eluci-
dation of them cannot be avoided.

The main objections from the social sciences might pertain
to the uses of secondary materials. Specialists might object
that there is nothing new here. Again, the objection is acknowledged as correct insofar as this is not a work in history,
anthropology, economics, or even applied sociology; there is
no claim to break ground in the sense of uncovering new
material in any of these disciplines. I have used data already
at hand from the social sciences to shed light on issues that
transcend the limits of any single discipline. What is new in
this work is not the materials used but the interpretations
given to them.

Also, sociologists will not find here exhaustive discussions
of the internal (form and content) and external (types of
audiences, forms of production, distribution networks, consumption patterns) aspects of literature. Internal and external factors are discussed primarily when they help clarify
central issues in the texts, which in turn help in understanding issues in the sociology of culture and the thesis being
developed here. Discussions of the rise of different types of
novels in Spanish America, for example, have not been circumscribed by factors leading to an understanding of literary
texts, but they include broader considerations that help to
place both the Indian and the author in their sociocultural
context.

Two final points: First, I use the term culture to refer to
ideals, values, collective images, expressions of world views
through art and philosophy, and the like. I distinguish this
definition from the much broader concept of culture used by
anthropologists, for example, which may also include dialects, diet, tools, kinship-based social organization, and so
on. Second, my study is limited to Spanish-speaking countries in Latin America; Brazil's sociocultural development is
not included for analysis since that would mean introducing
the black's presence as a crucial factor. Although the black

influence has been important in its own right in Spanish America, it has not been nearly as strong as the Indian's, which constitutes the basis of this study. Therefore, to do justice to Brazilian sociocultural development would necessitate a different orientation altogether.

Chapter 1 is a general introduction to the parameters for which, and context within which, the main thesis of the work is developed. Among other things, it specifically establishes the essential characteristics of the Spanish American Dream for unity and the nature of the Spanish American quest for cultural identity. Chapter 1 further shows that literature by and about Indians, particularly novels, can be used as social indicators of the fate of Indians in the process of cultural definition while, at the same time, shedding light on the pervasiveness of the search for identity and the Dream of unity among Spanish Americans in general. Chapter 2 develops the historical background against which a group of *indigenista* novels can best be understood. It includes examples of pre-Columbian literature and a discussion of two preindigenista novels of the nineteenth century.

Chapter 3 is devoted to the sociocultural factors underlying the rise of the indigenista novel in the Andes. Because of social, cultural, and ethnic similarities, the region is treated as a whole; further, since sociocultural developments in Peru during this period are symptomatic of those in the entire area, my discussion centers on the Peruvian experience. Within these limits, two major factors are explored: first, the position of the Indian in the labor force, an indication of the Indian's general position in the Andes; second, sociocultural developments in the indigenista writer's milieu, which shed light on the setting in which his message was fashioned. Chapter 4 discusses in detail the message of Andean indigenista novels.

Chapter 5 analyzes the only two indigenista novels written in Guatemala. Although both novels are by the same author, the analysis of them and the sociocultural factors that made them possible are central to my study. First, these novels present an important aspect of the indigenista novel in general, since it is possible to compare and contrast them with novels written elsewhere in Spanish America, thereby illuminating how novel and society are specifically related in the Spanish American literary tradition. Second, the Guatemalan literary production constitutes an important bridge between indigenistà and later magicorealist novels in Spanish America, for it is the Guatemalan writer Miguel Ángel Asturias who must be counted as the foremost writer of Indian magicorealist novels.

Chapter 6 is devoted to the sociocultural factors underlying the rise of the indigenista novel in Mexico, and the role of the Mexican Revolution is discussed in this connection. Chapter 7 explores the message of the Mexican indigenista novel, revealing that it has much in common with its Guatemalan and Andean counterparts but that there are also striking differences. Reasons for these differences and similarities are found in the sociocultural factors underlying the indigenista novels in each case.

Chapter 8 discusses the decline of the indigenista novel in Spanish America and the role of Indian magicorealist novels in the Spanish American literary tradition. Three magicorealist novels are examined in this context. Finally, Chapter 9 is devoted to the New Spanish American Novel. Having shown how the Indian was incorporated into the mestizo's culture, I note some of the literary and cultural developments that came on the heels of such an occasion. Following the thrust of this work, I discuss the structure and message of the New Novel against the sociocultural background that made it possible.

I would like to thank Magali Sarfatti-Larson for suggesting this topic for my doctoral dissertation and for her subsequent encouragement and helpful comments. I owe special thanks to Fred Block, who read the entire manuscript on more than one occasion and offered his insights. I am grateful to E. Digby Baltzell and Steven I. Piker for their continued moral support. To my late friend and teacher, José María Arguedas, with whom I spent many memorable hours in Chimbote, Peru, I am deeply indebted for having introduced me to the spirit of the Indian of the Andes. I would also like to thank Carlos Fuentes; although we may differ in our general conclusions, I am grateful to him for helping me to think through the New Spanish American Novel and understand its noble battle against cultural colonialism. I thank Swarthmore College for three consecutive Summer Faculty Research Grants that made possible the completion of this project. To my wife, Nancy, I am indebted for typing the different drafts of the manuscript, making crucial observations, helping with translations, and preparing the index. Without her assistance this work would not have been possible. Finally, thank you, Kevin and Michèle, for giving me a much needed sense of perspective.

Chapter One

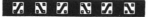

The Novel
and
the Dream

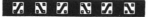

I charge and direct Martín Cortés, my son and successor, and all his heirs to my estate, to make every effort to learn what is appropriate to satisfy my conscience and theirs. . . .
—Hernán Cortés

It is a great idea to attempt to form of all the New World a single nation . . .
—Simón Bolívar

Let us engrave as the motto of our literature this synthesis of our propaganda and our faith: For the intellectual and moral unity of Spanish America.
—José Enrique Rodó

The Dream

By all indications, the Dream of sociocultural unity for what is today Spanish America did not exist before the arrival of the Spaniards. The people who inhabited that land were separated by vast territories and by ethnic, cultural, economic, and political differences that made the notion of a single nation impossible. Even within such highly centralized societies as the Inca and Aztec, different ethnic groups with different languages and political, economic, and religious institutions existed. Certainly, by calling all inhabitants of the land he found Indians, Christopher Columbus was twice mistaken: His hosts were neither Hindu subjects nor were they one people.

With the arrival of Columbus, Spanish America—the forced marriage between Europe and the newly found lands —came into existence. The concept of the New World, however, had been created before it had been fully discovered; it sprang as one entity from the European imagination. Long before Cortés met Malinche and Pizarro met Atahualpa, Europeans had envisioned a hitherto uncharted part of the world where utopia awaited discovery.[1] When the Spaniards finally reached the New World, they claimed it in its entirety. Not long after Columbus had landed, his king signed a decree promising insoluble unity to all lands his subjects would discover in the New World.[2] The unity thus promised became a proclamation for Spanish America as well and lasted about 300 years. Even though Spain's colony in America was governed through viceroyalties and captaincies general due to the vastness of its territory, Spanish America was viewed as one entity throughout its colonial period. The entire region was under Spanish monarchic rule and governed by common laws.

As the Spanish conquistador gave way to the hidalgo[3] of colonial Spanish America, a newly created elite claimed all

2

of Spanish America for Spanish culture. This claim, a powerful integrating force in Spanish America, was not decisively challenged until the latter part of the eighteenth century. The hegemonic claim, however, was never more than that; it hid the existence of alternative cultures throughout the colonial period, particularly Indian, but also that of black slaves, mulattos, and mestizos. Hegemony of Spanish culture during this period did not result from the consent of the ruled but from the realities of colonization; hegemony translated the power of colonial masters, both Spaniards and *criollos* (whites born in America), into the cultural realm. The cultural unity of Spanish America during this period was sustained by fiat; it rested on a borrowed culture. In art, for example, form overshadowed content, and art and letters produced in the colonies rang hollow. In their preoccupation with belonging, Spanish American writers and artists aped their Spanish counterparts, while original artistic creation in this period was left to *castas* (nonwhites) and was, therefore, denigrated or ignored. But for all this, during the colonial period, the idea was established that a single Spanish America was not only possible but highly desirable.

During the nineteenth-century wars of liberation, the unity of Spanish America, sustained up to then by colonial rule and cultural dependency, was rejected, and Spanish America began to search for new forms of social relations to maintain its unity. It is a great idea, wrote Bolívar, the clearest exponent of a Spanish American nation, "to attempt to form of all the New World a single nation, with a single tie that could pull the parts into a whole, given that [the Spanish American people] have the same origin, language, customs, and religion. . . ."[4] But his idea was never realized due, in large measure, to two interrelated factors: the fractionalization of the internal colonial structure, which reached its breaking point at the dawn of the nineteenth century, and the failure of the criollo caudillos to carry out drastic socioeconomic changes at all levels throughout Spanish America.[5]

The practical problems of ruling a vast colony, especially during the seventeenth and eighteenth centuries, made it imperative for Spain to create smaller administrative units to regulate commerce and colonization. Around these administrative units there soon developed small but powerful and aggressive commercial and agrarian groups. On the eve of the wars of liberation, these groups constituted decisive political and economic blocks. Some of these groups looked kindly at efforts toward liberation from Spain. Yet many, fearing that their power bases would be undermined by the changes the liberating forces proclaimed, opposed them vigorously. Eventually, however, as these groups lost confidence in the ability of the Spanish crown to protect their interests, they also moved to proclaim their independence and worked toward conserving and consolidating their power within limited boundaries.

Thus, colonial institutions became the blueprints for the boundaries of the nineteenth-century republics. The caudillos of the liberating forces were either unwilling or unable to override local forces in the interest of the Nation by thoroughly restructuring their society. Having left local interests to control sections of Spanish America, especially the ports, the caudillos defeated their Dream of unity; for these reasons, the idea of a Spanish American nation was stillborn. In 1826, the last attempt in the nineteenth century to realize a Spanish American nation miscarried. At the Congress of Panama of that year, delegates from several parts of Spanish America who had gathered to discuss the future of the Nation failed to provide a framework for unity; later attempts to revive the congress were also ill-fated.

The balkanization of Spanish America was concomitant with replacing the caudillos of the wars of independence with lesser figures who served local economic interests. With political independence secured, the old caudillos and their ideas of unity were no longer welcomed by the newly emerging national elites, and in their rush to seize a piece of the crumbling Nation, these elites hastened the old leaders' departure from the political scene. Simón Bolívar (1783–1830), José de San Martín (1778–1850), José Gervasio Artigas (1764–1850), and Bernardino Rivadavia (1780–1845) were either ostracized or died in exile; Antonio José de Súcre (1795–1830) and José Bernardo de Monteagudo (1789–1825) were assassinated. The idea of a Spanish American nation was definitely truncated. In South America, wrote Bolívar, bitterly against the Spanish American elites, "There is neither trust nor faith either among men or among the various states. Every treaty is here but a scrap of paper, and what are here called constitutions are but a collection of such scraps."[6] Bolívar died convinced that he had plowed the sea.

Although the moment for realizing the Spanish American nation was missed, the Dream of unity lives on. It is not surprising that after Bolívar's failure, political action gave way to literary action, as the Dream of unity retreated to the cultural realm. Ever since, throughout the history of Spanish America, the need and the desire for unity have been emphatically sustained by the cultural elite, who constituted itself as keeper of the Dream.

The often romantic position held by the leaders of the wars for liberation did not withstand repeated rebuttal by reality. Shortly after independence had been obtained, the most prominent leaders, including Simón Bolívar and José de San Martín, fearful that the Nation would fall into anarchy turned to monarchic forms of government for salvation.[7] Such a desperate gesture was, of course, to no avail; the Nation did not survive. But as the generation of Bolívar was overtaken by events, new cultural leaders appeared in Spanish America who continued to argue and call for unity. This new generation, too, was afraid of anarchy, but its proposed solutions were different. It no longer based its views on romantic French ideas but on Anglo-Saxon positivism. The fear of anarchy that prompted Bolívar to advocate monarchic forms of government led the followers of Darwin and Spencer to advocate unity and progress.[8] "Let us be the United States," exhorted Domingo F. Sarmiento (1811–1888) from Argentina. His harangue echoed throughout Spanish America, and many followed him in his desire to build a United States of Spanish America.

Positivism in Spanish America developed in opposition to the romantic naïveté of the liberators and the colonial legacy, particularly its religious aspects.[9] Positivism considered the colonial period to be the Middle Ages of Spanish America; that is, a period when obscurantism, intolerable fanaticism (exemplified by the Inquisition), and oppressive paternalism prevailed with the blessings of kings and popes. Against this legacy, the positivists opposed their faith in reason, science, and progress. To many positivists, the future seemed bright and bountiful in view of the material and human resources that a united Spanish America, free from the blinders of religion, possessed. But as positivists were rushing to rescue a Spanish America they believed to be prostrated before a tyrannic Catholic tradition, a "counter-reformation" was in the offing.

The antipositivist movement was led by the Uruguayan writer José Enrique Rodó (1871–1917) and his "Arielista" followers, who, at the end of the nineteenth century, unearthed the specter of Spanish humanism.[10] The movement had particularly deep roots in Mexico, where its battle against the positivist supporters of the Díaz dictatorship typified the clash between the two movements. José Vasconcelos, Alfonso Reyes, and Antonio Caso, deeply influenced by Rodó's proclamations, became influential figures in the Mexican Revolution. As for the caudillos of the nineteenth century, the sight of revolutionary soldiers in march fostered among the new leaders the hope for the birth of a New Man, the mestizo, in Spanish America. The Peruvian Alejandro Deustua and the Argentine Alejandro Korn, together with many others across Spanish America, joined in the crusade. In place of Sarmiento's harangue to be the United States of America, Rodó and his followers bid Spanish America to return to the Catholic values bequeathed by Spain during 300 years of domination.

The heated controversies that resulted from the clash between positivists and antipositivists did not destroy the Dream of unity, for at the core of the counterreformation, too, there lay the Dream of a united Spanish America. The tone for the counterreformation movement was set by Rodó in 1896, years before he published his famous *Ariel*. In a letter to his friend Manuel Ugarte, he wrote: "Let us engrave as the motto of our literature this synthesis of our propaganda and our faith: For the intellectual and moral unity in Spanish America."[11]

And in the twentieth century, the Dream of unity is still cherished by the cultural elite in Spanish America. Furthermore, not all have followed Rodó's tacit acceptance of the political and economic disunity implied in his letter to Ugarte; rather, the Dream of unity has been reaffirmed on two fronts. The Dream of total unity (that is, political, economic, and cultural) has been advanced by such liberal figures as Víctor Raúl Haya de la Torre and his followers since the 1920s and by such socialist leaders as Fidel Castro and Ché Guevara since the 1950s. The Dream of cultural unity, on the other hand, has been affirmed by writers and humanists throughout Spanish America, not that they accept economic and political disunity; rather, they believe that cultural unity is closer to being realized and that eventually this cultural unity will impose itself as the basis for total unity. One of the most prominent humanists in Spanish America, Octavio Paz, argues, for example, that the divisions that now exist in Spanish America are the result of "calamities and circumstances alien to the profound reality [*realidad profunda*] of our people."[12] The balkanization of Spanish America is seen by Paz as something superficial, an unfortunate accident that came about due to the acts of caudillo and imperialist interests. Were those forces to disappear, he argues, "there would be other frontiers."[13]

Contrary to the views of some commentators,[14] socialists in theory and action must be counted among the most ardent supporters of Spanish American unity. Their support is revealed most clearly in their international political thought and view of Spanish America as an entity to be eventually liberated in toto. The United States' accusation that Cuba contemplated "exporting revolution" had its basis in reality: After all, Ché Guevara was born in Argentina, fought in Cuba, and died in Bolivia, and he, more than any other, represents the socialist in Spanish America. What irritates some liberal commentators is that the unity contemplated by socialists is based on socialist politicoeconomic thought. In their theory and action, socialists attempt to furnish Spanish America with the political program that they believe more truthfully represents its wishes and hopes.

As must already be clear, my work focuses on the cultural elite's development as keeper of the Dream. Recurring efforts toward economic integration, such as the common markets, are not discussed here, since the cultural dimension suffices to show the pervasiveness of the Dream of unity in Spanish America.

The Search for Identity

The 300 years of so-called cultural hegemony in Spain's American colonies had important consequences for the development of Spanish American culture. The creole "hidalgos" always knew that they could lay claim to only a copy of, and, therefore, to something inferior to Spanish culture, and herein lay the beginning of the long history of the Spanish American elite's inferiority complex vis-à-vis Europeans. This class of "hidalgos" measured itself against its Spanish counterpart as a surrogate elite for Western culture. Contrary to the European, writes Leopoldo Zea, "The American has never felt universal. His preoccupation has been, precisely, a preoccupation to incorporate himself into the universal."[15] And the universal means here Western culture.[16] Today, as Spanish America reaches toward "plenitude of conscience" it does so "crippled by *resentimiento*."[17]

The preoccupation that Zea points out has often led to total acceptance or total rejection of Spanish culture; in either case, there has usually been a tendency to apologize for Spanish American culture. In other words, the search for identity during most of Spanish American history has meant searching for a way to fit into Western culture—to be European. During the colonial period, for example, the eagerness to be a part of Spanish culture was such that the "hidalgos" tended to denigrate all things not Spanish; of course, by doing so they denigrated themselves. This feeling of inauthenticity has deeply scarred the Spanish American mind.[18]

As noted, cultural borrowing by Spanish American elites had significant economic and political consequences: The cultural dependency of Spanish America maintained the unity of the colony and ensured compliance with the colonial power's economic and political demands. Cultural dependency was by no means the only factor supporting asymmetric relations between America and Spain, but it certainly was a powerful one.[19]

The realization that cultural dependency was central to colonial rule led creole liberators in the nineteenth century to attack Spain on two fronts: militarily, economically, and politically on the one hand; culturally, on the other. Bolívar attempted to shake Spanish America loose from its cultural dependency, arguing that Spanish America was mestizo; in doing this, Bolívar shattered centuries of traditions and penetrated the secrets of his class. His attempt to free the Spanish American cultural elite from its inferiority complex by bringing to the level of consciousness what was unnamed and untold, however, was not successful. The inferiority complex was briefly unveiled, contemplated, then left to sink once more beneath the surface of Spanish American culture.[20]

Bolívar's failure was inevitable insofar as he and his class in general tried to attain cultural emancipation by copying other Europeans, particularly the French. Given that French intellectuals furnished much of the ideology of the caudillos who rose against Spain, cultural independence from Spain did not mean cultural independence for Spanish America. During this period, the idea of a Spanish American nation was based on French conceptions of politics and government and was embellished with French romantic fervor. This was clearly evident in the coupling of literary romanticism and political action by the caudillos in revolt, for example, appealing to the Inca past as a justification for cultural independence.[21] In short, identity during this period, too, was sought within the Western European tradition.

Because of its decisive influence during the formative period of republican Spanish America, it is not surprising that French cultural developments influence Spanish America to this day. But by the middle of the nineteenth century, the strong French influence had become only one among several others influencing Spanish America. From the 1860s, Anglo-Saxon culture became increasingly influential; today, the United States and Eastern European influences vie for supremacy. Thus, the cultural dependency that began in the early days of colonial life has continued to the present with more or less intensity.

The Mestizo as Basis of Unity

In one of his earlier masterpieces (*Cortés and Malintzin*, 1926), the great Mexican muralist José Clemente Orozco made the clearest statement of the search for identity and the Dream of unity in Spanish America. Cortés is depicted as a powerful new Adam, firmly holding the right hand of Malintzin, the new Eve. Malintzin, who represents the Indian people, casts down her eyes in a sign of submission. Such a gesture earns her Cortés's protection, which Orozco symbolizes by portraying him shielding his lover with his left arm, the arm of the heart, the compassionate arm. This new Adam and Eve, the leader and the led, the protector and the protected, are shown rising above the fallen bodies of the Indian people—a testimony of the birth pangs of a new culture. The offspring of Adam and Eve, the mestizo, is present in the work as the promise of this union, a hope for the birth of a New Man—a man Orozco thought he recognized in the midst of the Mexican Revolution.

This mural shows the Spanish American thrown into the future by the clash of two worlds. He has definite historical origins but an uncertain future. This uncertainty is further accentuated by the sense of guilt resulting from the destruction of Utopia by conquest.[22] And the mestizo, the New Man, bears the guilt in his very being, for he is the product of rape, partaking of both his father's violence (Cortés—Spain) and his mother's suffering (Malintzin—America). The historic record reveals the mestizo's oscillation between rejecting his father and anger toward his mother, a vacillation that often translates into a denial of his Indian heritage. Yet, this vacillation itself indicates a quest for inner peace. Neither white nor Indian, forlorn in a cultural limbo, the mestizo feels himself in possession of a "haunted soul."[23]

Under these circumstances, the mestizo's quest for identity and inner peace entails coming to terms with the original violence, freeing himself of the trauma of birth. To find peace, the mestizo must acknowledge, and thus appropriate, his origins; he must assert himself as a New Man by asserting his *mestizaje*.[24] Only in this way can his future be free of ghosts. According to the cultural elite, the quest for identity is shared by Spanish Americans from Patagonia to beyond the Rio Grande; all Spanish Americans are mestizo, brothers in suffering since the conquest. The lessons taught by Bolívar, Martí, Rojas, and countless other cultural leaders are clear in Orozco's vision. Furthermore, by the time Orozco painted his masterpiece, the signs of Spanish America's cultural unity were believed to be there for all to see in the songs, the faith, the language, but most of all in the faces and the blood of Spanish Americans.

The Mexican Revolution overlapped both the First World War and the Soviet Revolution in 1917. By the time the

armed phase of the Mexican Revolution ended in 1917,
Europe lay in ruins and Western intellectuals searched for
non–Western world views to repair their battered faith in
human progress. For some, the Soviet Revolution offered
hope. Spanish Americans, having seen unparalleled numbers
of Indians and mestizos in the Mexican revolutionary armies,
turned their eyes to their Indian roots. The four decades
that followed witnessed a growing appreciation of ancient
and contemporary Indian cultures in Spanish America; painters, musicians, philosophers, and writers all hailed the
coming of the mestizo New Man in Spanish America. And in
the concept of the New Man, the search for identity merged
with the Dream of Spanish American unity.

The mergence of the search for identity with the Dream
of unity was effected by Bolívar himself in his revolutionary
movement. But Bolívar's francophile tendencies, the absence
of a large and organized mestizo class, and the long tradition
of cultural dependency, rendered his notion of mestizaje
largely rhetorical. Later in the century, José Martí (1853–
1895) pushed the ideas of a mestizo America further; but
he, too, his manifest love for *nuestra América* notwithstanding, never fully developed a social program and philosophy
explicitly based on mestizaje. It was only in the twentieth
century, after the armed phase of the Mexican Revolution,
that men like Víctor Raúl Haya de la Torre, José Carlos
Mariátegui, and José Vasconcelos had the social conditions
necessary for politicophilosophic and programmatic exaltation of mestizo culture. From that moment on, the search
for identity in Spanish America meant the search for the
identity of the mestizo. Also, from that moment on, the
mestizo was seen as the basis of unity in Spanish America.

From the viewpoint of cultural leaders in the twentieth
century, the mestizaje is the only viable culture in Spanish
America. But how was the mestizo conceived by the cultural
elite of the time? Who was this latecomer to the American
scene?

The Cosmic Race

The conquest of the New World by the Spaniards, according to the keepers of the Dream, initiated a fateful mixture of the races whose end product became the mestizo. During the nineteenth century, but particularly during the first half of the twentieth, the mestizo was considered to be coming to terms with his past and claiming a future. Certainly, it was argued, the process of mestizaje was "far from completed,"[25] but it was well under way; indeed, in this sense, the future of Spanish America mirrored the future of humanity. In this vast land, a new cosmic, integral, definitive race was emerging from the mixture of "the blood of all people."[26] This race was the race of all races, the "human race."[27] The idea of a New Man in Spanish America owes much of its optimism to this conception of mestizaje.

At least up to the middle of this century, however, there was strong evidence against this basic aspect of the Dream: Indians, blacks, and orientals refused to be melted away. As a consequence, many kept the Dream by denying reality; the denial was often accomplished through racist arguments. This was José Ingenieros's position, for example, which argued that in Argentina, "emancipated a century ago by the ideas and deeds of one or ten thousand Euro-Argentines," there would live a race composed of 15 to 100 million white people who, in their leisure hours, would read the chronicles of the extinct indigenous races, the stories of the gaucho crossbreeding that retarded the formation of the white race.[28] Trying to uphold the Dream, Ingenieros turned his back on history. The gauchos, under the leadership of Güemes, and blacks had been a significant force in liberating Argentina.[29]

More significantly, I find a theme in Ingenieros's position that is at the core of the Dream of unity in Spanish America: the biologic absorption of the dark races by the white. (In the case of Argentina, Ingenieros's hopes have been realized to an extent due to a heavy European immigration and the original and war-produced sparcity of Indians in much of the territory.) Even those who regarded the total amalgamation of the races as the basis of unity were unable to resist their cultural tendency to see the white race as ultimately superior. Maybe, conceded José Vasconcelos, himself a mulatto, white traits will predominate in the cosmic race after all. But this predominance will come about, he argued, as a result of free taste and not because of violence or economic pressures. This is crucial: In Vasconcelos's view, even if economic injustice or violence of any sort were to be eliminated, the cultural tendency in Spanish America would be to become not mestizo but white. This view of mestizaje, related, no doubt, to the long-standing inferiority complex vis-à-vis Europeans, is deeply embedded in the minds of the Spanish American elites.[30] In literature, the cultural elite's realm par excellence, the "impertinent Indian," the "black intruder," and the "inscrutable oriental" had to be dealt with; the Dream had to be upheld. This goal forms the very essence of the indigenista novel itself, which set out to save and redeem the Indian.

The Spanish Language

It should not be surprising to find that from the very beginning the Spanish language has been seen as one of the most irrefutable indicators of the possibility, if not the reality, of the cultural unity of Spanish America.[31] It was a matter of course to postulate language as a basis of unity, closely connected to ways of viewing the world, thinking, and feeling. But here, too, there was counterevidence: During most of the colonial period, the white Spanish-speaking people in Spanish America were a minority. The vast numbers spoke languages other than Spanish, mainly Indian languages. In some areas, in fact, the Spanish-speaking population did not constitute a clear majority until at least the first decades of this century; such was the case in the Andes and Guatemala and large portions of Mexico, for example.

At all costs, in order to claim cultural unity, this evidence had to be neutralized, its existence denied. During the nineteenth century, for example, there was little or no discussion of Indian languages in Spanish America as living languages. In the twentieth century, when intellectuals finally talked about Indian cultures—as a direct result of the Indian's role in the Mexican Revolution—they often considered these Indian languages, as did Alfonso Reyes, to be "anthropological relics."[32] But even in the early 1940s, when Reyes made this statement, more than half the population in the Andes and Guatemala and millions in Mexico (Reyes's own country) spoke a language other than Spanish. The issue here is not whether these Indian languages are disappearing but that the *pensadores* were all too eager to see them neutralized.[33] In their eagerness to uphold the Dream, these intellectuals ended up denying reality.

This does not imply that all members of the cultural elite saw the common language of Spanish America as something positive. Juan Bautista Alberdi, for example, viewed it as something that tied Spanish America to its colonial past, to the Middle Ages of Spanish America. He believed such legacies should be, if not eliminated, at least sublated or complemented with a good dose of English, the language of "liberty, industry, and order."[34] Others argued for the formation of a new language appropriate to the realities of the New Man, a prospect that alarmed many an intellectual.[35] These debates and possibilities came on the heels of the revolutions for independence. As the nineteenth century progressed and the revolutionary elites became settled in the comfort of their influential circles, these possibilities were soon forgotten. The time had come for those who argued for the universality of the Spanish language in Spanish America while accounting for contrary evidence. Such well-known

writers as Augustín Yañez, Lezama Lima, José María Arguedas, and Miguel Ángel Asturias, for example, took the
position that Indian and black languages, having interpene-
trated a Spanish base, gave the Spanish language, as spoken
in the Americas, additional flexibility.[36] It is important to note
that these writers never seriously attempted to write in the
Indian languages;[37] instead, they have tried to incorporate the
Indian Weltanschauung, as expressed in their language, into
the Spanish American experience.

Ultimately, as in the case of biological mestizaje, the tendency of the Spanish American cultural elite has been to
incorporate the language of the dark people into that of the
white. It is absolutely impossible, wrote the Mexican phi-
losopher Antonio Caso, "to form a country [patria] possess-
ing that splendid unity perceptible in France or Italy if the
Spanish language does not realize its definitive supremacy
over the indigenous languages."[38] Clearly, no new language
was thought possible in Spanish America, for were these
intellectuals to have worked toward creating a new language
for the New Man of Spanish America, they would have had
to minimize, if not sever, ties with their basic European
literary and cultural tradition. And who among them was
willing to go that far?

The claim of the universality of the Spanish language
in Spanish America laid the ground for a further claim,
namely, that the literary tradition of Spanish America forms
an indivisible unity. Not one important writer in this century
has challenged this basic postulate; even those who have
endeavored to produce a national literature have not seriously disclaimed the relevance and relation of their work
to the entire region. Because in Spanish America literature
is produced by members of the same elite that keeps the
Dream of unity alive, this latter claim is closer to the truth.
Spanish American literature does constitute a corpus; the
most cursory acquaintance with it will confirm this. Besides,
all those who create it affirm it as such.

The Catholic Religion

Most intellectuals in Spanish America would agree that the Catholic religion made possible to a large extent the unity of Spanish America, at least during the conquest and colonial periods; they would disagree, however, as to how this was accomplished. Some elite members argue that from the beginning Spanish conquistadores believed themselves to have been entrusted by Providence to carry out the evangelization of the New World and that consequently they saw the task of conquest and colonization as an affirmation of faith. The conquerors' deeds, they hold, were carried out under the aegis of a Catholic monarchy that gave the enterprise a sense of cosmic purpose.

Others point out, however, that Sepulveda's unearthing of Aristotelian racist arguments to classify Indians as natural slaves and, therefore, subject to being bought, sold, and even killed indiscriminately did not stem from a high sense of charity.[39] Pizarro did not affirm the Catholic faith by massacring the Indian for gold. Nor was the random rape of Indian and black women during the colonial period an affirmation of faith; for centuries biological mestizaje in America has been the result not so much of holy matrimonies but of rape.[40] For these critics, religion during the colonial period and after has served the powers that be by justifying their claims over the heavily exploited population. Be that as it may, no serious thinker would deny the fact that religion has been a cementing force throughout the centuries in Spanish America.

The religious dimension of the Dream sheds additional light on the cultural elite's conception of the mestizo New Man and his culture. In the religious dimension, too, the superiority of the Spanish heritage is clearly upheld; in other words, there never was room for a new religion (religious mestizaje) in Spanish America. It matters very little that Peruvians claim the first mulatto saint or that Mexicans worship a dark virgin; for at the bottom of all this, the Christian God is white and central to the affirmation of Western culture. Syncretism is only tolerated, never truly accepted.

In short, it is quite clear that in Spanish America mestizaje, the basis for the Dream of unity and cultural identity, entails whitening the dark races and Europeanizing the native culture. Only under these conditions is mestizaje desirable for the keepers of the Dream.[41] Wherever European colonialism has taken place, there has been little attempt by the colonizer in Spanish America to adopt the culture of the colonized. Rather it is expected that the exploited would adopt the ways of the exploiter; in reality, this has not always been possible. Large Indian, black, and Asian cultural niches can still be found in Spanish America; but then, it might be argued, the Dream is not yet fully realized.

The Dream and Utopia

One of the most fundamental aspects of the Dream of unity and the search for identity has been the utopian quest, which has nearly always accompanied statements on identity and unity and given them their futuristic aura. In fact, to an extent, the Spanish American Dream of unity can be interpreted as an extension of the utopian vision brought to America by the Spaniards.

As noted, from the very beginning, the New World was regarded as a possible utopia, whose discovery promised a resting place after the long search for Shangri-la. But the discovery of utopia entailed at the same time its destruction, so that feverish searches for El Dorado or the Fountain of Youth were futile attempts to reach and hold onto a utopia that was already largely destroyed. They merely testify to the fact that utopia slipped through the conquerors' fingers while searching for treasure. For, and this must be clear, the destruction of America did not come as a surprise to the Spaniards; rather, it came as an often regrettable but nonetheless calculated enterprise. This is one of the major reasons why there never was a truly epic account of the conquest of America. The gods to whom the conquerors prayed had abandoned them in view of their colossal yet reprehensible undertaking. The epic is possible only when the soul feels secure in its journey, not when the hero's conscience squirms as he prays.[42] The chronicle, a mixture of confession and epic, became the only true literary form for the literature of conquest.

The utopian element belied by the destruction of America was not completely absent after the conquest; there always remained a question of what might have been had the encounter between the two cultures been more auspicious. Even more, amid the havoc caused by genocide in America, utopian thought survived by retreating to ever smaller social islands. The attempt by the Bishop of Michoacan, Vasco de Quiroga, to implement Moore's utopia in Mexico and the Jesuit experiment in Paraguay testify to the permanence of utopian thought. When Bolívar and his generation rose against Spain they found the utopian element in Spanish American culture to be an ally of their cause.

The search for identity and utopia were intertwined in Bolívar's Dream of unity. When Spanish America, finally free from tutelage and centuries of oppression, constituted a mestizo Nation, then, and only then, would social prosperity, justice, and harmony among brothers be possible. For men like Bolívar, all the evils of the present were due to injuries suffered in the past. Only a new Nation and a New Man could renew and make old dreams of Arcadia come true. Following Bolívar, every great Spanish American thinker from Martí to Ché Guevara has paired the Dream of a united mestizo America with a utopian element.

The Dream of a united mestizo Spanish America, however, has developed dialectically as a mixture of good and evil, and insofar as it has been paired with utopia, it has been a positive category. In fact, it can be argued that in this sense the Dream of a united mestizo Spanish America has been the most revolutionary sociocultural category Spanish America has ever had. By pointing to the future, the Dream allowed Spanish Americans to distance themselves from the present and define its oppressive nature; thus, through the utopian Dream, an oppressed humanity projected its hopes for a better life. In this sense, abandoning the Dream of unity could very well mean abandoning the hope for a better future and resorting to utter pessimism for Spanish America; it could mean accepting the given state of affairs. This is one of the reasons why contemporary intellectuals find the partial (that is, cultural) unity, which is becoming increasingly evident, dangerous; it may cloud the need for a total social transformation.

But with all this, it must not be forgotten that the utopian Dream was imported to Spanish America. Those who suffered the most from attempting to realize it were never consulted either about its viability or desirability. There are good reasons why the Indian may want nothing to do with a utopia that from the very beginning was based on his exclusion; utopia, in fact, means banishing the Indian as an Indian. First, utopia belonged to the white conqueror, later to the mestizo under whom the Indian was to be subsumed. In the latter case, the Indian was to participate in the utopian Dream vicariously through the mestizo; but vicarious participation is never enough. The joys of the mestizo can never be those of the Indian.

Thus, like the two faces of Ometeotl, the utopian Dream has always been dual: It has held out a promise while delivering destruction. Because the New World was destroyed to make room for the white man's dreams, the utopian Dream has been a thorn in the mestizo's flesh. How the Spanish American elite attempted to reconcile destruction with creation is evident in the literature discussed in this work.

The Spanish American Writer's Calling

Having acknowledged the centrality of the Dream of unity and the search for identity in the Spanish American cultural world, to what extent is it reflected in Spanish American literature, particularly in the novel, which is my main social indicator? However, I cannot use literature as a fruitful social indicator before analyzing the position of those who produced it within their given sociocultural context. In this section, I discuss the role of the writer in Spanish America, since it is he who translates the dreams of his culture into particular works of literature.

A note of clarification is needed here: Since most of the literature considered in this work was produced either before the middle of this century or by writers influenced by sociocultural developments that took place during this period, my discussion pertains specifically to the role of the writer as conceived by Spanish Americans until roughly the 1950s. The changing role of the Spanish American writer in the last 25 to 30 years is discussed together with issues pertaining to the nature and extent of the cultural unity of present day Spanish America in the last chapter of this work.

The Nonprofessional Writer: An Ideal Type

A discussion of the Spanish American concept of the social role of the writer and his production up to the middle of this century must begin by elucidating an apparent contradiction: In this period, the area produced very few of what modern readers would consider "great" works; yet, writing was one of the most valued activities in which Spanish American cultural elites were engaged. How can such a phenomenon be explained? In the past, native and foreign critics of Spanish American culture focused their attention on the pervasive racial mixture of the population. The argument was often made that the mestizo and his culture were a handicap in producing great literature. But racist arguments are no longer tenable—at least not in sociological discourse. I believe the reasons behind this apparent contradiction must be sought in social factors underlying literary production in Spanish America.

The role of the Spanish American writer was clearly delineated at the time of independence from Spain at the turn of the nineteenth century. But the defining characteristics of the writer's social role were forged through three basic traditions. The first laid the ground for the writer's role as the witness of unjustice. This was a legacy handed down by the Indians who translated the birth pangs of a new culture, forged during the genocide days of the conquest, into a written testimony. Indeed, the Indian's nostalgic presentation of what had been, however apologetical, constitutes the first protest delivered through literature in Spanish America. Inca Garcilaso de la Vega, a century into the colonial period, continued this tradition by protesting against the destruction of Indian civilizations by those searching for spiritual and material rewards. Contrary to common opinion, then, protesting against the exploitation of man by man in Spanish American literature is not a recent development; it is, in fact, as old as Spanish America itself.

The second tradition developed in Spanish America during centuries of European domination; I call this the Iberian legacy. Two aspects worthy of noting here are the conception of charity and the distinction between manual and mental labor. In Spanish America, charity has always been considered a cardinal aspect of the good life. This conception of charity is related to that of salvation, for it is believed that personal salvation may be obtained through charitable acts.

Furthermore, what is most important in Spanish American tradition is the belief that acts carried out for the salvation of others constitute the most sublime charitable acts.[43] In this sense, every individual is somewhat like a priest. This conception of charity sustained many humanists who came with the conquistadors and who, at times, disagreed with their policies. When pressed to their limits, they fell back on the notion that more important than the protection of the Indian's body was the salvation of his soul. The cosmic purpose of which some elite members speak in connection with the conquest lies in this concept of charity. In the present day, this concept of charity is helping Spanish American theologians bring about social change, and the "theology of liberation" presently being developed in Spanish America has essential connections with this tradition.[44]

Such a conception of charity, with its obvious connection to Catholic mysticism but often shy of its religious character, supported the image of a writer who saw his task as a calling. The writer was to write in full view of a wrecked humanity; he was to offer advice; he was to measure up to the role of the savior. The writer's calling was seen as fraught with temptations (for example, political co-optations, economic considerations) and danger (for example, imprisonment, exile, death); but the writer was to thrust himself forward to help those in need from a deeply felt sense of charity.

The second aspect of the Iberian tradition supported the view that those whose work was intellectual were superior to those who worked with their hands, regardless of the economics involved.[45] Throughout the colonial period and after, Indian and black forced labor spared most criollos from physical labor and afforded them the time to imitate the Spanish *gentilhombre*. During this time, the priesthood and law were the preferred occupations when the hacienda was not sufficient to guarantee a comfortable life. The sciences and technical professions, on the other hand, were looked down on as not proper ways of engaging the time of a "hidalgo." The dichotomy between mental and manual labor has been maintained to this day.

As a consequence, the image of the writer was that of an Olympian figure, of someone who knew. This conception was at once flattering and awesome, for the privileges of the Olympian posture carried with them burdensome responsibilities. The writer was expected to understand the world in all its complexity and be able to translate that understanding into counsel for his audiences. The writer was, in other words, an opinion leader in the broadest sense. Versed in politics, economics, theology, philosophy, and so on the writer's pronouncements on important matters were expected and given the consideration due the words of one who knows. *Mutatis mutandis,* the writer approached Walter Benjamin's image of the storyteller and the *tlamatini* of the pre-Columbian world.[46]

The third tradition that influenced the Spanish American writer was that of writers as misunderstood geniuses, messianic and romantic figures, popularized by French letters in the late eighteenth and early nineteenth centuries, precisely when Spanish American authors were asserting their Spanish Americanism.[47] Heavily influenced by this conception, Spanish Americans often saw the writer as idealistic in the sense that he always seemed to be ahead of his time. When the writer received the rebuttal of reality, there was always reason to argue that it was reality and not the writer's conception of it that needed changing. However, there is a crucial difference between French and Spanish American romantic writers. Contrary to his European counterpart, who was reacting against, and attempting to escape from, the world he saw engulfed in the evils of capitalist growth, the Spanish American writer sought involvement in the world and became a revolutionary, advancing the progressive forces of the criollo elites in revolt against colonialism. Thus, from its very beginning, Spanish American romanticism was allied to progressive forces aimed at changing the social structure of society along liberal lines.

Supported by such a sociocultural milieu, the self-image of the Spanish American writer of this period recalled Don Quixote: a crusader against the evils of the world, wherever those evils might be found. The history of Spanish American letters during this period documents the writer's polemics for or against Catholicism, colonialism, capitalism, communism, atheism, and a host of other isms, including caudillismo. And, the writer saw all the sacrifices demanded and endured by him or his audiences as justified by a personal sense of honor and calling.[48] Thus, an aura of mysticism surrounded the Spanish American writer, an aura claimed by his self-image and validated by the audience's praise.

All these factors—the quixotic self-image, the sense of charity, and so on, together with the real and perceived sordid reality that was the basis of all these claims and attributes—made possible the concept of the Spanish American writer, by both himself and his audiences, as *social critic*.[49] Whether he wrote for his class or for the people, the Spanish American writer during this period always saw his primary role as critic of the past and the present in light of a promising future that he envisioned. This is one reason why literature is a particularly strong indicator of the nature and extent of Spanish America's utopian Dream.

Having in mind the role of the Spanish American writer as he and his audiences understood it in this period, it is not surprising that the aesthetic element was of secondary importance to the writer. During this period of Spanish American history, literature was a means of socioethical ends. In a world of poverty and violence, art in general and literature in particular were the realms where dreams, anger, hope, pride, and shame were deposited and examined. It is no accident that the only original literary genre created by Spanish Americans in the nineteenth century, that is, when they had attained political independence, was socioliterary. In fact, the literature of even later writers such as José Martí cannot be understood unless it is placed within the context of his political views and programs.[50] This close relationship

between literature and social criticism had important consequences for the nature of literary works produced in this
period. Literature was didactic, and herein, above all, lies
the reason for the absence of what modern readers would
call great literary works in Spanish America during this
period.

Finally, the fact that whatever the writer's calling he is
always affected by his position in society must not be overlooked. Until the middle of this century, the writer was a
member of an elite, not only culturally (a position shared by
writers everywhere) but economically, politically, and socially as well. Between the writer and the majority of the
citizens of the Nation for whom his calling demanded his
concern, there was the inevitable gulf between the "civilized" and the "barbarians."[51] Under such circumstances, the
writer claimed privileges for himself that members of the
masses, for whom he was often the self-appointed spokes-
man, could not. This split, which followed class lines, added
to the burden of the writer's calling. To be true to his calling, the writer was often asked to turn against class, family,
and friends to denounce the shortcomings of the status quo.
At the same time, he had to come to terms with his own
superior social position vis-à-vis the masses. His calling, in
fact, demanded that he distance himself from his class while
still being unable to be one with the masses, who saw him
not as a friend but as a mistrusted protector, not as a partner
but as a *patrón.*[52]

Attempts to solve this problem varied from writer to writer. Many ended up accepting a guest position among the
elite along with the privileges it afforded them; they learned
to live with guilt. Some descended to the people, tried to
become another, wrote in an elementary fashion; few were
successful.[53] But whatever the solution, the position of the
writer, torn between calling and class, made him truly the
conscience of his own class—the ruling class. The ambivalence inherent in the nonprofessional writer's calling must be

kept in mind as I proceed, for it forms the very core of his creations.[54]

The Novel as a Social Indicator

The novel is one of the most recent major literary forms to be created; its development, as with everything that reflects culture, is an indication of underlying social processes. As such, the novel, according to the young Lukacs, "is the epic of a world that has been abandoned by God."[55] That is, it is the product of a world that had departed from the bosom of religion at the dissolution of the Middle Ages.

The rise of the novel coincided with the acceleration of two social processes in Europe: increasing social mobility aided by a new sense of individuality and the delineation of national cultures. Reflecting these processes in modern society, the novel's characters are in constant search, and their lives can be understood in terms of essentially bourgeois careers and followed as they question, ascend, and descend in their social world. Their careers, furthermore, are guided by value systems of the national culture with which the characters themselves identify. The novel could not have achieved its definitive form in a society where social structures allowed little mobility and a developed sense of national culture did not exist.

Its very inception, then, betrays the spirit that moves man to write novels. The novel is the product of an age whose ethos is constant questioning; it was the outgrowth of the situation of European man, who, with the security of the Middle Ages gone, found himself alone in a world whose meaning was becoming increasingly problematic. The novel, a product of an age in search of meaning, as Michel Zeraffa suggests, took the guise of oracle.[56] More directly than other forms of art, the novel confronts man with the meaning and value of historic and social experiences. The novel defines

itself as an art that searches for the solution to man's predicament in the world, not in terms of either-or, good-evil, but
in terms of choice, action, compromise; in other words, in
terms of history.

Thus, in the novel, all temporal modalities of human existence are significant. It is this approach to temporality that
makes the novel a privileged literary form for shedding light
on the Spanish American utopian Dream for a united mestizo Spanish America. Spanish American man is regarded as
the product of two cultures with different and receding pasts
—and, consequently, as thrown into the future. The search
for being—an aspect of the utopian Dream—is carried out
within the temporal flux that is history, and for this reason,
like no other literary form, the novel reveals the depths of
Spanish American culture. The sociological view that literature illuminates underlying and adjoining cultural processes has here one of its most promising instances.

The Novel in Spanish America

Spanish America did not produce a single novel during
the entire colonial period of about 300 years (ca. 1500–ca.
1800).[57] Although many overzealous priests attempted to
deprive Spanish America of Quixotes and Celestinas, this
should not be taken as the reason for this absence; the reasons can be found only in the nature of Spanish American
society itself. The feudal institutions that Spain exported to
her colonies in the New World lingered long after equivalent institutions in Europe had disappeared. During the colonial period, Spanish American society was highly stratified
and governed by officials sent from Spain who were directly
responsible to Spanish institutions. The majority of the
Spanish American population made up of mestizos, Indians,
and blacks were subject to severe restrictions that prevented
not only their social mobility, but often their physical as
well. On the other hand, the Spanish American cultural

elite was content to follow the dictates of the Spanish rulers and looked to Spain for cultural guidance and a sense of nationhood. This state of affairs prevented the growth of a collective consciousness that could have been the foundation of a Spanish American culture. The novel had, in fact, no social basis for its appearance.

It is no accident, then, that the rise of the novel in Spanish America coincided with movements toward liberation (1800–1830) aimed at changing colonial institutions and allowing criollos and wealthy mestizos to assume government of the land. The first Spanish American novel, *El periquillo sarniento* (1816) was a picaresque novel written by a Mexican patriot on the eve of Mexico's independence from Spain in 1821. Criticism of colonial rule and search for a Nation were the twin forces that made the novel possible in Spanish America. Indeed, the novel did not really flourish until the 1950s, when the middle class in Spanish America bid for power through alliances with foreign interests.

In addition to the central treatment of temporality, then, the novel sheds light on the writer's role in Spanish America as no other literary form has done. For surely if literature in general has been a means of socioethical ends in Spanish America, it is the novel that has been the most utilized literary form in this function. "Epic of a society that is founded in criticism," writes Octavio Paz, "the novel is an implicit judgment of that reality. In the first place . . . it is a question about the reality of reality. This question, which has no possible answer, because its own asking excludes any answer—is the acid that corrodes the entire social order."[58] Indeed, the novel has been the tool par excellence of the Spanish American critical mind. With reason, John E. Englekirk, writing in 1935, called Spanish American novelists in the nineteenth and early twentieth centuries "patriots, political exiles, essayists, pamphleteers, rather than novelists."[59] The nature of the writer's calling made this judgment possible: Aesthetic elements were often overshadowed by social criticism.

The Centrality of the Indigenista Novels

To demonstrate the nature and extent of the utopian Dream of a united mestizo Spanish America by examining the Spanish American novel in general surpasses the scope of this work. Rather, I focus on a selected group of novels, Indian novels, particularly indigenista novels written between 1919 and 1964 in Bolivia, Ecuador, Peru, Guatemala, and Mexico,[60] which reflect the very core of the utopian Dream.

There are two reasons for selecting indigenista novels: First, these novels were part of a broader sociocultural movement in Spanish America concerned with the "salvation" of the Indian people. The movement, *indigenismo* (ca. 1919–1970), touched every aspect of Spanish American society and culture as it swept across different nations, even those where the Indian was but a memory. Further and most crucial, in its attempt to liberate the Indians, indigenismo by necessity dealt with their race and culture; that is, with one of the essential components of Spanish American being. Through indigenismo, the Spanish American cultural elite attempted to acknowledge and appropriate its origins. Essentially, indigenismo was an attempt to return to the original act; it constituted reliving the violence of the father and the rape of the mother. Just how successful the cultural elite was in its attempt at going beyond the original trauma will become clear as I proceed. The point is that insofar as the indigenista novel partook of the indigenismo movement, it was a vehicle for reliving history.

Second, since the indigenista movement dealt with Indian cultures, Spanish American elites confronted head on the most important challenge to Spanish American mestizo culture. Given the characteristics of the role of the writer and literature in Spanish America during this time, an analysis of the indigenista novel illuminates how the cultural elite defended and asserted its cherished utopian Dream.

How, for example, was counterevidence of the Indian's presence dispelled? More to the point, given the cultural elite's tendency to see the mestizo—and a white-mestizo at that—as the New Man of Spanish America, what was their vision of the Indian's future? For, as should be clear, to the cultural elite, the future of the Indian as Indian presented itself as a problem whose solution was imperative if a mestizo culture was to be upheld.

In addition to these more central considerations, an analysis of the indigenista novel should also reveal the ambivalence, burden, and guilt that envelop the writer's calling. Did the indigenista writer demand the liberation of an entire people who had been considered barbarians prior to the twentieth century? If so, how was his work affected? For among all types of novels in Spanish America, indigenista novels must be counted as some of the most didactic. Given all these reasons, analyzing indigenista novels is crucial for my purposes. Indeed, if I am able to demonstrate the strength of the utopian Dream through a literature that was ostensibly reacting to traditional Spanish American culture and, in fact, supportive of the Indian's culture in general, my case can only be the stronger. As this work unfolds, it will become clear that those very writers who set out to save the Indian ended up by demanding his cultural death. By proclaiming the banishment of the Indian for their own ends, these writers affected the incorporation of the Indian's culture into the mestizo world for which they were spokesmen.

Chapter Two

The Indian
and the
Literary
Tradition

Broken spears lie in the roads;
we have torn our hair in our grief.
The houses are roofless now, and their walls
are red with blood.

Worms are swarming in the streets and plazas,
and the walls are splattered with gore.
The water has turned red, as if it were dyed,
and when we drink it,
it has the taste of brine.
                    —Visión de los vencidos

Defining the Indian

The treatment of the Indian in indigenista novels is the culmination of a long literary tradition developed by Indian, Spanish, and Spanish American writers. Over the centuries, this tradition has shown important continuities as well as ruptures caused by different views of the Indian and his world. The main continuities and ruptures in the literary tradition up to the end of the nineteenth century are discussed in this chapter with reference to the underlying social factors that affected them. Before proceeding, however, it is important to state as clearly as possible who is considered Indian in this work in order to avoid a possible misunderstanding of the discussion that follows.

Figures concerning the actual size of the Indian population before the Spanish conquest vary, and no definitive one has been reached; estimates range from about 13 million to about 150 million. What is certain is that a large number of Indians died during the first decades of colonial rule due to massacres, plagues, and forced labor. Calculations prepared by the Berkeley school of historians and demographers show that in Central Mexico alone there were an estimated 25,200,000 Indians in 1519, the year Cortés landed in Veracruz; 13 years later, there were 16,800,000 Indians left. By 1580, 60 years after the conquest, the Indian population had been reduced to only 1,900,000![1] These figures give an idea of the genocide that accompanied the conquest of Spanish America.

Despite the tremendous demographic collapse, Indians were able to endure. This was particularly the case where they had developed large and integrated societies; that is to say, in the regions generally referred to as nuclear America: the Andes zone in South America, Central America, and central and southern Mexico. After the first centuries of colonial rule, the bulk of the Indian population was circumscribed in these areas, where their demographic density made possible the retention of their culture as they retreated from the coastal regions to the less accessible highlands. Where their numbers were small, as in large portions of present-day Argentina, for example, the Indians dissolved both culturally and biologically into the mestizo within the first centuries of colonial domination.

Population estimates of present-day Indians also vary. Some argue that there are only about 10 million Indians left in Spanish America compared with about 160 million or so whites and mestizos.[2] But these estimates should be viewed with caution, for there is no general agreement as to who is Indian in Spanish America. Are, for example, those who walk barefoot Indians? Those who do not speak Spanish? Those who are dark? Those who dress like Indians? Indeed, as it has been pointed out by several writers, figures concerning existing Indian populations vary according to the criteria each investigator uses in calculations.

There are three basic criteria for classifying a person as an Indian: biological, cultural, and social. Biologically speaking, there are few pure Indians in Spanish America; yet, phenotypically speaking, no one can deny their great number in the area. In fact, were Spanish Americans to classify Indians phenotypically, as blacks are classified in the United States, for example, the majority of Spanish Americans could be classified as Indian; Haya de la Torre and his followers based their claim for an Indo-America on these grounds. The biologic basis for classification does not, however, do justice to the complexity of the Indian problem in Spanish America. Phenotypic characteristics are crucial classification factors only when used in conjunction with other cultural and social criteria.

The interpretation of the Indian problem as a cultural one has been widespread in Spanish America since the first years of indigenismo, the movement whose goal was to redeem the Indian. Racial prejudice, it has been argued, is really cultural prejudice. If Indians were to learn Spanish, dress in western fashion, and so forth, they would cease to be Indian and become mestizo; their Indianness would fall off like a change of skin. No doubt, this view of the Indian problem has some basis in reality, but it ignores too much. Deculturation is not sufficient for a change of skin. As a mestizo, the deculturated Indian will still be discriminated against by the whiter population and remain at the bottom of his nation's economic ladder.

The noble battle waged by indigenistas against those who argued for a biological interpretation of the Indian problem soon became spurious. For sociologically speaking, one of the things to remember when dealing with discrimination in Spanish America is that there are people who look, think, feel, and live differently from Westerners and who are considered Indians by these Westerners. While it may be true that pure Indians are slowly facing biological extinction, be it through intermarriage or rape, it is also true that less pure Indians encounter discrimination in Spanish America because of their phenotypic appearance. Sociologists would do well to remember W. I. Thomas's insight: If the situation is defined as real, it is real in its consequences. In Spanish America, if a person is defined as Indian, he is treated as one and discriminated against whether or not he is biologically pure. Biology does play a part in discrimination in Spanish America, however mistaken its basis may be. In attempting to disprove racist arguments, adherents of the cultural conception of the Indian problem downplay its biological aspects.

Ever since the famous essays by Mariátegui, there have been social scientists who argued that racial prejudice hides unequal and unjust economic relations between two groups of unequal power.[3] This thesis, too, has basis in reality, and the most cursory view of Spanish American history bears it out. Today, for example, the majority of the poor are darker skinned than the privileged few. The Indian problem was clearly used to mask economic interests in the case of the *científicos* in Mexico who, following positivist and evolutionist philosophies, argued that by natural laws the white (fittest) rose to the top of the economic ladder and the Indian (unfit) remained at the bottom. Exploiting Indians and dark mestizos for the benefit of the small oligarchic group was thus justified. But to argue from there to a purely economic interpretation of the Indian problem in Spanish America is to be guilty of bad faith, and the staunchest proponents of the thesis know this and acknowledge the limitations of their analysis. Even if racial discrimination is often fostered and sustained by the class system in Spanish America, the fact that there is discrimination based on phenotypic characteristics can not be ignored.

What seems clear is that neither of these factors alone sufficiently explains the Indian problem in Spanish America. Phenotypic characteristics and cultural prejudices make it possible to justify an unjust economic order where the Indian is usually at the bottom. Alternatively, the low economic position of the Indian supports the ruling class's negative attitude toward the Indian's culture and the phenotypic characteristics that single him out.

With these issues in mind and for the purpose of this study, I shall adopt the following criteria when referring to Indians: Indians are those so defined by the rest of the Spanish American population and who evidence phenotypic characteristics and cultural traits associated with the definition.[4] This concept of Indianness follows from that of race as a social rather than a genetic category while at the same time allowing for the impact of phenotypic characteristics on classifying people into distinct races.

Pre-Columbian Spanish America

A brief excursus on pre-Columbian history is necessary for two reasons: First, the role of the writer and literature in

Spanish America can be understood only when seen in its sociocultural context of which the ancient world and its demise are a part; second, many Indian novels in the nineteenth century and particularly the twentieth century cannot be understood without reference to Indian life before Columbus.[5] The major problems of much of the research on Spanish American society and culture stem from the basically ahistoric approach of the research. What everyone knows must be rescued from what is taken for granted: The fact that the Indian's life has involved endless suffering with little or no change for the better over the centuries must not prevent historians from recounting it. We cannot close our eyes to what has been and expect to grasp what is.

The evidence so far suggests that the inhabitants of the New World were not natives of it; rather, it seems that they came in successive waves, probably through the Bering Strait, and scattered throughout the vast continent searching for adequate habitats. For about ten thousand years before the arrival of Europeans, these people were basically unaffected by human development elsewhere. The discussion of pre-Columbian culture that follows is limited to what has been referred to as nuclear America.

Olmecs, Toltecs, and Aztecs

From about 1500 to 400 B.C., there arose around the gulf coast lowlands of Mexico the precocious and enigmatic Olmec civilization. The Olmecs laid the foundations for the great cultural effervescence that has been called the Classic Period of pre-Columbian America. Olmec culture decisively influenced the cultural development of Indian groups in the central Mexican plateau and Central America. The Olmecs' technical, artistic, and scientific achievements are truly impressive; however, despite their achievements, the origins, development, and subsequent disappearance of the Olmec civilization remain a mystery. It seems that its fall was due to a combination of internal civil strife and natural disasters. Following the classical period, there came a time of chaos and civil turmoil dominated by militaristic and expansionist ideologies; this chaotic period lasted until about A.D. 1000.

Out of this period emerged the Toltecan empire, an impressive civilization that radiated from Tula, its capital city, located about 50 miles from Mexico City. The Toltecs, too, contributed greatly to the sociocultural development of the area, but by 1174, the Toltecan king Huemac, confronted with internal civil disorder, drought, and external pressures, apparently committed suicide. With his death, the Toltecan state also disappeared. Years after the disappearance, however, people of the region celebrated the legend of the Toltecs' grandeur and the almost paradisiac socioeconomic order they had established in the region. Legends of the Toltecs' brilliance survived up to the time of the conquest, fueling legends about hidden Indian treasures.

One source of external pressure that eventually brought about the destruction of the Toltecan empire was the coming of the Chichimec, the barbarians from the north. Among the late waves of barbarians to arrive were the Aztecs, basically a hunting and gathering people who had minimal acquaintance with agriculture. They settled in the valley of Mexico in about 1218, occupying an inhospitable and poor area around Lake Texcoco. From Texcoco, they began to build their empire helped by a militaristic ideology.

By the time Cortés arrived, the Aztecs had extended their dominion beyond the valley of Mexico to include areas from the fringe of the arid northern plateau to the lowlands of Tehuantepec and from the Atlantic to the Pacific. The Aztecs ruthlessly exacted tribute from subjugated Indians within their area of domination; only the fierce Tarascans, who inhabited the city-state of Tlaxcala, maintained complete independence from the Aztecs and their allies in that area. Other lesser kingdoms, such as the Cholula, managed to strike a bargain so that they were left in peace in return for cooperating with the Aztecs. The ruthlessness with which

the Aztecs waged wars and their treatment of prisoners
(taken for sacrifice) explain in great part the ease with which
Cortés conquered Mexico. When Cortés arrived to take Te-
nochtitlan, the capital of the Aztecan empire, he was followed by an army of disgruntled Indians hoping for revenge.

On the eve of the conquest, the Aztecs' political system
was a mixture of royal despotism and theocracy. Political
power was concentrated in a ruling class of priests and
nobles over whom the emperor presided as absolute ruler.
The priesthood was perhaps the main integrating force in
Aztecan society; the priests, a celibate and austere group,
accumulated and transmitted the lore and history of the
Aztecs. Through their possession of a sacred calendar that
regulated agricultural tasks, priests also played a key role
in the lives of the people, intervening between them and
their gods and counseling them in times of personal or collective crisis.

The nobility consisted of warriors and bureaucrats (such
as tribute collectors, judges, ambassadors, and the like) who
had gained power through war and political concentration.
The warrior nobility's source of wealth was largely landed
states that continually expanded during the Aztecan rule.
The bureaucrats were paid with revenues from the public
lands assigned to support them. At the bottom of the social
ladder and making possible the large noble class were the
serfs tied to the land (*meyeques*) and a sizable number of
slaves. The latter had become slaves as a punishment for a
variety of offenses, including failure to pay debts; often, too,
people were forced to assume slavery in return for food.

The social stratification of Aztecan society was rigid and
reinforced by numerous means: Aztecan clothing, for example, differed according to social status; education was also
segregated in terms of class. The *telpochcalli* (house of
youth) was attended by sons of commoners, merchants, and
artisans, whereas the *calmecac* (priests' house) was a school
of higher learning reserved for sons of the nobility, although
there is evidence that some sons of commoners and mer-

chants were admitted. In this latter educational institution, the Aztecan sages (*tlamantinime*) taught their vision of the cosmos and man's place in it.

Mayas, Quichés, and Cakchiquels

The splendid Mayan civilization extended from southeastern Mexico and included almost all of Guatemala, all of Belize, the western part of Honduras and the western half of El Salvador. But the Mayan civilization flourished particularly in the Petén region of Guatemala at the base of the Yucatan Peninsula from A.D. 300 to 900. As with other cultures of the area, the rise and fall of the Mayan civilization remains a puzzle. It seems likely that there, too, internal dissension coupled with natural disasters (soil erosion and earthquakes) and external pressures from expanding Indian groups were at the root of the Mayas' fall. By the sixteenth century, when the Spaniards arrived in the area, all centralized rule had disappeared in Central America.

Like their Aztecan counterpart, Mayan society was highly stratified; the population was divided into four classes: nobility, priests, commoners, and slaves. These classes were ruled by a hereditary priest-king with civil, military, and religious functions. The class lines were rigid and reflected in the type of dress, diet, and housing allocated to the population. As among the Aztecs, the priests were in charge of education and other intellectual pursuits. The Mayan priests taught that the world creator was Hunab Ku who, after a number of unsuccessful experiments, finally molded man out of maize. Like the Aztecs, the Mayas believed that a number of worlds had been successively created and destroyed in cataclysmic convulsions and that their present world would also end in a final convulsion. Their conception of the afterlife also resembled that of the Aztecs. The priests taught that souls traveled through an Upper World consisting of 13 layers and an Under World of nine in search of a final resting place. But the Mayan priests' greatest

achievements were in mathematics; they developed, for example, a place-value method of calculating based on a sign
for zero, thus anteceding the European use of zero by at
least a millennium.

With the collapse of their empire, the Mayan people scattered throughout meso-America and built new empires. The
Quichés and Cakchiquels, whose descendants make up a
large portion of the Guatemalan Indians, were two of these
empires. The Quichés and Cakchiquels came to Guatemala
from the north sometime after the tenth century and, on
entering Guatemala, subjugated native Indian tribes and
exacted tribute from them. By the fourteenth century,
through wars and alliances, the Quichés had consolidated
their political hegemony throughout the entire region; in
about the second half of the fifteenth century, however,
Quichés' rule was relaxed due to internal political turmoil.
The Cakchiquels took advantage of the situation and moved
to the areas around Lake Atitlan. From then on and until
the arrival of the Spaniards, these two empires fought recur-
rent battles for control of the territory.

The Incas

The Incas ruled over several nations in the Andes like a
small caste that was in turn governed by an even smaller
aristocracy. Even though all Incas claimed direct descent
from the sun, the supreme god of the land, the Incan nobility came mostly from one kinship group, the *capac ayllu*,
and constituted a minority of the Incan people. Between the
Incan caste and the rest of the empire, there existed an
unbreachable gulf.

The success of the Incas' rule was due in great part to two
interrelated factors: their military excellence and their socialist policies. Militarily, the Incan army was a unique phenomenon in the pre-Columbian Western world. Although it
was occasionally reinforced by provincial militias composed
of non-Incan soliders, the Incan army, always officered by

professionals from the nobility, had at its core two pure Incan regiments. The Incas' efficient military machinery was dependent on intelligence-gathering mechanisms made possible by a highly sophisticated road system. Thanks to their system of communication, Incan nobility was kept abreast of events in the empire and could dispatch within days or even hours military expeditions against pockets of unrest anywhere in the empire. Building and maintaining the roads were done by the people of conquered nations as part of their tribute to the Incan emperor.

Backed by military power, Incan rulers did not allow dissension among their subjects, and when it did take place, the rulers moved quickly to arrest it. Incan military repression was generally bloody and unmerciful for the rebels. In cases where rebels were numerous and thought to be a latent danger to the empire's security, Incan armies were directed to break up entire nations and move them in groups to different parts of the empire. On their departure, more dependable and acculturated groups from other nations were brought in to occupy their place. Under this system, the Incas practiced a kind of social engineering that allowed them to remain in power by dividing the subjugated nations into scattered groups from which no concerted efforts against the empire could be mounted.

The Incas could not have been as successful as they were in ruling the various Indian nations in the Andes had they relied solely on the force of arms. Their military might was complemented by their genius for devising and implementing social programs that generally improved the lot of the Indian living under Incan protection. Their political and economic power was concentrated in Cuzco, the capital of the empire and the center of courtly life as well as the center of culture and social planning. From Cuzco emanated the imperial social policies that maintained the empire's unity by holding internal dissension at a minimum. There was also a group of wise men and educators called *amautas* in Cuzco, who formed part of the Incan nobility and whose function it

was to educate the young nobles, keep the vital statistics of
the empire, advise the Incan emperor in all matters, and
generally be responsible for the growth of the arts and sciences.

In the absence of a written language, the enormous task of
the amautas was carried out with the help of the *quipu*, a
mnemonic device consisting of a master cord on which other
cords depended. The subordinate cords varied in length and
color, and by tying knots on different cords, the amautas
kept records for different categories, such as: tribute (for
example, grains and labor power) given to the Incan emperor from different parts of the empire; movement of the
population in terms of sex, age, occupation, and so on; income and disbursement of all items stored in the empire's
warehouses throughout the empire; and other statistics. In-
ventories were kept throughout the empire and combined
into provincial tallies, which were sent to the central archives of the empire in Cuzco.

Tribute was at the core of all imperial planning. Advised
by the amautas, the emperor knew exactly how much grain,
labor power, gold, and so on, he was due in tribute from
various parts of the empire, and failure on the part of local
nobles to produce the required amount was tantamount to
treason. With his armies ready to march, the Incan emperor
exacted tribute from the smallest provinces with utmost
punctuality. On the other hand, close supervision of the
empire's socioeconomic state enabled the emperor to move
swiftly and efficiently to protect the welfare of his subjects.
Only part of the collected tribute was sent to Cuzco for the
enjoyment of the Incan ruling caste; the rest was stored in
warehouses alongside roads that crisscrossed the empire.
These provisions were always available to the population at
large in case of wars or natural disasters, the occurrences of
which were immediately reported to the emperor.

In addition to the amautas, the land-tenure system was a
factor in providing for the security and general welfare of
Incan subjects. As the Incas extended the boundaries of

their empire, they imposed on conquered territories their own system of land tenure based on collectivist principles. Under this system, land was not individually owned but held communally by kinship groups (*ayllus*). All lands were controlled and managed by the ayllu, which periodically met in council to decide who should and should not use the land and how the plots were to be allocated. Under this system, every newborn member of the ayllu was assigned a plot of land sufficient to provide for his or her well-being. In the case of the elderly and those unable to work, the ayllu took responsibility for cultivating their land communally. Ideally, everyone in the empire was thus assured his or her livelihood, and extreme cases of wealth and poverty were nonexistent. These collectivist principles also governed the labor process in the Incan empire: Everything from planting and harvesting crops to road construction was done communally. Work was usually connected with religious or quasi-religious practices that served to renew and maintain the communal spirit; in short, work was almost a communal rite.

In sum, pre-Columbian nuclear America was governed by a succession of small groups of people who cemented their power through force. The majority of the Indians did not enjoy the full benefit of their labor, and many suffered the consequences of being a conquered people. Even in the Andes, if the Indians were not slaves, they also were not free. It is important to keep in mind that tribute, repression, and even slavery were not brought by the Spaniards to the New World; there never was a utopia in nuclear America. The twentieth-century novelist's exaltation of pre-Columbian America hides the truth about the past in order to criticize the present more. But for all this, it must not be forgotten that the Spanish conquest cut short the development of a remarkable people and condemned them to perpetual suffering. The coming of the Europeans did not bring respite to the Indian; rather, it augmented oppression to unheard-of proportions.

Pre-Columbian Literature

The literature of nuclear America, marking the onset of
Indian culture, shows a remarkable development.[6] To be
sure, as in most societies of that time (ca. 1000 B.C.–A.D.
1500), literary production and enjoyment among the Indians
reflected the social stratification of the society between the
aristocratic few and the rest of the population. The most
accomplished pre-Columbian literature was basically a literature of theopolitical ruling classes.

From the remnants of this literary tradition, it can be
deduced that pre-Columbian literature lacked what might
be called a critical tendency. Tragedies, for example, which
involve a close analysis of the sociocultural complexities of
society are conspicuously absent. Even the fable, perhaps
one of the most indirect ways of criticizing ruling powers,
did not develop here in that direction. Moreover, due to its
theopolitical character, thematic changes in literature within
regions (for example, Aztec and Incan societies) seem to
have developed as different cultures competed with one another. This is one of the factors supporting the view that
cultural unity of what is now Spanish America was not even
remotely considered in pre-Columbian times. Finally, it
should also be noted here that pre-Columbian literature did
not develop as literary genres, such as poetry, drama, epic,
and so on; the Indians combined theology, medicine, history, myth, and literature in a single work.

Written pre-Columbian literature was developed to the
highest degree by the Mayas. In addition to inscriptions on
stone, the Mayas had a large number of sacred books or
codices. Evidence so far indicates that they did not develop
an alphabet; the characters of the codices represent ideas or
objects rather than sounds. But like Aztec writing, Mayan
writing was moving toward syllabic phonetics through the
use of rebus writing, where sounds of a word are represented

by combining pictures or signs of things whose spoken names resemble sounds in the words to be formed. Unfortunately, most of these codices were burned by the conquering Spanish priests; only three are extant today.

Besides written texts, the Mayas, Aztecs, Incas, and other pre-Columbian people had a large body of myths, legends, poetry, and traditional history that was transmitted orally from generation to generation. The excerpts on philosophy and art that follow are examples of the few remnants of ancient nuclear America's cultural developments. They are part of an oral tradition that was finally written down during the early days of conquest. The first text relates Quetzalcoatl's vision of Ometeotl, the dual god and fundamental being in Nahuatl cosmology. He is depicted as having a masculine countenance and features that are at the same time feminine. Ometeotl is master of what is near and far, master of everything that is. He is the origin; he dresses in stars like a maiden and vests himself in black and red, colors symbolizing wisdom.

> *And it is stated and said that*
> *Quetzalcoatl called upon, as his*
> *proper god, one who dwells in the*
> *interior of the heaven.*
>
> *He invoked her, surrounded by a skirt of*
>   *stars,*
> *him who gives light to all things;*
> *Mistress of our flesh, lord of our flesh,*
> *She who clothes herself in black,*
> *He who clothes himself in red,*
> *She who established the earth firmly,*
> *He who gives activity to the earth.*
>
> *Thither did he direct his words,*
> *thus did he know himself,*
> *toward the place of the duality*
> *and of the nine crossbeams*

in which the heaven consists.
And as he knew,
He called on him who dwelled there,
directed supplications to him,
living in meditation and in retirement.[7]

The second text concerns the Aztecs' conception of knowledge, tradition, and of those who develop and transmit it. The figure of the tlamatini, he who knows something, prefigures the more modern Spanish American writer-critic. Master of black and red, the symbols of wisdom, the tlamatini illuminates the world and man as "a full torch that does not smoke." He thinks and writes down his thoughts in the sacred books of paintings. He is a teacher who attempts to give humans a proper face, a proper personality and character so that they "become prudent and careful." He desires to know and guide his pupils on the path to the mysteries of the Upper World (*Topan*) and Under World (*Mitlan*); he shows forth his light over the world and knows what is above us and the region of the dead. It is thanks to him that men humanize their desires, fortify their hearts, and receive a strict instruction.

The tlamatini: a light, a torch,
an ample torch that does not smoke.
A mirror pierced through,
A mirror full of holes on both sides.
His is the ink black and red,
his are the codices,
he is the master of the books of paintings.
He is himself the scripture and the wisdom.
He is the way, the true guide for others.
He leads persons and things,
he is the guide in human affairs.

The good tlamatini is careful (like a doctor)
and guards the tradition.
His is the wisdom handed down,
he is the one who teaches it,

he follows the truth
and he does not desist from counseling.
he makes strange faces wise,
he makes them develop it.
He opens their ears, he illuminates them.
He is the master of guides,
he gives them their path,
and one depends on him.

He puts a mirror before the others,
he makes them prudent, and careful;
he makes them acquire a face.
He establishes things,
regulates their path,
disposes and orders.
He turns his light upon the world.
He knows that which is above us (Topan)
and the region of the dead (Mitlan).

He is a thoughtful man;
everyone is comforted by him,
is corrected, is taught.
Thanks to him, the people humanizes its
*   desire*
and received a strict instruction.

Comforter of the heart,
comforter of the people,
help and remedy,
he brings healing to all.[8]

Among the many tlamatinimi who enlightened pre-Columbian America, the best known was Nezahualcoyotl. Born in
1402, the son of a king, he became one of the most influential
men of his time. He opposed the Aztecan practice of human
sacrifice and the wars of flowers, while seeking the possibility of overcoming death. He searched for a root that
would allow man to escape time and change. The third text
shows Nezahualcoyotl's awareness of the effects of time on
man and world.

*Perhaps one with root truly lives upon the
  earth?
Not forever on the earth;
Only for a short time here.
Even if it be of jade it will be broken,
even if it be of gold it will be shattered,
even if it be the plumage of a bird that rends
  itself.
Not forever on the earth;
only for a short time here.*

*Only for an instant does the meeting endure,
for a brief time there is glory. . . .
None of your friends has root,
only for a short time are we given here as
  loans,
your lovely flowers. . . .
Everything that flourishes in your mat or in
  your chair,
nobility on the field of battle,
on which depends lordship and command,
your flowers of war . . .
are only dried flowers.*

*I am inebriated, I weep, I am afflicted,
I think, I say,
within myself I find it;
if I would never die,
if I would never disappear.
There where there is no death,
there where death is conquered,
there will I go.
If I would never die,
if I would never disappear.*[9]

Nezahualcoyotl's fears and anxiety foreshadow the fate of
his people a few years after his death: With the arrival of
the Spaniards, Indian cultures disappeared. In their haste to
dominate, the Spaniards were swift to destroy, not only na-

tive political and economic structures, but the Indian's cultural world as well.

Fortunately, not all Spaniards came to destroy; some came to salvage what was being destroyed. Among the latter were priests and other humanists, who guided the efforts of young Indians writing down some of their fading literature.[10] To be sure, precisely because of this guiding effort, the literature written down by the Indians for the most part treated their destroyed culture nostalgically and made excuses for that destruction. (In these works one finds the earliest manifestations of the Dream of a mestizo Spanish America.) Even recording pre-Columbian history was aimed at preserving and incorporating it into the new ideology supporting the new order. Nonetheless, among the bulk of recorded history and lore, there are crucial remnants that are an awesome testimony of the conquest. This testimony remains in the Spanish American memory, bearing witness to the fact that the mestizo culture was born of rape. To forget this past would entail the mestizo's self-denial; a self-denial that has never been possible, despite many attempts.[11]

In their testimony, the Aztecan cultural elite, for example, tell how the Spanish conqueror treated the treasures of their civilization. In a naïve attempt to save his empire, Moctezuma took the Spaniards to his treasure house in Teucalco; there, the Spaniards carried out all the cultural treasures. "Immediately, the gold was taken from war shields and from other emblems. They made a huge mound of gold and set everything else afire. They burned, burned everything that was not gold, no matter how valuable: Thus everything went to ashes."[12] Unable to stop the ransacking of their cultural world, the tlamatinime contemplated the destruction of their ancient knowledge of the world, the vision of the heavens. The books of Chilam Balam preserve the lament of the ancient teachers over the destruction of their lessons by a horde of "damned bearded foreigners: Lost will be science, lost will be wisdom"[13] and they describe the violence and destruction of the gods:

You tell us
that our gods are untrue.
This is a new thing
that you tell us,
it disturbs us,
it fills us with grief.
For our ancestors,
those who were before us,
those who lived on the earth,
were not accustomed to tell us so.
And now should we destroy
the ancient rule of life? . . .
Truly we cannot believe it,
we do not accept it as the truth
even though it offends you.[14]

In the end, however, an end that came centuries later, the Indians had to admit the death of their gods; the destruction all around them demanded it. Their fears were to become prophecies:

Let us die then,
Let us perish then,
For our gods are already dead![15]

True, beneath their vision of doom, the Indians kindled a hope of enduring, of returning—a forever truncated hope. "This is our genealogy," says the testimony of the Cakchiqueles, "which will never be lost because we know our origin and shall never forget our forefathers."[16] But remembrance is a double-edged sword; when the past becomes a refuge, the future turns opaque. Memory can be a catapult to action, but it is also the pastime of a people without a vision of the future. In the long travail that constitutes the Indian's history since the conquest, the effects of memory of the past have alternated like Ometeotl. For long periods, it has been a sedative: The Indian and his descendant, the mestizo, have retreated to the memory of better times and failed to act in the present. At other times, memory has spurred the same Indian and mestizo to rebellion. (By prohibiting Indian plays where the Incan past was recalled, as in Peru in 1782, the Spaniards showed awareness of the revolutionary potential of collective memory.) Over the years, however, the Indians have lost even the memory of their past. In the twentieth century, the Indians are a people with almost no conscious history; whites and mestizos have become the keepers of the memory. Consequently, the potential for liberation stored therein has left their hands. Here lies one of the reasons why Indian rebellions in the twentieth century have increasingly been directed by mestizos and not by Indians themselves.

Pre-Columbian literature is an important aspect of the literature of today's Spanish America; it records the Indian's glory, hopes, fears, and fate. Surely, pre-Columbian literature translates the vision of a world that neither a white nor a mestizo can totally penetrate, but it constitutes a voice from the past that present-day Spanish Americans can hardly ignore. As such, this literature has become a source of pride as well as shame, guilt, and hatred for modern Spanish Americans. In these testimonies, Spanish America relives the conquest and colonization. As things stand, it is highly unlikely that today's Indians will ever produce a literature that presents a vision of the world in terms other than Western. Indian literature production ceased in the early days of the conquest and, from then on, the literature of Spanish America was to be written in Spanish or by individuals with basically a Western world view.

Two important aspects of the Indian's literary legacy should be stressed. First, much of this literature already points to the coming of a mestizo culture, which was permeated by an apologetic tendency from the very beginning. This effort to forgive and forget the violence of origins began with Spanish American history, since the audience intended for these works was not the Indians themselves but their white masters. Secondly, it must also be stressed that the literature of protest in Spanish America and the role of the writer as social critic began with using literature as a testimony of the genocide days of conquest. The tradition began, therefore, with the protest, however veiled, of a disintegrating civilization aware of its tragedy. And the dual tendency to apologize while protesting that is present in the first Spanish American literature has permeated all subsequent literary production by or about Indians in the region.

The Conquest
and Colonial Literature

A detailed account of the Indian's social conditions during the 300 years of colonial domination is not possible here; suffice it to note the following: The Indian's welfare deteriorated drastically as colonial rule became more secure. As a subject to the Spanish crown, the Indian was required to pay tribute either in gold or work or both, a situation from which Spaniards living in America profited by making the Indian work without wages. Millions of Indians died because of disease, wars, and physical exhaustion resulting from extreme forms of forced labor under the *mita, repartimiento,* and *encomienda* systems. Moreover, the Spanish conquerors saw themselves as racially superior, and, therefore, they exploited the Indian not only physically by securing his labor without payment but psychologically as well by demanding the obedience and submission of a slave. In other words, the genocide days of the conquest were extended to the colonial period. For centuries the social, economic, and political privileges of colonial society rested on the servitude of the Indian people.

In the literature of conquest, the Indian was depicted as a mixture of warrior and savage. Through this literary image, the Spanish chroniclers sang of Spanish courage and the triumph of civilization.[17] In their literary vision, the writers of this period transformed the Indian's culture and psychology to fit preconceived models. Alfonso de Ercilla y Zúñiga (1533–1594), the most gifted writer of this period, for example, presented the Indian in his long poetic work *La araucana* (1569–1589) as an unhappy cross between a European classical mythopoetical being and a savage. In this work, it is not uncommon for savages to deliver their thoughts in the most classical Spanish, and less gifted writers were equally inaccurate in their portrayal of the Indian. This image of the Indian remained in Spanish American literature for centuries to come.

This view of the Indian was a matter of course, given the literary tradition and the audience of the time. As were most writers of the period, Ercilla was a Spaniard who wrote for a Spanish audience for whom the classical form was required for writing good poetry. As Concha Meléndes has noted in her well-known analysis of literature about Indians written during this period, the authors carried with them their classical culture "intercepted between the physical object and their vision."[18]

During the ensuing years of colonial domination, the Indian's image did not change substantially; however, elements introduced in the literature of Spanish America by Indians who survived the demise of their society were further accentuated. As noted, the work of Indian chroniclers was tinged with nostalgia and apology for the violence committed by the Spaniards. One hundred years into the colonial period, Inca Garcilaso de la Vega, the illegitimate son of an Incan princess and a Spanish captain, fully developed this dual tendency in his famous *Comentarios reales*, published in 1609.

Garcilaso's work is one of the most knowledgeable accounts of Incan culture, but, like the work of all Indian chroniclers, the *Comentarios reales* tends to apologize for the conquest. In fact, Garcilaso viewed the conquest of the Incas by the Spaniards as the end of a long process of preparing the Andean Indians for salvation—a preparation that had begun with founding and expanding the Incan empire

itself. Some of the passages most critical of the Spanish conquest deal with the lack of missionary zeal on the part of
Spanish conquerors. Conquest and colony were thus justified by an appeal to the sublime Christian God and superior
Western culture. It is no accident that Garcilaso presented
his case to whites and no longer to Indians; that he did so in
a highly stylized and erudite Spanish (he identified Cuzco
with Rome in the preface and in several places within the
text, and biblical and Greek references abound) shows to
what extent he had internalized his father's culture as his
own.

As did other chroniclers, Garcilaso emphasized the past,
not the present or future of the Indians: The beautiful narrative of the *Comentarios reales* is nostalgic. But in a mas-
terful dialectic move, Garcilaso transformed this nostalgia
into a vision of utopia;[19] in this work, Incan leaders appear
godlike, and their society approaches perfection—except for
a few drawbacks such as their pagan religion. In transform-
ing the past into a utopia, Garcilaso made one of his most
important contributions to Spanish American culture. For
by positing an Incan utopian past, Garcilaso subtly but force-
fully protested against the injustice of the Indian's conditions in his time. True, Garcilaso's protest was devoid of
militancy and did not seek to marshal soldiers for a cause; it
only attempted to enjoin the sympathies of the conquerors.
Nonetheless, showing the Spaniards that the Incas had had a
complex culture and a high sense of justice, honor, and
pride constituted a tacit act of protest against the Indian's
present state and the Spaniards' arrogance.

This view of a utopian Indian past has been used again and
again as an ideological weapon; it was used by Bolívar and
his generation in the nineteenth century and by the indigenista movement and various political parties in the twentieth century. In this sense, Garcilaso's work must be seen
as one of the foundations of the indigenista novel. Also, by
maintaining the dual tendency noted, Garcilaso contributed
to developing the Spanish American tradition of the writer

as critic (witness to injustice) and literature as a means to socioethical ends, while maintaining ambivalence toward the benefactors of this protest.

The Romantic Period

If Garcilaso wrote with nostalgia, Fray Bartolomé de Las Casas, a Spanish Dominican priest, did so with compassion.[20] Of all those who defended the Indian throughout Spanish American history, none surpasses Bartolomé de Las Casas in kindness, perseverance, and courage. His denunciation of the violence that accompanied the Spanish conquest of America has always inspired intellectuals, men of science, and social revolutionaries and influenced their attitude toward the Indian problem in Spanish America.

Bartolomé de Las Casas's work, however, situated as it was in the period of conquest, could not free itself from some idealization of the Indian and his world. In his passionate defense, the Dominican priest presented the Indian as virtuous, innocent, and submissive. He set Indian life before conquest in a quasi-utopian world, in a state of social tranquility reminiscent of the childhood of the human race. With the pangs of civilization not having reached such a world, the Indian was thought to live in a most harmonious relationship with nature in a self-contained paradise.

No two other men were to influence ideas about the Indian of the Americas held by the nineteenth-century European romantic writers as did the Dominican Bartolomé de Las Casas and the mestizo Garcilaso de la Vega. They gave European writers the image of the noble savage, the uncorrupted, happy, natural man. This image of the Indian before his encounter with the civilization that put him in chains helped European romantic writers to rise above history to the realm of abstract human nature.

When nineteenth-century Spanish American writers rediscovered the Indian, such a rediscovery did not involve

the Indians around them, that is, the poor and exploited
Indian. Rather, it involved the Indians of the French intellectuals; in other words, the virtuous, noble, savage Indian
whom their European mentors first knew through the work
of Bartolomé de Las Casas and Garcilaso de la Vega. As a
consequence of this importation, the Indian of literary creation in nineteenth-century Spanish America was the transformed, rarefied, ahistorical Indian presented in the works
of Voltaire, Rousseau, Saint-Pierre, Chateaubriand, Marmontel, and others. Thus, the real Indian was overlooked by
the Spanish American literary imagination and was largely
supplanted by an imagined Indian—a poetic Indian extracted
from the works of conscientious and pious men. In this importation of the Indian character, the profound cultural dependency of the Spanish American cultural elite during the
nineteenth century is most clearly seen.

This romantic rediscovery of the Indian by Spanish American writers coincided with movements for independence
from Spain; in fact, both political ideology and literary romanticism were mutually reinforcing. The leaders of the revolutionary movement were romantic visionaries who made
the Indian a symbol of their cause. In their manifestos, programs, and personal correspondence, these caudillos evoked
a romantic Indian past; a poem by the Venezuelan patriot
Andrés Bello (1781–1865) is significant:

> Not for long would the Spanish foreigners
> usurp the Kingdom of the Sun,
> nor, in seeing his throne in such disgrace,
> the ghosts of Manco Capac moan.[21]

To reiterate, the wars for independence in Spanish America were led by members of the creole and mestizo elite who
claimed the political and economic power that had always
been in the hands of the Spanish king and his representatives. Ideologically, the wars for independence were fought
with vague notions of liberty, equality, and fraternity that

Spanish American elites had learned from the French Revolution. These revolutionaries advanced the interests of creole and mestizo elites who were guided by tenets of economic liberalism because they found colonial rule fettered their economic development.

The changes in political and economic power that took place during the wars for independence did not, however, substantially change the lot of the majority of the Spanish American people. The Nation became fragmented, largely due to the lack of radical social transformations. Indians, blacks, and the majority of poor mestizos, who had fought the war, gained little or nothing either as a class or an ethnic group. When, in February 1825, Bolívar claimed in Lima that the revolution had broken the Indian's chains, he was carried away by his own rhetoric.[22] In fact, in the transfer of power from the Spanish kings to the local oligarchies, the Indian lost both economically and politically. For, if in the past, the Indian had been exploited, he at least had had the protection of colonial laws that gave him some security for his lands. With the abolition of the legal colonial structure, the Indian was more thoroughly exploited by his new masters who introduced laws aimed at dispossessing him of more of his lands.[23] In the ensuing years, through deception and outright violence, the Indian lost much of his land to creole and upper-class mestizo landlords.

It is important to emphasize that during the period of activity to found a united Spanish America, the Indian was used not only physically as a soldier but symbolically as well. In both cases, he was used to advance the interests of his eventual exploiters. Of course, since real Indians were an indispensable support for the revolutionary armies, the leaders of these revolutions did not ignore the Indian's situation while the fighting was going on. Some steps were taken to better his lot although, more often than not, these steps were ineffective and even counterproductive. After the revolution, when the transfer of power permitted old aristocrats to become presidents of new republics, the Indian was no longer a viable political or military force. And once his symbolic and military role had been exhausted, the interest granted his condition by the elites also began to fade. Thus, the Indian reverted to his position of beast of burden in the eyes of the new Spanish American society.

As political activity to found a united Spanish America gave way to the Dream, so, too, the combination of symbolism and reality, literature and politics, which the Indian represented, gave way to a purely literary romanticism. Significantly, the Argentine Esteban Echeverría (1805–1851) laid the foundation for the romantic literary movement in 1834.[24] That is, the romantic movement achieved a comfortable separation from politics and a degree of cohesiveness as a literary school only when the local oligarchies were secure in their positions of power. The Indian, whose image during the wars of independence supported a call to combat, throughout the rest of the nineteenth century became a purely nostalgic and exotic element in Spanish American letters.

Due to its abstractness and generalities, when the romantic notion of human nature that fostered the brotherhood of mankind was transported from Europe to Spanish America, it enabled the Spanish American writer to disregard the Indian's real situation. As a literary movement, romanticism in Spanish America failed to deal with the Indian's psychology, culture, or objective social position. Bent on proving their national pride, many of the postindependence romantic writers took flight into the Indian's golden past. And by doing so, they idealized the Indian until he was little more than a product of their imagination. In this context, the Ecuadorian writer Juan León Mera (1832–1894) was able to write that "everything indigenous exists as a historic remembrance, and I do not see any inconvenience in its being useful in a poetic work, be it as a principal or secondary theme."[25] There can be little doubt that for the romantic writers the Indian was long since dead. One of the last writers in this tradition, the Uruguayan Juan Zorrilla de San Martín (1855–1931), presents the romantic writers' view of the Indian:

> *He is silent*
> *Silent forever, like time*
> *Like his race,*
> *Like the desert*
> *Like a grave that the dead has abandoned.*[26]

The Indian seemed to be no more than a memory. But if this view could be held with some justification by Argentine or Cuban writers in whose countries the Indian population during the nineteenth century was small and rapidly disappearing, the fact that Juan León Mera was able to share such a view is indicative of the romantic period as a whole—his Andean country Ecuador was one where the majority of the population was Indian.

Two Novels

Novels in the nineteenth century did not seriously explore the socioeconomic factors that were fast corroding Indian cultures and the Indian's efforts to survive as an Indian in Spanish American society. Writers of this period viewed the Indian through charitable eyes, as encased in a golden past, at best; as an exotic and barbaric creature, at worst. To illustrate the nineteenth-century novelist's treatment of the Indian in Spanish America, I discuss two novels that are representative of the epoch. The first, *Cumandá, o un drama entre salvajes* (1879) by León Mera is representative of the romantic novel; the second, *Aves sin nido* (1889) by the Peruvian Clorinda Matto de Turner, represents the turning point from nineteenth-century romanticism to twentieth-century realism.[27]

Cumandá

León Mera's *Cumandá* is one of the best nineteenth-century Indian novels in Spanish America. León Mera himself was a very active political figure in Ecuador, where he was a militant in the conservative party; he was an ardent supporter of Gabriel García Moreno, who governed Ecuador (1860–1875) with an iron fist and the blessings of the Catholic Church. A devout Catholic himself, León Mera often found himself a defender of the faith and at odds with his compatriot and contemporary, Juan Montalvo (1832–1889), an influential nineteenth-century liberal leader in Ecuador.

León Mera's style was impeccable and seldom out of control (he founded the Academy of the Spanish Language in Ecuador) but yet always in tune with the literary canons of the romantic school that had influenced him. He had always been interested in the Indian as a literary theme and before *Cumandá* had written long poetic works dealing with the subject (*La virgen del sol,* 1861; *Las melodías indígenas,* 1865). But it was with *Cumandá* that he became the clear representative of the nineteenth-century romantic writer in Spanish America.

The plot of *Cumandá* is simple. In 1790, the family of José Domingo Orozco perishes at the hands of Indians who, tired of the innumerable injustices committed against them by the landlord, rise up in rebellion and set fire to the landlord's house. The destruction of Orozco's hacienda is almost total, and only he and his son Carlos are able to escape the assault. Desperate and spiritually exhausted, Orozco leaves his hacienda to seek solace as a priest in a Dominican order. Several years later, Orozco seizes the opportunity to travel as a missionary to the Ecuadorian jungle accompanied by his son, Carlos, now a poet. Once in the jungle, Carlos meets a beautiful Indian girl, Cumandá, with whom he falls in love. Carlos writes poems to her, and after some surreptitious meetings, the lovers are discovered by Cumandá's family, which does not approve of the relationship. There follow several attempts on Carlos's life, who escapes unharmed thanks to Cumandá's timely interventions.

Cumandá's father, Tongana, confronted by her determination, decides to offer her in marriage to the chief of the tribe, the formidable Yawarmaqui. Yawarmaqui accepts and plans to marry Cumandá and expel Carlos from his territory. Before Yawarmaqui can marry Cumandá, however, his tribe is attacked by a neighboring one, and he is mortally wounded. He decides to carry out the marriage ceremony anyway, but he dies on his wedding night. At his death, the Indians must perform a ritual in which the chief's most beloved wife is poisoned so that she may accompany her husband on his travels in the afterlife.

Realizing that she is the one to be sacrificed, Cumandá escapes from the tribe to the nearby Christian settlement where Orozco is a missionary. The Indians of her tribe follow her and demand that Orozco return her so that the ritual may be performed. They inform Orozco that Carlos is their prisoner and they are seeking an exchange. While Orozco broods over the problem, Cumandá escapes and gives herself up in order to save Carlos's life. Realizing this, Orozco follows the fugitive and finds his son tied to a tree; he also finds the dying Tongana being attended by his wife. Orozco liberates his son and notices a leather bag that Cumandá had tied around Carlos's neck before she was taken to be sacrificed. Orozco opens the bag to find a gold locket and the picture of his dead wife. He asks Tongana's wife for an explanation, and she confesses that she is, in fact, Orozco's former servant who had saved Orozco's daughter, Julia, from the assault 18 years before. She had found refuge in the jungle from the government forces that carried out a bloody repression after the uprising. Orozco and his son hurry to save Cumandá from sacrifice, but it is too late: They find her dead body at the feet of Yawarmaqui. "Ay, my daughter!" exclaims Orozco; "ay, my sister!" exclaims Carlos. A few months later, Carlos dies of grief, and Orozco returns to the monastery.

In this novel, the influence of French romanticism, especially Chateaubriand, is in full force. *Cumandá* reads very much like Chateaubriand's *Atala,* and the Rousseauian melancholic reflections while contemplating nature that permeate *Atala* are also evident in *Cumandá.* At the sight of the grandeur of Nature, for example, man realizes "how small, impotent, and miserable" he really is. His soul feels "oppressed by an undefinable and powerful grief," and he is forced to grasp "the truth of his momentary existence and his sad predicament in the world."[28]

It is no accident that León Mera's romanticism forced him to transport his drama from the white world where it begins to the jungle where the Indians live isolated from that world (the title itself indicates this intention). For had León Mera developed his plot around the Indian in the white world, he could hardly have idealized him as he did, since there the Indian lived exploited and oppressed by the conquering culture. Removing the drama from reality to an exotic place freed the author from the burden of dealing with the Indian's unfortunate conditions.[29] Instead of depicting the real Indian, which would have required a thorough analysis of the socioeconomic structure of Ecuadorian society, León Mera gives his readers a unidimensional picture of the Indian, a surface rendition of the world where the Indian is encased in beautiful plumage, war paint, and exotic jewelry. No attempt is made to penetrate the Indian's psychology, and the Indian is presented through clichés learned from the writer's European mentors.

León Mera's ardent Catholicism also permeates his work. In contrast to nearly all indigenista novels of the twentieth century, the priest is presented in *Cumandá* as a dedicated, humanitarian, and gentle individual, true to his calling. It is the priest alone who faces the task of helping the "ferocious animals who look like men"[30] and bringing them the light of civilization. Father José Domingo Orozco, former landlord and now devoted missionary, does not heed his son Carlos's warnings that their delay could cost Cumandá's life. Orozco calmly proceeds to administer the last rites to his old enemy, the Indian Tongana. Once Orozco has seen the Indian expire with the help of the sacrament, he exclaims, "I have saved a soul perhaps at the cost of my daughter's life!"[31] a supreme sacrifice in the name of the Christian god.

León Mera was not oblivious to the Indian's need for help; like other romantic writers, he stands within the Spanish American tradition of the writer as social critic. His demand for change is, however, based squarely on the Catholic notion of charity as exemplified by the missionary work of Father Orozco. The white man has the duty, León Mera argues, of Christianizing and thereby civilizing the savages, to incorporate them into national life where their lot would be bettered.[32] His call for change is limited to incorporating the Indian into civilization and does not include an analysis of the situation of the Indians who had already been incorporated into civilization and lived as virtual slaves to the white men.

Aves Sin Nido

While León Mera was writing in Ecuador, Peru was engaged in a war against its southern neighbor, Chile. The Pacific War, which lasted four years (1879–1883), turned out to be a very costly affair for Peru, which was defeated and occupied by Chilean forces. When Chile finally retreated after occupying Lima for three years (1881–1883), Peru had lost its southernmost province to the Chileans.

The total civil and military defeat of Peru during the war left the task of understanding its causes to Peruvian intellectuals. Outstanding among them was an aristocrat and leader of the iconoclasts and freethinkers of Peru, Manuel Gonzáles Prada (1844–1918). Initially influenced by scientific positivism and an anarchist in his old age, Gonzáles

Prada blamed Peruvian defeat on the utter inability of the governing elite to lead the nation to victory and, perhaps most importantly, on unjust social conditions to which this elite had subjected the majority of the population, the Indians. How could the Indian soldier, he asked, march to victory against an enemy he did not know in order to defend an enemy he *did* know, namely, the Peruvian governing class? How could this class expect the Indian to fight for a country of which he had no conception because he was isolated and exploited in his isolation, with no rights of citizenship at all?

These reflections forced Gonzáles Prada to reveal the existence of an Indian problem beneath the seemingly placid Peruvian highlands. And once he had uncovered the real Indian, he established himself as the Indian's defender. He defended the Indian with his poetry, his inflammatory oratory in the intellectual circles of Lima, and numerous essays in which he showed himself to be Peru's master of irony, wit, and intellect. However, although he sometimes advocated a violent solution to the Indian problem, he never developed a coherent and socioeconomically grounded solution. His role in Peruvian culture was not that of a builder but a destroyer. He took on the task of destroying such myths as the romantic Indian, which he believed was part of a hypocritical posture on the part of the ruling class.

Among Gonzáles Prada's famous disciples was Matto, the author of *Aves sin nido*. She was born Clorinda Matto Usandivaras in 1854 in Cuzco, the ancient capital of the Incan empire in the highlands of Peru, and educated in a teachers' college in Cuzco, where she married an English physician, Joseph Turner. Matto was an admirer of the great Peruvian writer and historian, Ricardo Palma (1833–1899) from whom she borrowed the style used in her early literary pieces.

Influenced by Gonzáles Prada, who saw the Indian exploited by what he called the trinity of terror (the priest, the landlord, and the government representative) and in need of redemption, Matto decided to write a novel in which she could present the Indian's condition as she had experienced it in her native Cuzco and surrounding areas. The result was *Aves sin nido*, a romantic indictment against the unnatural life of the clergy, the abusive acts government officials committed against the Indian, and the scars left on the Indian by mestizaje.

Aves sin nido is one of those novels that attained fame on its own merits as well as by the infamous acts committed against its author. In a gesture of resistance, Catholic powers in Peru attempted to neutralize Matto's message and influence by a show of force: The author was excommunicated from the Church and the novel burned in public. Matto was ridiculed and ostracized by the decent people of Lima and finally expatriated by the Catholic dictator Nicolas de Piérola (1895–1899); she died in exile in Buenos Aires, Argentina, in 1909.

As in *Cumandá*, the plot of *Aves sin nido* is simple. Fernando Marín, a wealthy stockholder and general manager of a mining company, arrives with his wife, Lucía, in Killac, a provincial town in the Peruvian highlands. There, Lucía, a warmhearted young woman, is approached for help by Marcela Yupanqui, an Indian woman whose family is being unmercifully exploited by the town's priest and a local businessman. Lucía, touched by Marcela's plight, decides to intercede for her with the priest and local governor, but she fails. Bent on helping the Yupanqui family, Lucía pays off the family's debt to the priest and the businessman.

Lucía's charitable act goes against the custom of the town where priest, governor, and judge live off exploiting the Indians whom they keep in their perpetual debt by extending credit. The Indians are not allowed to settle their accounts, thus the creditors are able to live off the interest on the loans. The town priest and the governor see a threat to their livelihood in Lucía's generosity which they must stop at any cost. They decide to kill the Marín family. Together with the help of other town notables, the priest and the

governor manage to arouse the town against the couple by
spreading rumors that thieves have sought refuge in their
home. The townspeople, now turned into a mob, attack the
Maríns' home in the middle of the night. Marín and his wife
are saved by the timely intervention of a young law student,
Manuel, the son of the local governor himself, who had
returned from Lima on a visit.

Hearing the noise of the battle, Juan Yupanqui and his
wife Marcela run to the aid of their benefactors. Yupanqui
is killed in the assault along with several other Indians, and
his wife is mortally wounded. Marcela is taken into the
Maríns' house where, before dying, she whispers a secret to
Lucía and asks the Maríns to look after her two daughters,
Margarita and Rosalia. Fernando and Lucía agree and make
the two girls their godchildren.

Meanwhile, Manuel, the law student, falls in love with
Margarita when they first meet after the assault; Margarita
returns his love. Their relationship, however, is complicated
by the fact that Manuel happens to be the son of the governor, who is indicated by all the evidence as one of the per-
petrators of the crime against Margarita's parents. To destroy
this barrier, Manuel intimates to Marín, now Margarita's
godfather, that he is really not the governor's son; but he
does not tell him who his real father is. The love between
Margarita and Manuel is allowed to grow.

After many unsuccessful attempts to obtain justice, the
Marín family decides to move out of the town and travel to
Lima, where Margarita is to be educated. Manuel, after
liberating an Indian unjustly charged with attacking the
Marín house, rushes to Lima in order to find Margarita and
ask her godfather for her hand. He arrives in Lima and
discloses the identity of his real father, Pedro de Miranda y
Claro, former priest of Killac, long since deceased. Hearing
this, Margarita is elated; she can now love Manuel freely.
Fernando and Lucía, however, are shocked. They must now
tell the lovers the secret that Marcela told Lucía before
dying: that Margarita's real father was also the priest Pedro

de Miranda y Claro, who had abused Marcela in her youth. Margarita, crying, falls into the arms of her godmother.

Without question, *Aves sin nido* marks the crossroad of the romantic and realistic treatment of the Indian in the Spanish American novel. Matto's novel began an effort to seek the real Indian and see his situation as a national problem. Straddling two radically different orientations, however, she more often than not succumbed to the lure of the romantic. The impossible love between brother and sister, for example, sets *Aves sin nido* in the tradition of *Cumandá*. The characters, especially the Indians, are no more than caricatures and are represented totally from the outside, with little effort to explore their psychology.

Given this romantic orientation in her work, Matto's approach does not lead her to scrutinize the social, political, and economic structures of Peruvian society, about which she makes only vague and general statements. Her analysis and protest are directed at small-town life in the highlands, and these small towns are not seen as microcosms of Peruvian society but basically as exceptional cases within a more just, more enlightened, and more charitable Peru. Her work, therefore, issues an emotional and vehement protest against conditions without basing it on a sober analysis of their causes.

Without grounding her work on a thorough socioeconomic analysis, Matto bases her hopes for the solution to the Indian problem on the good effects of education, which is in turn based on the Catholic concept of charity.[33] This concept, however, was waning in Peru at the turn of the century, especially as expressed in Matto's view, so greatly influenced by Gonzáles Prada's teachings. Such hope, therefore, eventually had to turn into disillusionment. Marín, after learning from Manuel that the Indians in Killac are still being exploited by the trilogy of terror exclaims in defeat, "It is plain, my friend, there is no remedy."[34]

This grasp of the Indian problem and the disillusionment over its solution is indicative of the struggle between the old romantic view of the Indian and the new approach based on a close scrutiny of socioeconomic processes. In this struggle, the concept of the Indian's future is at stake, and in the case of *Aves sin nido*, the old view finally reasserts itself. For, although it seemed clear to Matto, and to many of her contemporaries who were concerned with the Indian's plight, that charity was not the answer, she did not suggest an alternative. It was this predicament that forced her to visualize solutions to the Indian problem as either charity or death. At the end of the novel, Isidro Champi, an Indian unjustly imprisoned and robbed of his few material possessions by the trilogy of terror, repeats the narrator's comment stated some 150 pages earlier: "Death is our sweet hope to liberty!"[35] And here Matto articulates the underlying theme that permeates all subsequent novelistic production in Spanish America: The Indian must die.

There are two themes underlying nineteenth-century romantic novels that are pertinent to a discussion of the indigenista novels themselves: one is the theme of the Indian's passivity; the other, the theme of incorporating the Indian into the mestizo world. As both novels discussed suggest, for the romantic writer, the solution to the Indian problem rests solely on actions taken by whites. Whatever solution there might be, it must be based on charity by the civilized toward the uncivilized. The Indian is portrayed as a passive individual who does not constitute an actual or potential political force; in *Cumandá*, this is expressed by the actions of Father Orozco and, in *Aves sin nido*, by the actions of the Maríns. Secondly, in both novels, the assumption is that the only way for whites to save the Indian from oppression (other than death) is to incorporate him into their world. These views are expressed by the narrator in León Mera's novel and, among other things, by the hopes placed on education in Matto's work.

It is against this background that many indigenista novels (in the Andes, in particular) take form and deliver their message. Other novels (particularly in Mexico) continue in the tradition of Matto to straddle two orientations, although they most often succeed in breaking loose from the lure of the romantic.

Realism

A final point should be made before discussing the social factors that made indigenista novels possible. While Indian novels in the nineteenth century were basically romantic, indigenista novels in the twentieth century were basically realist. This literary rupture, as might be expected, followed in the footsteps of a similar rupture in the European tradition, namely, the broad transformation from romanticism to realism in literature.

European realism arrived in Spanish America in the 1860s. By the time it developed into a significant school there at the turn of the century, its influence in Europe, especially in France, where it had been the strongest, had diminished; nonetheless, the strong influence that French writers had on Spanish American letters during the wars for independence continued under realism. Like Chateaubriand and Marmontel in the romantic period, Balzac and especially Zola became the mentors of Spanish American writers of Indian novels during the realist period.

To be sure, transplanting European realism in Spanish America did not take place without fundamental changes. In Europe, for example, such French writers as Balzac and later Zola shared their eminence with the great realists of Russia, Tolstoy and Dostoyevsky. In Spanish America, the Spanish cultural elite, always fond of French letters, was not decisively influenced by Russian writers. Tolstoy's work, with its heavy dose of mysticism, did not constitute one of the pillars of realism in Spanish America, nor did Dostoyevsky's insights into, and fascination with, psychology gain many followers.

In addition to the Spanish American elite's predilection

for French letters, there were other reasons for the lack of influence by Russian writers. For one thing, at the time realism arrived in Spanish America, the cultural elite was going through a period of optimistic faith in science. And scientific positivism as a philosophy of art or politics was too strong to allow mysticism in Tolstoy's tradition. Influenced by Mexico's positivist thinkers (the científicos) and Peru's Gonzáles Prada, a wave of anticlericalism swept across Spanish America, announcing the age of enlightenment. Instead of mysticism, therefore, it was anticlericalism that later became one of the principal characteristics of the indigenista movement in Spanish America.

The near absence of Tolstoy's influence did not mean, however, that nonscientific concerns were unimportant to the indigenistas; even at the height of the movement, Spanish America's indigenista writers never ceased to preach morality. What happened was that the old individual morality, basically Catholic and mainly concerned with salvation and the soul, gave way to a kind of *social morality* concerned with the Indian's salvation. From the 1860s until at least the 1950s, realists, indigenistas prominent among them, were perhaps the most moral of all writers in Spanish America. In this sense, Zola, and not Balzac, became the true master of indigenismo. From its very inception, indigenismo was engaged in a moral crusade to stamp out the evils of society;[36] literature was a tool for regeneration. This original moral stance of indigenismo survived the demise of its initial ally, scientific positivism, and continued invigorated under Marxist socialism. It is true that socialist writers did not openly call for moral regeneration, nor did they draw their inspiration primarily from a religious conception of the world; nonetheless, a deep moral stance is evident throughout their work. Marxism in the hands of these writers, particularly in the Andes, became the light that showed how to destroy the evils of society. These writers endeavored to liberate man from social sins.

European realism underwent other changes with its introduction in Spanish America; two of these changes were the near absence of pessimism before the evils of society and the negligible treatment of sexual behavior. Spanish American indigenismo, for example, inspired as it was first by scientific positivism and its faith in science and progress and later by socialism based on Marxist thinking, could not have easily become pessimistic. In fact, as Marxism displaced positivism in the 1930s, indigenista literature became even more optimistic, so that the denunciation of social evils was paired, if not with a program, then with a hope for their solution and abolition.

As to the shady side of sexuality, Spanish American elites had not yet thrown away their long cherished *pudor,* their sense of shame. Naturalistic writing on sex was not in good taste; besides, to the indigenista writers, worse than sexual perversion was the corruption of social, political, and economic institutions, the exploitation by the rich of the workers in general, and the Indians in particular. The crudest scenes ever depicted in Spanish American literature up to the middle of the twentieth century were those in Jorge Icaza's *Huasipungo* (1934), a novel about the social, economic, political, and spiritual exploitation of Indians by the ruling classes in Ecuador. The Indians in this novel appear almost subhuman, with the result that such a presentation is an indictment against the ruling classes, which are portrayed as greedy and morally corrupt.

Perhaps the best way to characterize the changes in perspective that accompanied the shift from romanticism to realism in Indian novels is to view them as obeying different gestalts. On the one hand, the romantics view Spanish America as a country composed of beautiful and unexplored landscapes, noble and savage Indians, and heroes who die romantic deaths; in short, according to this view, Spanish America is suspended in an ideal world. The realist school, on the other hand, depicts a society led by a morally bankrupt elite supported by a corrupt military machine and clergy, all of whom live off the Indian's labor. According to this view, Spanish America is divided into a wealthy and corrupt minority and a sick, exploited, hungry, and dehumanized majority. To the indigenista writer, especially under the influence of Marxism, Spanish America had a long history of corruption and oppression; however, deliverance is foreshadowed, that is, the solution and transcendence of evil in the future.

Chapter Three

The Rise of the Andean Indigenista Novel

You will go to feed them; you will put on their clothing, use their hats; you will speak their language. But their actions will be actions of discord.

—Chilam Balam

Social Conditions
of the Indians:
1900–1950

Until the middle of this century, the Indian in the Andes lived primarily in the highlands and engaged almost entirely in agriculture. The Inca empire had been an agricultural society that was able to maintain itself due largely to its communal form of land tenure. With the arrival of the Spanish, this system was abolished, and the Indian was forced to work for the white man, while retaining less and less of his land. With the advent of the republican period 300 years later, the Indian lost more of the land he still held, so that by the 1900s most of the available land in the Andean highlands was held by a few white and mestizo landlords. The Indian was left to make a living from the small, unproductive plots he was able to retain.

As a subsistence farmer, the Indian's situation was precarious; a single year's drought or crop failure could affect the livelihood of an entire family or even an entire community. Given this situation, sometimes as a precaution but more often when already confronted with a bad year, the Indian was forced to supplement his income in the only other way possible in the highlands: as a peon on a nearby hacienda. This search for alternative sources of income, mainly to prevent starvation, pushed the Indian into disadvantageous economic relations with the landlord. Although not all Indians were forced into such relations, at the beginning of this century and continuing until at least the 1950s, most Indians had to maintain these relations. Consequently, most Indians suffered severe economic, political, and social constraints imposed on them by the landlord.[1]

There were various ways that the landlord set up his economic relations with the Indians: He rented plots of land to Indians for cash; he retained Indians as sharecroppers (with one-half of the crops usually going to the landlord); or he rented use-rights to Indians, such as water and irrigation, pasture, timber, rights of trespass, and so on, for which they paid with labor. These economic arrangements were usually carried out by members of Indian communities or towns whose lands, pastures, water supply, and wooded areas were not sufficient to maintain their already low standard of living.

It might appear that in these cases the Indian entered freely into economic relations that he could terminate at his convenience. However, since land was the primary source not only of food but of general income for the Indian, merely threatening not to rent a plot of land, grant use-rights or permission to sharecrop was used to obtain the Indian's compliance in social and political matters. Such compliance might involve maintaining a system of water distribution that favored the landlord, political demonstrations for the landlord or his candidate for congress, or supporting specific legislation in local politics. The supposedly free Indian was, in fact, under the landlord's control.

There was also another form of labor relation between landlord and Indian: debt-peonage. In this arrangement, the landlord gave propertyless Indians a plot of land for their own use and their homesteads, together with other advances, such as seeds, tools, building materials, or small amounts of cash. In return, the Indian was to pay off the debt by working for the landlord farming and herding and as a personal servant at extremely low wages or for food rations. This arrangement involved not only the head of the family but all of its members. The number of days each week that the peon and other members of his family had to work for the landlord varied form one to four but sometimes included the entire week. In addition to his labor, the peon was required to furnish his own animals for work done on the landlord's property.

The basis of this arrangement was the peon's inability to pay back the landlord's initial advances. Besides the fact that the peon's salary for his work was extremely low, he was seldom paid in cash but rather in goods from the landlord's store at prices set by the landlord himself. And in addition to the peon's original debt, there were fines incurred for his failure to carry out stipulated duties or assessments made against him for loss of animals or tools. When the peon died, his debt was transferred to his children and was thus handed down from generation to generation, making the peon a virtual slave of the landlord. The landlord, aided by the local police or the military, would not permit peons or their families to leave the hacienda until all debt was paid off; such practices afforded the landlord a stable and cheap labor force.

During the first half of this century, especially in the first three decades, the Indian in the Andes was subjected to other forms of forced labor, which were basically variations of the colonial mita and were just as detrimental for the Indian population. One of these variations was the so-called voluntary labor requested by national or local governments to construct roads and public buildings. This voluntary labor was obtained from Indians who were rounded up by the police and forced to march in groups from their villages to construction sites in distant towns or alongside national roads. The Indians thus forced to work were seldom paid or fed and died in large numbers due to accidents, inclement weather, or sheer exhaustion.

A second form of forced labor was the patriotic labor required by the state's military institutions, particularly the army. This involved using soldiers, most of whom were Indians, to construct roads in remote places as part of their obligatory military service of about two years. Through this practice, the state was able to build roads using cheap labor, and the army obtained some justification for its existence in times of peace.

In the first half of this century, Indian labor was the basis of private wealth as well as Andean solvency; in fact, forced Indian labor was an indispensable part of the socioeconomic structure of Andean societies. Given the Indian's position in the labor force and the fact that he was exploited by priests, landlords, local and national government officials, and other members of the white society and culture, for all practical purposes, the Indian was not truly a citizen with recognized rights under the law.

Indian Communities

The most important factor underlying the Indian's social, economic, and political conditions in the Andes has been Indian labor; however, not all Indians worked under these conditions. A significant portion of the Indian population managed to survive, partially sheltered from oppression by an ancient institution—the ayllu, or Indian community. Within the ayllu, Indians carried on a life more in tune with their ancient customs. This institution played a significant role in the indigenista writer's efforts to depict the Indian's world in the twentieth century.

Latin Americanist Carlos A. Astiz wrote in 1969 that the history of the Peruvian highlands could best be described as "the struggle for land between the landowner and the Indian communities, a struggle that the landowner has been consistently winning."[2] The same can be said of the entire Andean region, and as previous discussions suggest, the outcome of the struggle could not have been otherwise, since landowners had all the advantages. Despite the tremendous odds against Indian communities, they were, however, able to survive; by the 1950s, in Peru alone, there were approximately 4,500 Indian communities, of which the government recognized about 1,500.[3]

These scattered communities offered the highlands Indian an alternative to debt-peonage. To be sure, more often than not, the land in these communities was not as good as the land the Indian had lost to the landlord. Driven out by

the landlord's expanding haciendas, Indian communities had
to establish themselves in the hills, where access was difficult, and land erosion and irrigation always a problem. The
Indian leaders of these communities often used Indian labor
to enhance their personal wealth, or, alternatively, they
placed additional burdens on their fellow Indians in order to
maintain the integrity of communal lands.[4] But if life for the
Indian who lived in the community was not comfortable, it
was at least bearable. Within his community, the Indian
managed to eke out a living from the communal property,
procuring at least minimal shelter and food.

Certainly, the benefits of communal living for the Indian
could not be measured only in terms of his ability to achieve
a modicum of physical security. The psychological traumas
suffered by Indians at the hands of the conquering culture
were neither so many nor so extreme for those living in
communities as for Indians who, having lost their land, lived
in virtual slavery as debt-bound peons. A peon was, in fact,
often uprooted from his residence to herd the landlord's
cattle, transported great distances and for long periods of
time during harvest, or rented to the landlord's family or
friends in distant cities. Without communal support in times
of need, the debt-bound peon suffered alone the effects of
uncertainty about his future. The Indian who lived in a
community, on the other hand, at least had a sense of belonging; he shared a similiar culture and history with fellow
members of the community.

"Placing a high social value upon hard labor is clearly
an Indian cultural trait in the Andes," argues Henry F.
Dobyns.[5] And, if this characterization applies to all Indians in
the Andes, it is particularly true of Indians living in communities who still view the labor process as did their ancestors
—that is, as communal labor. While the peon had to labor
for other men with no hope of justly sharing in the product of his efforts, an Indian in a community labored for
himself and the welfare of that community. The high value
placed on physical labor by the Indian in the Andes was only

enhanced by the Indian's pride in his community's accomplishments. In the eyes of many indigenista novelists, this particular Indian custom of communal living formed one of the pillars on which rested the Indian's liberation and the advent of a new society in the Andes.

Indian Liberationist Movements

Given the nature of the Indian's life in the Andes, it is not surprising that he constantly rebelled against his white and mestizo masters. The history of the Andes, like that of Spanish America in general, shatters the common view of the Indian as passive and stoic in his misery. The fact that due to a lack of efficient organization and military equipment the Indian has never been able to overthrow the white-dominated sociopolitical structure in the Andes masks his constant militancy for a better life. And he has paid dearly for this struggle: Bloody repressions (*escarmientos*) by the military that began with the conquest continue in the present. The tragedy of these escarmientos in the Andes is still largely untold.[6]

Perhaps the best-known example of escarmiento in the Andes was carried out against Tupac Amaru II in 1781, a few years before the wars for independence. He had called for a general Indian rebellion to free his people from the extreme oppression of colonial rule, and after initial successses, he was defeated. All members of his extended family were methodically and publicly executed as part of the official policy to eliminate future Indian leadership.[7] A century later, Indian children still shuddered at the thought of having their own heads or those of family members mounted on the end of a spear at the entrance to their village.

A century later, in 1885, the Indian leader Attusparia led his followers in open rebellion against the central government from Huaraz, northern Peru. The reasons for the rebellion were basically the same: onerous acts by the prefect of the time (Noriega), heavy taxes, military contribution, demands for free Indian service for road construction and the upkeep of the city, and the general mistreatment of Indians throughout the region. Attusparia was successful in enlisting Indians for a general uprising in the north of the country, but he was finally defeated by military reinforcements sent from Lima. The bloody escarmiento that followed is still remembered in northern Peru.

Other Indian liberative movements took place in Ilave and Huanta provinces during the presidency of Piérola around 1896. On this occasion, González Prada accused Piérola of putting down the revolt with merciless butchery. Other movements followed later in Huancané, Azángaro, La Mar, Ayacucho, Puno. . . . As the last indigenista novel of the Andes was being written in 1963, Indians from central Peru were once again taking up arms to free themselves from oppression. But this time, too, the revolutionary movement failed, and the Indian paid the consequences, as the military, with the aid of foreign experts, eliminated Indian men, women, and children for a lesson to be remembered.

It is important to stress that philanthropic, liberal, and socialist solutions to Indian problems all followed rather than preceded the Indian liberative movements. That is, efforts by white and mestizo social reformers were in response to Indian rebellions—rebellions that were interpreted according to the reformers' own interests and future plans.

The Writer's Sociocultural Milieu: 1900–1950

The extremely poor living conditions of Indians in the Andes constituted necessary but not sufficient grounds for the rise of the indigenista novel; after all, these conditions had existed in the Andes since at least the times of conquest. It was only when these conditions were viewed by writers from the perspective of early twentieth-century sociocultural developments in the region that the indigenista novel was possible.

The Indianista Period: 1883–1917

In Chapter 2, Matto's novel *Aves sin nido* was situated at the crossroad of romanticism and realism, and it was noted that she did not have a clear alternative to philanthropy as a means of solving the Indian problem. Sociocultural developments during and following the publication of her novel played out Matto's predicament on a larger scale. The years between the end of the War of the Pacific in 1883 and the outbreak of World War I in 1917 saw the rise and decline of liberal-philanthropic efforts to ameliorate the Indian's condition. In order to distinguish efforts to solve the Indian problem during this period from the indigenista movement, I refer to the former as the *indianista* period.[8]

During the War of the Pacific, Indians in Peru and Bolivia were hunted down by the police, inducted into the army, and sent to the front lines as cannon fodder. Many of these recruits had no knowledge about the nature of the war; some believed it involved General Chile fighting against General Peru. These Indians often died of hunger or illness on the battlefields. In protest against this tragic fiasco, Gonzáles Prada pointed his accusing finger at the Peruvian elite; other leaders, too, questioned the Indian's lot in the region. When General Luís Carranza (a physician, geographer, politician, writer, and soldier, 1843–1898), for example, retreated with some of his forces to the Peruvian highlands after the Chilean occupation of Lima, he founded newspapers and used them to denounce the Indian's exploitation by landlords and priests. His writings became known and were highly influential in the Andes.[9] Thanks to these and similar efforts, the Indian question once again became a political issue.

After the war, these initial steps were further developed by positivist thinkers who cast a new light on the Indian problem by encouraging a scientific discussion of Andean culture. Indian cultural accomplishments, therefore, ceased to be a tabooed subject. Not surprisingly, the primary reason for this change was Europeans whose respective disciplines lent prestige, in the eyes of the "Europhile" Andean elite, to the subject. The work of Italian geographer Antonio Raimondi, for example, aroused interest in the natural resources of the region; the German archeologist Max Uhle suggested new areas in the study of Andean culture. Americans, too, contributed to this cultural effervescence: Hiram Bingham, for example, awakened interest in pre-Columbian Andean civilization, and Philip Ainsworth Means led the scientific discussion of ancient Peruvian art.

Following these and other foreign scientists, Peruvians began discussing the problems of the area in a new way, if not entirely according to scientific canons, certainly with a critical edge. As in so many other issues, foremost among the intellectuals establishing a new view of the Indian and his environment was Gonzáles Prada. He argued for an explanation of social phenomena in terms of race, milieu, and historic period (*raza, medio, momento*). Mariano Cornejo wrote a *General Sociology* (1908) exalting Spencer's theories; the book was well regarded in academic circles. Víctor Andrés Belaunde wrote treatises lamenting the lack of knowledge about Peruvian reality and urging young intellectuals to begin studying Peru with the modern methods of the social sciences. All this does not mean that the Indian had found in the followers of positivism enthusiastic allies to his cause; on the contrary, in most of Spanish America, including the Andes, positivism as a political philosophy was often highly

detrimental to the Indian because it encouraged racist attitudes. (This was the case with even the first indigenista novelist of the Andes, Alcides Arguedas.) But what positivism
did was to suggest Indian culture as a respectable area for
study. Later generations were to use the investigations encouraged by these positivists with the well-being of the
Indian clearly in mind.

In this general intellectual effervescence, there emerged
in Peru a pro-Indian organization (Asociación Pro-Indígena)
founded in 1908 by the philanthropist Pedro Zulen and his
wife Dora Mayer de Zulen. The declared purpose of the
association was to defend the social interests of the Indian in
Peru. The association set up branches across the country
and received reports from the smallest provinces. Despite
its impressive initial development, however, the association
was short-lived; due to the illness of Pedro Zulen, the association lasted only until 1915. Clearly, the major weakness
of the association lay in its completely personal and paternal
nature; so much so that as the leader became incapable of
assuming his responsibilities the rest of the organization collapsed.

The Pro-Indian Association was symbolic of indianismo in
general; it based its approach on the Catholic concept of
charity and the liberal notion of due process as a solution to
the Indian problem. Thanks to this organization, the Peruvian legal code was extended to include new laws protecting
the rights of Indians. But like the Laws of the Indies centuries earlier, these laws became dead letters as soon as they
were written because no realistic provisions were made for
their implementation. With the dissolution of the Asociación
Pro-Indígena in 1915, the liberal-philanthropic attempt to
solve the Indian problem ended. To be sure, this did not
mean that the Indian problem was forgotten altogether;
on the contrary, the Indian and his problems occupied a
greater and greater place in the consciousness of the cultural
elite of the region. But already by the 1920s, the liberal-
philanthropic approach was being replaced by a socialist ap-

proach that became increasingly militant; in other words, indianismo was being replaced by indigenismo.

With the demise of the Asociación Pro-Indígena and following in the footsteps of writers like Gonzáles Prada, Matto, and Carranza, there emerged in Peru the famed *Colonida* generation. The first issues of the periodical *Colonida*, from which the movement took its name, appeared in January 1916; among its contributors were such prominent men of letters as its founder Abraham Valdelomar, the poet José Santos Chocano, the novelist César Falcón, and the young social critic José Carlos Mariátegui. The movement was anticolonial in nature: It condemned the Spanish past and exalted a romanticized Incan period; it attacked the established academic circles of Lima as decadent and exalted the provincial culture and popular Indian and mestizo customs and practices.[10]

But despite its strident rhetoric, or perhaps because of it, the *Colonida* generation's concern with the Indian was basically literary and almost touristic. The denunciation of perceived Indian problems followed along rhetorical lines established by González Prada, who never carried out a sober socioeconomic analysis of the Indian's situation but, instead, based his denunciations at first on a deep sense of morality and later on anarchistic principles. It is not surprising that Mariátegui, who did carry out the necessary analysis, eventually left the movement and attacked it as hopelessly romantic and naïvely liberal.

In literature, indianismo, the exotic, decorative view of the Indian and his culture, was retained in the Andes until about 1930. Some writers were clearly influenced by archeologic works mentioned earlier, and in their efforts to revive Indian legends, they wrote historic novels set during Incan times. Perhaps the best example of this type of novel is Augusto Aguirre-Morales's *El pueblo del sol* (1925), which relates the fate of a local noble who attempts to rebel against the great Incan empire but fails. Other writers produced exotic works based on their short experiences among the

Indians; for example, Ventura García Calderón's *La venganza del condor* (1924) and Enrique López Albújar's *Cuentos andinos* (1920) and *Nuevos cuentos andinos* (1937) are exotic short stories written about Indians during this period. The influence of these indianista writers on liberal indigenista novels is apparent.

The Student Movement: 1918–1930

In the last years of the nineteenth century and the early years of the twentieth, the liberal ideas shared by such leading intellectuals as Prada and the Ecuadorian Juan Montalvo coincided with the development of modern capitalism in the Andean countries. During this period, which may be considered a period of gestation for the indigenista novel, small industry was beginning to take hold, especially in the coastal regions and around major cities. During this time also, mining industries began opening their doors to foreign capital. In contrast to the traditional capitalist system, based primarily on land ownership, there arose throughout the Andes a bourgeoisie composed of small entrepreneurs and members of the professions.

The rising bourgeoisie soon realized that all political power was controlled by a tightly organized oligarchy that had governed the Andes since the early days of independence. Finding it necessary to develop a political and ideological base from which to advance their own economic interests, the bourgeoisie used scientific positivism as their primary ideological weapon against this oligarchy. Under the aegis of scientific positivism, with its faith in science and progress, rationalism (in the Weberian sense) became the basis of the growing bourgeoisie's attack and defense. Rationalist principles were pitted against a system based on quasi-feudal economic relations between a landlord and his peons, a system whose ideological support was largely drawn from the now ailing conservative Catholicism.

The drive for political power on the part of the Andean

bourgeoisie expressed itself most clearly in their fight to control the universities. By the second decade of this century, the bourgeoisie had succeeded in opening up university education, once the privilege of a very few, to eager young men and women from larger sectors of the population. But if the nature of the student cohorts had changed by this time, the universities as institutions had changed very little; on entering, the new students found themselves inside a quasi-medieval system of higher education. Professors' appointments followed the dictates of personal influence and purity of doctrine (usually Catholic and conservative); required courses had little, and sometimes nothing, to do with preparing for the future as an engineer or medical doctor, and so forth. Confronted with these realities, the new students undertook an increasingly critical appraisal of the universities, examining their internal organization and their role in society. Armed with liberal ideas, these students concentrated on destroying the universities' isolation from the larger society. The ivory tower was to be toppled. This critical appraisal resulted in a series of fullfledged student rebellions, a phenomenon that has been present ever since in the Andes.[11]

At first, the issues at stake in these rebellions were purely academic; that is, they involved issues central to university life. But the students soon left the universities to take their demands to the streets. Since the universities reflected the lingering power of the traditional elites, this development was not unexpected. Any solution to the universities' problems had to come from the society at large, where the battle between the rising bourgeoisie and the landed oligarchy was being conducted. As one student cohort succeeded another, the positions taken by student organizations were radicalized. By the 1920s, powerful socialist groups had developed alongside liberal organizations. This process of radicalization, clearly affected by the Mexican and Soviet Revolutions, reached its peak in the 1930s. By this time, students were not willing to confine their militant posture to the university campuses; they now questioned the social, political, and economic organization of society as a whole.

In succeeding years, student organizations more openly became adherents of direct political and military action. In 1930, for example, Bolivian President Hernando Siles (1928–1930) was overthrown with the help of students at the military college. Bolivian students also helped in overthrowing President Gualberto Villarroel (1943–1946); this time, they attacked police headquarters and used the confiscated arms to assert their demands. In Ecuador, students intervened decisively in the revolution of 1944, and in Peru, students have participated actively in labor disputes and political crises.

As far as the Indian is concerned, the students presented themselves as pitted against landlord, priest, political functionary, and military leader. They stood for the people and often exhorted the Indian to assert his rights, to turn his attention to his socialist past. But if student rebellions affected the life of the middle classes, their impact on the Indian's life was minimal. In the eyes of the Indian, students continued to be members of the white or mestizo world; they remained little patrones who would eventually confront him as judges, priests, or government functionaries. Furthermore, since universities in the Andes were located in large urban centers, they were hardly a part of the world of the Indian, whose education was minimal, if he had any at all. Thus, when the reform movement shook the foundation of the universities, the Indian hardly noticed. And when more radical students spoke to the Indian about his socialist past and socialism in general, the Indian listened but often did not believe and seldom acted on the students' advice. It was not until the late 1950s that the Indian began to see in the student a leader and not a patrón. This change of attitude took place only when a growing number of students spoke the Indians' language, lived among them, and knew their culture. But even to this day, student leaders have not gained the Indian's full trust.

The gulf separating Indian and student was not due solely to the Indian's reticence. Until recently, intellectuals in general tended to view the Indian from their position as members of a cultural elite. These intellectuals—be they socialist, communist, or liberal—wanted to lead the Indian, but to lead him according to *their* own concept of justice and social, economic, and political processes. Few of these intellectuals tried to learn the Indian's views on these issues. In many ways, theirs was the role of the little patrón who wished to save the Indian from the big patrón, and the Indian was to be saved in spite of himself. This relationship between Indians and intellectuals was maintained and depicted in the indigenista novel in the Andes.

Two Revolutions

The student movement coincided with two great revolutions: the Mexican Revolution (1910–1940) and the Soviet Revolution of 1917. The outcome of these two revolutions decisively influenced the Andean cultural elite. The immediate influence of the Mexican Revolution on the radical wing of the cultural elites in the Andes is hard to assess. Because of its long duration, it overlapped with the Russian Revolution and shared its limelight. Ideologically, Mexico's example was in many ways overshadowed by the Soviet Revolution. In terms of political thought, for example, what in Mexico was haphazard presented itself in the October Revolution as a theoretical and ideological whole. For in their long struggle, the leaders of the Mexican Revolution did not follow a coherent ideology. In fact, most of the leaders of the Mexican Revolution were passing figures who articulated the ideas of a revolutionary moment that was soon followed by another. As a consequence, Mexican leaders lacked a unified vision of the future; the nationalist stance common to all revolutionaries of this period offered them only provisional and precarious unity. The passing revolutionary leaders sensed that the future of Mexico was at stake, but they were unable to direct the energies unleashed by the revolution to develop stable nationwide social, political, and economic organizations. Abstract unity in terms of national pride and honor gave way when leaders were confronted with actual policy implementation to internal struggles for power that lasted over 30 years with more or less violent results.

In contrast to the Mexican Revolution, the Soviet Revolution was viewed by young intellectuals in Andean countries as a successful revolution and a paradigm as well. Once Lenin had triumphed, he was able to claim that there was only one true revolution, a socialist revolution and that there was only one way to reach it, through the guidance of the community party, which based its strategy on the Marxist philosophy of historic materialism. Also contrary to the leaders of the Mexican Revolution, the Soviets regarded their revolution as a spearhead for further socialist revolutions that would eventually transform man's life. This is to say, the October Revolution had clear international overtones, and its triumph echoed around the world, the Andes included.

But for all this, the Russian Revolution did not totally overshadow the Mexican experience; it only complemented it. This was possible because while the Spanish American intellectual regarded the Russian Revolution as paradigmatic in terms of political theory and revolutionary strategy, its protagonists, the people who carried out the revolution, were seen as remote and even exotic. The Russian peasant, for example, was a man known only through the works of Tolstoy, Gogol, and other Russian writers, and not through first-hand experience. A predilection for Western European culture had prevented the Spanish American intellectual from discovering the Eastern world. The Andean radical wing of the cultural elite, in particular, was virtually ignorant of the land of the Soviets.

By contrast, the Mexican Indian and mestizo revolutionaries were very close to home; Mexico resembled the

Andean countries in terms of language, culture, and ethnic composition. What the Mexican Revolution had made clear to the Andean intellectual was that the Indian and mestizo in rural areas could be led to victory in a revolution. And it was clear that a revolution without a strong ideological unity would falter as had the Mexican Revolution. With proper guidance, however, these intellectuals saw the Indian as the determined soldier, the potential revolutionary who was stirring in the rural areas of the Andean region.

The image of the Indian as a potential revolutionary force made sense in terms of political practice as well. For, while the Marxist-Leninist path to successful revolution demanded the full participation of a strong proletariat, Spanish America, and especially the Andean countries, had only a very small and unorganized urban population, with very few potential proletarian strongholds. The bulk of the population was agricultural and lived in rural areas; any hope for a successful revolution, therefore, had to include the Indian as the spearhead of the movement. These considerations prompted socialists in Andean countries to follow the theoretical lead of the Russian Revolution while, at the same time, taking the Mexican experience seriously, especially the role of the peasant in that movement.

It is important to emphasize here that discovering the revolutionary potential of the Indian did not stem from a purely Marxist interpretation of Spanish American reality. Mexico's influence seems to have been, at least initially, a major impetus toward viewing the Indian as a potential revolutionary force. Besides, the Indian problem in Andean countries had been studied and its solutions sought along radical lines long before the inception of the first socialist parties. Gonzáles Prada's analysis, for example, although superficial, prompted him to advocate violence as the only means of solving the problem.[12] Luís Carranza wrote along the same lines, and the failure of the Pro-Indian Association had encouraged many liberals to seek more radical solutions.

This is not to say, however, that both socialists and liberals saw the Indian problem and its solutions within the same analytic framework. What it means is that the difference between liberal and socialist thinkers did not lie in the centrality or noncentrality of the Indian problem to the overall solution of social problems in Andean countries. Their differences lay rather in their approach to the Indian problem and the solutions offered. Both liberals and socialists agreed that in order to solve the problems of these countries it was necessary to solve the Indian problem and, conversely, that the Indian problem could not be solved without restructuring societies at large. Liberals, however, took a moderate approach and wanted the Indian to be allowed to vote, to have access to education, and to participate in a liberal political process. Socialists, on the other hand, took a radical position and bade the Indian to abolish the liberal system itself and return to the ancient practice of communal living.

Two Andean Leaders

Student rebellions and the first two great revolutions of this century deeply affected the sociocultural development of the Andes. As would be expected, however, the nature of the influence varied according to the people and groups affected. This can be seen most clearly in the lives and work of two great Spanish American leaders, Víctor Raúl Haya de la Torre and José Carlos Mariátegui.[13]

Haya de la Torre (1895–1978) came from an old and respected family in northern Peru. His own home environment impressed on him at an early age the meaning of foreign penetration; in fact his own family's fortune experienced a reversal due to the expansion of Gildemeister interests in and around Trujillo, Haya de la Torre's native city. While a student at the University of Trujillo, Haya de la Torre was strongly influenced by the works of Gonzáles Prada. A few years later, he and Mariátegui, then a close friend, were received and taught by Gonzáles Prada himself in his own home. In Lima, Haya de la Torre became a popular student leader and collaborated with Mariátegui in publicizing the demands of the student movement in the pages of *La razón*, a periodical founded by Mariátegui and César Falcón, an indigenista writer.

Because of his involvement with the student movement, Haya de la Torre was imprisoned by the dictator Augusto B. Leguía in 1923 and then sent into exile. From this moment on his political path and Mariátegui's diverged. During his exile, Haya de la Torre traveled to Panama and visited the canal zone; there, he experienced United States imperialism first-hand. After Panama, he traveled to Mexico, where he participated briefly in the revolution and came to appreciate the revolutionary potential of the Indian and mestizo peasant. From Mexico, he annunciated the basic principles of a new political party, the American Popular Revolutionary Alliance (APRA): (1) antiimperialism, (2) political unity of Latin America, (3) nationalization of land and industries, (4) internationalization of the Panama Canal, and (5) solidarity among all people and classes in the world.

The crucial principle to this discussion is the second. In his early writings, Haya de la Torre, echoing José Vasconcelos, Ricardo Rojas, and others, argued that a New Man was coming into being in Latin America. And the coming of the New Man was concomitant with the rise of a new civilization, which, while rooted in the older Western culture, would make its own and unique contribution to the development of mankind. More significantly, the new civilization and the New Man would have at its core a decisive Indian element. Indeed, Haya de la Torre argued, all current terms designating the sociocultural realities of people from the Rio Grande to Tierra del Fuego were misnomers; they now represented dated stages in the development of America itself. The term Ibero-America or Spanish America applied to the colonial epoch and Latin America referred to the republican era so dominated by French and Spanish ideas; Pan-America, in turn, applied to the economic policies of United

States imperialism; only Indo-America expressed the new revolutionary concept of America. It designated a continent ready to develop into a unified whole and build definite economic, political, and social organization.

Thus, like Bolívar and Martí before him, Haya de la Torre envisioned a Spanish American nation founded on the creative potential of the Indian, who, finally incorporated into an overarching sociocultural organization, would participate in the new order as producer and consumer. The actual form that such an organization would take was never fully spelled out, but it is clear that its fundamental principles were neither purely socialist nor capitalist. Haya de la Torre, unlike most Spanish American thinkers in this century, sought to develop a socioeconomic organization suited to the realities of mestizo Spanish American and thereby avoided copying models developed in other lands in accordance with other circumstances. Unfortunately, the project was abandoned by Haya de la Torre and his followers all too soon due to national and international political considerations.

But despite all rhetoric to the contrary, it must be emphasized that Haya de la Torre never really understood the Indian and his culture. In fact, more than anything, his views—like those of many Spanish American intellectuals during this time—reflected a turning away from Europe to non-Western cultures in search of inspiration to combat the disillusion that resulted from World War I and the apparent collapse of Western rationalism. In the final analysis, his true political constituency was the mestizo petite bourgeoisie, some sectors of the old declining landed aristocracy, and some proletarians. At first, the Indian image was used by Haya de la Torre to infuse his political platform with a critical edge. In this, he followed those of the *Colonida* generation who attacked political organizations that catered mainly to Lima's establishment; later, Haya de la Torre used indigenismo to advance his own political career. It is not surprising that he never developed a large following in the

highlands or overcame the peasants' suspicion. His solution
to the Indian problem was basically a liberal one grounded
on his hope of developing the internal market of the future
Indo-America. This very solution is found in many liberal
indigenista novels of the Andes, some of which (for example,
Serafín del Mar's *La tierra es el hombre*, 1943) were written
by avowed APRA followers.

Mariátegui (1895–1930) was in many ways Haya de la
Torre's opposite; he was born in Lima of a poor family and
did not attend a university as a regular student. Ironically,
one of the most ardent supporters of the university-reform
movement was an autodidact. In his early years, Mariátegui
was associated with Abraham Valdelomar and the *Colonida*
generation; there, he gained much of his journalistic exper-
tise and sharpened his critical capacities. On the death of
Valdelomar in 1918, Mariátegui continued to work on *La
razón*, the periodical he and César Falcón founded in 1919,
until *La razón* was closed down by President Augusto B.
Leguía, who, in a conciliatory gesture, offered Mariátegui
government aid to study in Europe. Mariátegui accepted
the offer and traveled extensively in Europe, writing articles
for Peruvian periodicals based on his experiences.

Mariátegui returned to Peru in 1923; unlike Haya de la
Torre, he came back convinced that only socialism could
save Peru from stagnation and poverty. In 1926, Mariátegui
founded *Amauta*, a highly influential magazine that immediately became the mouthpiece for socialist, vanguard,
aprista (APRA followers), and other left-leaning intellectuals.
But as the political scene changed, *Amauta* was radicalized:
It increasingly carried mostly socialist essays, and collabora-
tion with liberal groups was drastically curtailed. The split
between the *Amauta* group and the APRA party was inevitable. The rupture became final when Mariátegui founded
the first socialist party in the Andes in 1928.

In the same year, Mariátegui published in book form
some of the most influential essays in Spanish American
history; these essays, based on a Marxist analysis of society,

were particularly influential with respect to the Indian question. In these essays, Mariátegui argued that the Indian problem rested on an unjust land-tenure system in the Andes and that consequently no solution to the Indian problem was possible until, and unless, the land-tenure system was radically modified. Further, he argued, the modification must be along socialist lines; the Indian must be allowed and encouraged to own and work the land communally. With these essays, a Marxist interpretation of the Indian problem was definitively established in the Andes, and the creation of Marxist political parties throughout the Andes gave this viewpoint a permanent place in Andean politics.

The demand for a redistribution of land was indicative of the socialist interpretation of the Indian problem in general. Mariátegui and other socialists argued that the Incan empire had been socialist to the extent that it was based on an economic and social organization that emphasized a communal land-tenure system, communal labor, and social security systems. That is, to the socialists, the solution to the Indian problem inextricably involved the Incan past. The existence of a socialist Incan legacy was taken as an incentive to penetrate the Indian's world, to study the Indian's past in order to illuminate his present and his future. Very much like the leaders of the wars for independence in the nineteenth century, these revolutionaries turned to the Incan past, searched for, and found an ally for their cause. For the socialists of the 1930s, the Indian's past proved that a modern socialist form of government was compatible with his tradition. In fact, in their view, modern socialism represented a return to those traditions, however enlightened that return may have been. The socialists argued that ancient socialist ideas and practices survived in the highlands as a testimony to the Indian's spirit and that socialism was a dream of the majority of the people in the Andes—the Indian and the mestizo.

Armed with this conviction, socialist intellectuals urged

already rebellious Indians and mestizos to return to their Indian roots, convinced that such a return was in the not-too-distant future since it was already a reality in scattered Indian communities in the highlands that still retained communal land-tenure systems and labor practices. All that the Indian needed in order to claim his future was to be shown his past. Thus, socialism in the Andes meant politicizing the Indian. This socialist position was one of the most powerful underlying currents in the indigenista novel in the Andes.

Andinismo

In addition to liberal and socialist political views, an assorted group of organizations advocating Indian causes kept the Indian problem at the level of consciousness in the Andes. Again, the Peruvian experience suffices to show the extent of their influence in the region. In January 1927, for example, *Amauta* announced the creation of an organization, *El Proceso del Gamonalismo*, that was to follow in the footsteps of the defunct Asociación Pro-Indígena, except that it would no longer be based on charity but on political grassroots organization. The organization planned to publish a *Boletín de defensa indígena* and encourage the Indian to form autonomous republics as a first step toward regional political power. However, the organization never got off the ground. In the same year, a group gathered around *La sierra*, a periodical that expressed what may be loosely translated as "highlandism" and continued the *Colonida* generation's attack on the established, white, European cultural domination. Magazines with similar tendencies appeared in the highlands at this time: *Attusparia* in Huaraz; *Editorial kuntur* in Sicúani; *Chirapu*, *Waraka*, and *Sillar* in Arequipa; *La región* in Lima; and *Inti* in Huancayo. Also in 1927, Luís E. Varcarcel published his famous book, *La tempestad en los Andes*, where he announced the advent of a new civilization in the Andes and the resurrection of the

Indians there. He later organized a group known as *grupo resurgimento* made up of laborers, professors, writers, artists, and professionals who were to lead a new crusade for the Indians.

In sum, these sociocultural developments in and around the indigenista writers' milieu gave them the necessary support to develop a basically didactic novel on behalf of the Indian people. The cost of this didactic effort to the Indian people was very high.

Chapter Four

The Message of the Andean Indigenista Novel

You should not forget us, my son,
Never should you forget us.
You go searching for our blood,
You should return to our blood
Strengthened;
Like a hawk who sees everything
And whose flight no one reaches.
                    —Todas las sangres

In short, I have nothing with which to
express my life except my death.
                    —César Vallejo

The Temporal Dimensions

The Andean indigenista novel displays two fundamental characteristics that are crucial to the present discussion. First, in contrast to earlier writers, indigenista novelists did not view the Indian as still living in a golden past or in a remote and exotic region of his country. They saw the Indian as thoroughly integrated into the white and mestizo world of the Andes, but they also saw that integration was thoroughly oppressive for the Indian. Second, the indigenista novelists were concerned with the Indian's future liberation from such oppressive conditions.

The combination of these characteristics made it imperative for the indigenista writer to deal with all temporal modalities of Indian life. In order to present ideas about what Indian life should be in the future, it was necessary to reckon with the Indian's experience in the past and the present. Consequently, the indigenista writer devoted much energy to studying the social, economic, and political conditions of the Indians in the Andes during the first half of this century. In this sense, the writer's work can be viewed as continuing the tradition of literature as testimony, which began with the indígena literature in the first years of conquest.

But the indigenista writer also undertook an analysis of the Indian's history in the hope that it might shed light on problems in the present and indicate future solutions. The indigenista writer turned to the pre-Columbian world and, from there, followed the Indian's experience to the present; in other words, in these works, Spanish Americans relived the conquest and its aftermath, and in doing so, they gained a position from which to attempt to appropriate history. One consequence of reliving the past was the reevaluation of pre-Columbian Indian culture coupled with a total denunciation of the evils the white man had brought to the Indian from the days of conquest to the present. In this sense, these writers *reinterpreted* their nation's history (which they rightly believed had been written by whites for whites and where the Indian appeared either romanticized or not at all) in an attempt to destroy such national myths as the image of the Indian in the romantic novels.

But if the indigenista novel of the Andes is both a reinterpretation of history and a testimony of the present, the essence of its message is not to be found in either of these aspects. In fact, both aspects are secondary to the overwhelming concern with the Indian's future liberation. Indigenista writers were not interested in a detailed treatment of either the Indian's past or present for its own sake. Whenever they dealt with these two facets of Indian experience, they did so in light of the Indian's future liberation; consequently, these writers treated only selected aspects of historic and present Indian experiences. Furthermore, the criteria for selecting certain aspects of the Indian's experience to be treated depended on the writers' particular views of the future. The clear advocacy for Indian liberation in these novels makes it imperative to discuss their message within a temporal framework. In that context, the writers' hidden wish for cultural unity is unveiled, for in searching for a solution to the Indian problem, these writers had their own salvation in mind as well.

As noted, an exhaustive analysis of indigenista novels in terms of form and content is clearly beyond the purpose and scope of this work; literature is used here as a social indicator of the cultural development of Spanish America and, in particular, the position of the Indian in such a development. It is also important to keep in mind a point made earlier to the effect that alongside the overwhelming majority of indigenista writers who were socialists there existed a small group of writers who were still very much influenced by the liberal ideas of the turn of the century. The most accomplished of these liberal writers wrote before 1930, and their views on the Indian's future set them apart from the rest of the Andean writers.

The Mythic Past

Indian life before the white man is portrayed by indigenista novelists as a kind of lost Arcadia whose temporal dimensions are not clear. Some writers, such as the Peruvian César Vallejo, see the mythic past as comprising all Indian experience before the white man, regardless of when such an encounter took place. His novel, *El tungsteno* (1931), is set during the first decades of the twentieth century; Vallejo describes Indian life before the encounter with white and mestizo entrepreneurs in much the same way as Bartolomé de Las Casas had done about 300 years before: "They absolutely lack the notion of utility. Without calculation or worries about the economic results of their acts whatsoever, they seem to live life as expansive and generous play."[1]

Other novelists give a utopian image of the mythic past that is highly ambiguous in its temporal dimensions. In Ciro Alegría's most famous novel, *El mundo es ancho y ajeno* (1941), for example, an Indian elder tells a story that had also been told to him: "Before, everything was communities. There were no haciendas on one hand and enclosed communities on the other. But there came some foreigners who abolished the system of communal land tenure and began to divide the land into pieces and appropriate those pieces. The Indian had to work for the new owners."[2] In this case, the reader is left wondering to what time the passage refers; is the elder contrasting the time of Incan rule ("everything was communities") with the arrival of the Spaniards ("but there came some foreigners")? Or is he contrasting the colonial past ("there were no haciendas . . .") with the time of the wars for independence, when laws were enacted to abolish Indian communities ("there came some foreigners who abolished . . .")? It is not altogether certain. "Before" here refers to a vague and undetermined period of time. For other novelists, however, it is clear that the mythic past refers to when Incan emperors ruled the Andes. Alcides Arguedas, for instance, in *Raza de bronce* (1919) sees the period of Incan rule as a quasi-utopia when "the supreme law was to produce and to search for perfection."[3]

Despite the vagueness regarding precise temporal limits of the mythic past, however, all indigenista novelists saw this golden period of the Indians abruptly terminated by the encounter with the white man. In most cases, this encounter means the arrival of the Spanish conqueror; this is Fernando Cháves's position, for example. In his novel *Plata y bronce* (1926), the narrator states that a landlord, heir to Spanish conquerors, saw in the dark and sad eyes of an Indian girl whom he eventually rapes "the golden ostentation of the sensual and divine Indians, of that magnificent Atahualpa who was sinking with his golden throne in a sea of blood in the legendary distances of the history of his country."[4] With the death of the last Incan emperor at the hands of Spanish conquerors, a new period was born. This new period, Cháves suggests, was born in blood and continues by shedding Indian blood, as symbolized here by the landlord raping the Indian woman.

Evaluation of the Mythic Past

The vagueness with which indigenista novelists approached the mythic past is indicative of their intentions. They were not concerned with the mythic past per se but sought, rather, something to show their audiences that the Indian had not always been a slave. In this sense, the mythic past had an important function in the overall message of the indigenista novel: It offered novelists the occasion to claim that Indians in the Andes constituted a people who should be treated as such. Just as in the works of Indian chroniclers during the colonial period (particularly Inca Garcilaso de la

Vega), the image of a golden past, however vague, enabled indigenista novelists to judge the Indian's present condition to be the result of centuries of unjust treatment by whites and not the Indian's fault.[5]

The image of the Indian's golden past also made it possible for indigenista writers to think of all Indians in the Andes as having had a homogeneous culture that had flourished with the support of a socially, politically, and economically integrated society. Furthermore, these writers claimed that such a culture was not merely a thing of the past but still existed throughout the Andean highlands. Despite the real political, economic, and social disintegration of present Indian life, they argued, the Indian still held fast to his ancient culture through some kind of collective unconscious and telluric force that he felt in his very being. In other words, during the first half of this century, indigenista novelists believed that Indians in the highlands were still culturally united, even though they themselves may not have been fully conscious of such unity.

Having reached this conclusion, it was a matter of course for indigenista novelists to see the Indian as yearning, however vaguely, to exchange his present conditions for something approaching his ancient customs, where he lived in peace amidst more or less comfortable material surroundings. It is in this sense that most of these novelists saw the Indian's culture as a subterranean force. But why had the Indian not used his latent energies to solve his problem? Pondering this issue, novelists came to the conclusion that the Indian's culture presented conflicts that hindered as well as enhanced his future liberation. Consequently, they were unwilling and unable to view Indian culture as totally positive.

Not being able to exalt all aspects of Indian culture, novelists were faced with the prospect of sorting out what they considered to be the positive from the negative aspects of the culture. They were able to carry out such an evaluation because they stood outside the Indian's culture and, therefore, were free from the impediments of either custom or subjective appreciation. Indigenista novelists, concerned with the Indian's salvation, eventually demanded that the Indian eliminate those aspects of his culture that the novelists judged to be detrimental to the Indian's future.

It must be emphasized here that whenever Andean indigenista novelists discussed Indian culture, they did so by referring to the Indian's mythic past. That is, for these writers, present Indian culture exists thanks to the hardy spirit of the ancient culture; it is the ancient culture itself, however transformed. For this reason, the discussion of indigenista novelists' treatment of Indian culture is in relation to their treatment of the Indian's past, and not their treatment of the Indian's present conditions.

The Positive Evaluation of Indian Culture

One of the positive aspects of pre-Columbian Indian culture that indigenista novelists saw still extant during the first half of this century and that constituted a definite potential for liberation is what they variously called Indian courage, energy, or spirit. This ancestral spirit springs from the time when the Indian was master of his own destiny and may be detected in the present during moments of despair, exaltation, or daring—when Indian passivity is shattered. At such times, the Indian undergoes drastic character changes: By summoning his ancestral energies, he can transform himself from a melancholic or suffering peasant into a proud man or a determined and fearless warrior.

In their novels, indigenista writers present the Indian summoning his ancient energies through various symbolic devices, the most important of which is music. Indian music is seen as a powerful medium through which energies from the past reach the present. Dances, and especially festivities where musical instruments are used, are times when transformations take place. José María Arguedas discusses these transformations in his novel *Los ríos profundos* (1958), where the Indians "play *pinkuyllo* and *wak'rapuku* [Indian musical instruments] at the installation of new leaders of the community, during ferocious fights among young men, at carnival time, cattle branding, and bullfights. The voice of the pinkuyllo and wak'rapuku dazzles and exalts them, unleashes their strength; they defy death while listening to it. They confront savage bulls, singing and cursing; they build long roads or tunnel through rocks; they dance without rest, heedless of the change of light or the passage of time."[6] These transformations associated with festivities are very much internal Indian affairs; as such, they do not directly affect the Indian's relations with the landlord.

There are other times, however, when the Indian summons ancestral energies to carry out specific acts of rebellion against his oppressors. In these instances, the Indian uses the *pututo*, a kind of horn made from a bull's horn with a silver mouthpiece to call for rebellion. The sound of the pututo is depicted as having the power to summon ancient energies and transform peasants into warriors. This is illustrated in Alcides Arguedas's *Raza de bronce*, for instance, where, because of the landlords' repeated violence against his people, an old Indian leader decides to sound the pututo to call for rebellion. "I am already old and have lost my vigor, but I shall always find strength to blow so loud that even the nearby communities would hear me; and remember that Choquehuanca, the just, sacrifices his own in trying to loosen the fetters that enchained his race."[7]

The Indian's ancestral energies may also be summoned through language. Jorge Icaza, for example, describes the Indian's transformation from peasant into warrior in *Hijos del viento* (1948). In this novel, an Indian community is threatened by the continuous encroachment of the mestizo world. The Indians gather to defend their community with the cry, "Huairapamushcas!" (Sons of the Wind!). This is a word that, according to Icaza, "was the—lash and vengeance—that burned in the blood of the Indians since the obscure fantasy of Lord Wiracocha [Inca god], since the tragic memory of the appearance of the bearded men who came with the bad wind—suddenly on the wings of chance—who came up from the desert, from the *marigua*, from the sea. It was the wound of the soul. The wound rotting in the *encomienda*, in the *concertaje*, in the hacienda, suppurating suspicious, strange rancors against all people not of their refuge."[8] Over the centuries, the word came to mean Indians without a conscious history, deprived of their culture, dispersed across Spanish America by the winds of change.

It should be noted here that in all these cases the Indian's ancestral energies are potential liberating forces only insofar as they are symbolically summoned by the Indian. These energies act on the present only sporadically, and their presence depends on specific acts by the Indian. Therefore, these potential liberating forces are in constant danger of being forgotten by the Indian who must live under very oppressive conditions and may purposefully silence these forces lest he threaten his own survival by summoning them. The Indian, having decided not to rebel from fear of future reprisals, may relegate these energies to the past.

At this point, the first major difference between liberal and socialist indigenista writers becomes evident. In addition to these positive traits, socialists see energies from the Indian's past reaching the present in another important form: They see an ancient communal spirit infusing the Indian's everyday life. Further, these novelists see great potential for liberation in Indian communal activities since, in this case, energies from the past do not require specific summoning to be significant in the present. These energies infuse Indian life in such a way that its impact cannot be stopped except by the death of the Indian himself.

Liberals, in contrast, do not view such communal practices as potentials for future liberation; no doubt, this different emphasis has much to do with differing world views. To liberals, communal practices are just another aspect of Indian culture, whereas to socialists, these practices are the core of the new society that they hope to bring about in the

Andes. The consequences of this different emphasis will be discussed further when the novelists' view of the Indian's future is presented. Suffice it to point out here that the revolutionary potential of communal living is less significant to liberal novelists.

That the ancient value placed on communal living is still present among the Indians is exemplified in the indigenista novel in various ways, one of which is the treatment of agricultural labor. Alegría says in *El Mundo es ancho y ajeno*, for example, that at the end of a day's labor "the sound of the harp lingers on somewhere. Someone sings. Everyone is happy and, without wanting to explain it, lives the truth of having conquered the land for the common good."[9] Other novels show communal living other than farming: In Jorge Rivadeneyra's *Ya esta amaneciendo* (1957), for example, the narrator associates building a home for a newly wed couple with ancient Indian practices. He describes how the Indian labors happily in such situations (as opposed to when he works for the landlord) and explains this by the fact that "the *minga* [collective work] is the only free, enthusiastic, and voluntary labor, a feast of collective labor with *chicha* [an Indian alcoholic beverage] and love, an ancient custom as old as the Indian people, as rooted as centenary trees grappled to the land and the rocks."[10]

But in what sense do these communal practices indicate a potential for liberation? The novelists suggest that such potential lies in the fact that communal practices keep alive the Indian's memory of better days. These practices enhance the Indian's yearnings for a life where the fruits of his labor and his land would belong to him, and not to the landlord who reaps the benefits of planting and harvesting without contributing to the labor process. The Indian's hopes of recovering his land are seen by many novelists as one of the most powerful potentials for liberation. In *Ya esta amaneciendo*, for instance, the narrator, betraying this hope, exclaims: "Oh, that all labor were collective!"[11]

It is not only in the communal practices of land tenure

and labor that socialist indigenista novelists see potential for liberation. The Indian's collective spirit itself constitutes a positive force according to most of these novelists, who see this spirit as the very core of Indian life and strength. If the Indian has been able to survive 400 years of oppression, it has been due to his collective approach to life. This evaluation of Indian strength is illustrated by an example from José María Arguedas's work. In his first novel, *Yawar fiesta* (1941), Arguedas describes the decision of one Indian community to search for and bring down a wild bull from the hills to the town's plaza. The local landlord attempts to dissuade the Indians, whom he considers to be getting into a dangerous situation. He argues that the bull "belongs" to the hills and that no one could possibly take him from there. On hearing this, the Indians laugh and answer:

> "There is nothing impossible for the community, sir. Maybe even a high mountain could be transported to the sea [if the community decided to do so]."
> "There is nothing impossible for the community."[12]

The idea in this passage is that if, instead of confronting death by daring (here, bringing down the bull), the community decides to rebel, there will be no force capable of stopping it.

The Negative Evaluation of Indian Culture

Andean indigenista novelists (and all indigenista writers of Spanish America, as will be evident later) considered the Indian's belief in magic to be the most negative aspect of his culture. And they saw this belief in magic as a major handicap in the Indian's dealings with the white and mestizo world. In most of these novels, the Indian is presented as tenaciously clinging to a magical world in which he seeks

solace and the causes underlying his present condition. Relying on magic, and its association with fatalism and superstition, the writers point out, prevented the Indian from
recognizing the real causes for his condition; magic, in short,
kept the Indian from solving his problems.

The negative evaluation of the Indian's magical world is
illustrated in Alcides Arguedas's *Raza de bronce*, where he
portrays the Indians as holding fast to their beliefs in magic
against all odds. The novel describes the predicament of a
group of Indians who are about to lose their crops due to a
prolonged drought. Their attempts to influence the weather
by performing acts of magic are to no avail, and they finally
realize that they must find food elsewhere. They all counted
on the nearby lake that for centuries had provided food in
similar situations. However, they soon realize that the fish
in the lake are few and could not sustain the entire community.

Faced with the prospect of hunger and eventual exodus,
the Indians make one last attempt to influence their world
by performing an ancient rite. They wait until nightfall to
sail onto the lake. There, they manage to catch some fish,
and after the appropriate magical chants and motions, they
introduce alcohol and coca leaves into the mouths of the fish
while urging them to return to the depths to multiply. The
narrator continues with bitter sarcasm: "Each species received its stupendous commission and its ration of coca and
alcohol while the drum was beating and the flute was shriek-
ing; but no sooner had the fishermen retreated toward their
homes than [birds] fluttered, giving high-pitched squeals
around the poor drunk and wounded fish, and knocked one
another down . . . to devour the fish who carried the mission of reproducing in order to placate the hunger of the
'poor unfortunate men.'"[13]

In this novel, the Indians do not seek a rational explanation for either the prolonged drought or the near absence of
fish in the lake. Neither do they turn their attention to the
landlord's mansion, where abundant food is stored—food

that the landlord has obtained by making the Indians work without pay on the land he had previously stolen from them. The Indians' reliance on magic prevented them from recognizing the real causes for their hunger and suffering—unjust socioeconomic relations with the landlord.

The Indian's belief in magic and the magical world is, according to the indigenista novelist, the most powerful weapon of the white and mestizo ruling minority in the highlands against the Indian in all aspects of his life. In these novels, it is not uncommon to find instances where the Indian's superstition and beliefs in magic are used to exact from him compliance with the demands of his exploiters. Priests, for example, are often portrayed in these novels as preaching to the Indian that earthquakes, floods, plagues, and other similar disasters are specifically sent by an angry God against the Indian, who must then placate God's anger by carrying saints in processions, paying for special masses, bringing more gifts to the church or to the priests, or obeying the wishes of the landlord.

The Indian's Relation to Nature

The positive and negative evaluations of the Indian's culture by the indigenista novelist are not always as clear-cut as the previous discussion may suggest. In some instances, the writer sees the Indian's experiences as having both negative and positive aspects simultaneously, and this ambiguity informs his entire attitude toward the Indian's culture. The Indian's relationship with nature reflects this ambiguity.

On the one hand, the writer portrays the Indian as living in close relationship with nature. The narrator in José María Arguedas's *Yawar fiesta* states, for example, that in the Indian's heart "the rolling hills are laughing and crying; in his eyes live the sun and the sky; in his insides the rolling hills are singing with their voices of morning, noon, afternoon, and evening."[14] And this relationship is compared to the white man's experiences with nature, the white man who is so concerned with material possessions and so selfish that he feels forlorn in a strange world, alienated from nature to the point that he can no longer appreciate its beauty. "From the mountain peaks come four rivers and they pass near the town; in the waterfalls the white waters cry out, but the white men do not hear it. On the slopes, in the plains, on the mountain peaks, with the low wind, yellow flowers dance, but the white men hardly see."[15]

On the other hand, however, the Indian's total identification with nature, when seen in terms of his future liberation, leads the novelist to interpret this identification as a reactionary force. The identification with, and love for, a piece of land, for example, is considered by some writers as making the Indian vulnerable to manipulation by landlords: Reluctant to migrate to cities and away from the land, the Indian often accepts the landlord's unfavorable terms. Alcides Arguedas in *Raza de bronce* describes how the Indians had been dispossessed of their land and comments: The Indians, "subdued by misery, vexed by their indomitable nostalgia for the land, resigned themselves to accept the yoke of the mestizo and became peons to then become, as they were to be from then on, slaves of slaves."[16] Moreover, the Indian's total identification with nature, together with his belief in magic, according to these novelists, prevents the rational utilization of whatever land he has left. The Indian is, in fact, often portrayed in these novels as reluctant to change ancient agricultural techniques or as totally opposed to using portions of lands that are considered either enchanted or sacred, even when facing starvation.

The mythic past, then, according to the indigenista novelist, reaches the present through the Indian's culture that still existed during the first half of this century. This mythic past has both positive and negative aspects in terms of the Indian's liberation. The task of the writer is to discern between the two and encourage the abolition of reactionary elements.

The Historic Past

While indigenista novelists see both good and evil in the mythic past, they are convinced that no good has come from the Indian's encounter with the white man. In fact, they view this entire period as a continuation of the conquest and argue that throughout these years the Indian has suffered the consequences of belonging to a conquered people. The narrator in José María Arguedas's *Todas las sangres* (1964) sums up the Indian's experience during this period: "In the times of the Spanish king, the land was of the Spanish king and so was [the Indian's] life. . . . Since the republic, each landlord was a Spanish king."[17]

Moreover, the experience of 400 years of white oppression itself, the indigenista novelists suggest, is a negative force in terms of the Indian's liberation. These years of traumatic experiences have left the Indian with psychological scars; many Indians have become afraid even to defend themselves, so they suffer the tyranny of the landlord in silence. These Indians know, the novelists maintain, that all their rebellions have ended in failure and that, as the Indian leader states in Alcides Arguedas's *Raza de bronce*, "a single drop of white blood we pay for with torrents of our own."[18]

Under these conditions, the potential liberating force represented by the Indian's ancestral spirit might be stifled, if not totally suppressed. As generations pass, the Indian's spirit sinks deeper and deeper into his subconscious to surface only in sporadic acts of rebellion. This is one of the writers' explanations for the Indian's seeming passivity. How this fear of reprisals is transmitted from generation to generation is illustrated by José María Arguedas in *Yawar fiesta*. When the Indians were pushed to their limit and could no longer endure the white man's injustice, they gathered in anger, "encircled the white men and the abusive mestizos: Then,

the white men ran, or they were stoned. . . . After, came
the escarmiento; uniformed soldiers in the highlands, killing
old Indians, women, and children; and the plunder. . . .
Years later, the old Indians made the children tremble, telling the stories of the reprisals."[19]

One of the principal reasons this accumulated fear stifled
the Indian's spirit was that it led him to believe in his own
worthlessness and to deface himself before the white culture
and race. Ultimately, the Indian might believe himself to be
inferior because he was Indian and not dare to speak up for
his rights and demand to be treated as a human being. In
Huasipungo (1934), Andrés, the Indian leader, would like to
rebel instead of brooding about his forced separation from
wife and child, but he is unable to do so. "Who was he to
shout, to ask? Who was he to inquire about his family? Who
was he to display his feelings? An Indian. Oh! The fear of
the whip."[20]

While novelists may denounce the entire 400 years of
white-Indian relationships in the Andes, they are particularly interested in pointing out that during the republican
period the Indian was most oppressed. Here, they take
issue with all those revolutionaries of the nineteenth century, such as Bolívar, who claimed to have broken the Indian's chains and made him free. The claims of the ruling
classes that they headed democratic nations where liberty
and the pursuit of happiness were realities during the republican period were, according to indigenista novelists, a
farce. Because indigenista novelists found the theories and
historic writings of the nineteenth century to be totally false,
since they never dealt with the history or the rights of the
majority of the people—the Indians—the novelists were bent
on rewriting the history of their nations. They wanted it
known that the political and economic processes of their
nations during the nineteenth century were the affairs of a
small, inept, and corrupt elite, who wrote its own history
and argued about the rights and duties of a minority.

As a consequence of these efforts, indigenista novels are full of actions against the Indian that took place in the republican period; in fact, the novelists used these accounts as background for the Indian's present conditions. Alcides Arguedas, to use the first indigenista novel from the Andes as an example, in *Raza de bronce* tells how the once free Indians became debt-ridden peons. He is particularly interested in the presidential term of Mariano Melgarejo (Bolivia, 1864–1871). "By force of tears and blood, there were dissolved in three years of ignoble fighting, almost one hundred Indian communities, which were given to a hundred new proprietors. . . . More than three hundred thousand Indians were dispossessed of their land and many migrated, never to return."[21]

Perhaps the only positive result of the Indian's past experience may have been the lesson that the type of rebellions that were carried out during these years were ineffective and that new strategies should be explored. But, according to the novelists, even this lesson was not learned by the Indian due to his almost total ignorance of his own history. The Indians, in the words of Jorge Rivadeneyra, are "beings who know very little of their past, who probably believe themselves to be sprung from the earth, from the furrows open by the wind that blows from the beginnings of time."[22] Whatever knowledge the Indians had of these rebellions were vague memories that accentuated the repressive consequences.

In sum, according to the indigenista novelist, Indian history included the potential for liberation as well as reactionary forces preventing this potential from becoming a reality. How indigenista novelists saw these two factors affected by societal processes during the first half of this century is the next topic of discussion.

The Treatment
of the Indian's Present:
1900–1950

As I have indicated, the Indian's situation during the first half of this century was difficult, since his forced labor made possible the white man's privileges in the Andes. It does not seem necessary to review the nature and extent of the Indian's oppression; let it suffice to emphasize here that the Indian's present depicted by indigenista novelists is largely in agreement with the actual state of affairs at the time they wrote. The accounts that follow are not purely propaganda on the part of indigenista writers; what may appear to be exaggerations are only too well-documented occurrences. In this sense, indigenista writers are among the most realistic authors in Spanish American letters.[23]

Much of the effort of all indigenista writers was aimed at portraying the Indian's present conditions as a continuation of the historic past, that is, conditions under which the Indian suffered the consequences of a conquered race. Ever present in these novels is what Gonzáles Prada referred to as the trinity of terror: the landlord, the priest, and the government representative (judges, subprefects, local political bosses, and the military) who oppress the Indian in the Andes. Members of this trinity of exploiters are usually shown to be working closely with one another when dealing with the Indian.

One example that gives an idea of how the trinity was viewed by indigenista novelists as an efficient machine unleashed against an entire people is Icaza's *Huasipungo*, set in the Ecuadorian highlands during the first decades of this century. Here, the author describes the intentions of a landlord to construct a road to his hacienda in order to please some international investors and thereby avoid bankruptcy. Without much effort, he is able to convince the local priest and political boss (*teniente politico*) that they will share in the benefits that the road will bring to the town. Both the priest and political boss agree to join in the venture, and united in their efforts, they decide to construct the road by using free labor from both Indians and mestizos. For this purpose, they exploit an ancient custom of communal labor (*minga*), calling upon all able-bodied Indians and mestizos to help with the project. To ensure the assistance of all Indians and mestizos, members of the trinity assign themselves particular responsibilities. The priest preaches from the pulpit the blessings that participating in the project will bring. "One hundred days of indulgence for each meter the work advances," he promises, noting that "only thus will the Divine Maker give his great blessings to the town." The local political boss, on the other hand, taking advantage of the priest's specially prepared mass and festivities to attract as many Indians and mestizos as possible, orders his policemen to seal off the town and requests that those caught in the dragnet contribute their voluntary labor in the name of the nation. As for the landlord, he is to provide his Indians (peons) for the project as well as alcohol and small amounts of food.

After careful planning, the construction gets under way. Soon, however, a storm hits the countryside, and some workers without shelter or adequate garments fall prey to pneumonia; some die. The trinity insists that the work continue: More rum is provided by the landlord, more prayers and admonitions are given by the priest, more threats are made by the political boss, and many more Indians die.

Finally, after several months, the road is completed. By this time the priest has managed to buy a truck and begins to make money by replacing animal transportation of goods in and out of the town; the landlord avoids bankruptcy and invites his new partners from Quito to search for oil on his property; the political boss receives an increase in salary from the government for working in a town with a road.

As for the Indians, who had lost their money (used to pay for special masses), their time, and even some of their loved ones on the project, the completion of the road means that they will also lose their plots of land that the landlord has claimed for himself. The Indians rise in rebellion at the prospect of losing their land. Finally, the road that has cost the Indians so much is used by the military who come to put down the rebellion. The novel ends with a massacre of Indian men, women, and children at the hands of the forces of law and order.

All Andean indigenista novels (in contrast to those of Mexico and Guatemala) depict relations between members of the trinity of terror and the Indian. In fact, it is through this relationship that the novelists discuss the broader relations between the Indian and white-mestizo cultures. A discussion of the specific portrayal of members of the trilogy in relationship to the Indian should prove fruitful to understanding how indigenista novelists viewed the Indian's situation during the first half of this century.

The Indian and the Law

Isolated in the countryside, usually unable to speak Spanish (the language of the law), the Indian was seldom granted the same legal rights as whites or mestizos. His lack of legal protection was most serious in his relations with the landlord, who used the legal system to secure the Indian's compliance with the unfair social structure in the highlands. Working in harmony with legal authorities, the landlord never feared that justice would be done on the land; thus, much of the Indian's land and the benefits of his labor were legally usurped by the landlord. Needless to say, if the Indian could not get the authorities to uphold his rights to the land and labor, his other rights were even more easily circumvented. And although his rights to simple justice were violated daily, the Indian usually refrained from bringing the wrongdoer to court for fear of being punished himself.

The impotence of the Indian before injustice is portrayed in Raúl Botelho Gosálvez's novel, *Altiplano* (1945), where an Indian and his family are forced to migrate from their community due to a prolonged drought. The family, after much travail, ends up in a town where they are total strangers. Within a few days, local mestizos deceive them and steal their cows. Angered, the head of the family decides to bring the wrongdoer to court to recover his property. He cannot afford a lawyer, however, and he is helpless by himself before a court of law. He decides to seek help from a *tinterillo*, a man who either because of his prior work in lawyers' offices and courts or his good local political connections acts as a lawyer for a fee.

> *"Look, son, here there are two books,"* said the tinterillo, pointing to a Penal Code *and a* Manual of Civil Procedure. *"With which would you like me to defend you? With the big one or the little one? The big one, as you will see, has more legal and juridical weight than the little one."*
> *"Yes, lord, with the big one."*
> *"With the big book my fee is 600 bolivianos, half in advance. The little one costs less, but, son, I do not advise it: The cheap ends up being costly. . . ."*
> *"Yes, lord. But if I lose?"*
> *"That is not humanly possible. With this heavy book, there is no one who may dare to take away your rights. Not even the most respectable."*[24]

Needless to say, the Indian ends up with a double loss, his cows and the tinterillo's fees.

The exploitation of the Indian in the name of the law is

not carried out only by the tinterillo, who even though he is an inextricable part of the legal process in these nations is not officially recognized as such. The Indian is also exploited by representatives of the law who accept bribes or are otherwise co-opted to act in favor of the landlord against the Indian. José María Arguedas, for example, in his first major novel, *Yawar fiesta*, portrays the readiness of a judge to support the landlord's appropriation of Indian lands. The Indians are never brought to court; they never know that their possession of this land is being contested. When they realize what has happened, it is too late. The landlord rides to the Indian village and announces that he is taking possession of the land. To make such a property transfer legal, the landlord brings with him a judge, who tells the Indians, "Señor Santos is the owner of these lands, of everything. . . . Remember that . . . Indians! Señor Santos is the owner of these lands."[25] And with that, the issue is closed.

The law, then, is correctly interpreted by the indigenista novelist as a white man's tool for exploiting the Indian. In these novels, the legal process in the Andes is portrayed as a systemization of injustice against the Indian people.

The Indian and Politics

White and mestizo members of the ruling classes have always viewed the Indian's participation in politics as a threat to their privileges and have managed to keep the Indian outside the decision-making process. The political segregation of the Indian has usually been done legally. During the first half of this century, for example, one way of keeping the Indian out of politics was to require literacy of all voters. Since most Indians were illiterate, they were automatically excluded from electing their representatives. Other legal measures were enacting laws or emergency regulations preventing the formation of such Indian organizations as community federations through which the Indian attempted to influence the political process. Whenever such legal maneuvers did not work, the police or the army were called in to dissolve organized resistance by arresting Indian leaders and carrying out repressive measures against the Indians in general. These and other exclusionist policies took place not only in national politics but also throughout small towns in the highlands.

Indigenista writers realistically portray the Indian in the Andes as a political outcast, seldom allowed to voice opinions, and never permitted a modicum of political power. None of the indigenista novelists, for example, portray government representatives (that is, the *teniente politico*) as Indians; they are, instead, usually local mestizos who see their position as intermediaries between landlord and Indian. In fact, government representatives in these novels are among the cruelest exploiters of the Indian.

The Indian's position as an outsider is accentuated when the writer deals with the higher echelons of the political hierarchy. Subprefects, for example, are usually depicted not only as non-Indian but also as foreign to the region they come to govern; the subprefects are thus contemptuous of the backwardness of the territory under their command. In *Yawar fiesta*, for example, a subprefect complains about the town he rules: "Towns from another world! Only necessity, money, could bring one to suffer in this hell."[26] Money is, indeed, the primary motive for taking the post of subprefect in remote towns in the highlands; the salary of these political appointees, however, is often very low and not sufficient compensation for their trouble. But, by taxing the Indians or making them work without pay, the subprefect can provide for his necessities. In addition to money, indigenista writers find only one other motive for taking up the post of subprefect—the inability to do anything else—and subprefects are often portrayed as inept, relying on government jobs to keep from declining in socioeconomic status.

Other wielders of political power are no less insensitive to the Indian's problems. In *Los eternos vagabundos* (1939), Roberto Leytón describes an official sent by the Bolivian government to check on the working conditions of Indians in the mines. He is bribed by the mine administrator with liquor and other amenities, so that his report does not indicate the real situation. The Indians, discussing the incident, conclude that he does "what all from the government do—lie, steal, and get drunk."[27]

As for the electoral process, writers portray it as a mockery of democracy: The police prevent members of the opposition from casting their votes in César Falcón's *El pueblo sin Dios* (1929); local political notables manage to elect candidates by means of such illegalities as allowing dead people to vote in *Ya esta amaneciendo*; or representatives duly elected in the highlands with the help of the Indians are defeated in the nation's capital in *El mundo es ancho y ajeno*.

The Indian and the Church

The Catholic Church has, until recently, supported the privileges of the ruling classes in Spanish America, and its relationship with the Indians, up to at least the middle of this century, has been one of paternal guardianship. As an institution the Catholic Church exploited the Indian from the very beginning: It not only took away the Indian's land (until recently, the Catholic Church constituted one of the wealthiest landowning corporations in the Andes) but the benefits of his labor as well. As a religion, Catholicism preached passivity and acceptance of the status quo and gave solace to the Indian who in his desperation sought respite in an afterlife that transcended the cruelty of reality.

The indigenista novelists' attack on the Catholic Church is double-edged: They attack the Catholic Church as an institution and the Church's representatives in the highlands, the rural priests. The attack on the Catholic Church, it should be pointed out, is not always criticism of religion per se—although some writers, especially Marxists, do make such criticism. Indigenista writers are primarily concerned with attacking the uses that are made of religion by representatives of the organized religious system, regardless of the validity of given dogmas or beliefs.

As an institution, the Catholic Church is always portrayed as taking the landlord's side against the Indian, a practice that offers the landlord moral and ideologic support. In some cases, this support becomes the Church's militant posture against the Indian's demands for justice. Jesús Lara portrays this militancy in *Yawarninchij* (1959), which deals with the first peasant movements that culminated in the Bolivian Revolution in 1952. Fearing dispossession of his land, a local landlord enlists the help of a priest from the urban areas, who comes to preach to the Indians against receiving part of the landlord's land that a revolutionary government is parceling out. The priest tells the Indians:

> "*Suppose, beloved Christians, that a man comes, and showing me a beautiful piece of land, he tells me: 'This land is yours. Take it!' What should I answer? I should answer: 'No, sir, that property is not mine. It belongs to another by the grace of God and I could not take it.' The other insists and tells me: 'I am a high authority and I give it to you.' Then I, if I am a good Christian, should reply: 'No, God forbids me to usurp another person's land. You, like Caesar, can only dispose of what is yours and not of this land, which does not belong to you.'*"[28]

As the novel unfolds, the Indians, now determined to regain their lands, march in armed rebellion against the landlords. In their offensive movement, the Indians must contend with the united forces of Church and landlords. This is symbolized in the novel by a building belonging to the Catholic Church that stands between the Indians and the cities and from which the forces of the landlords present their last resistance.

As for the rural priest, in these novels, he is one of the

basest human beings whom the Indian encounters. The rural priest is often greedy, sexually degenerate, cynical about his role, and inclined to use his authority to exploit the Indian both spiritually and physically. Virtually all priests are portrayed as having succumbed to the temptations of the flesh, as Matto's protest against the unnatural life of the rural priest is continued by the indigenista novelist. Most of these priests have "nieces" and "nephews," that is, permanent concubines and bastard children; when such regular concubines are absent, the priest satiates his sexual appetite by raping Indian women.

The theme of the priest's cupidity is as pervasive as that of his sexual corruption. Driven by greed for money, the priest will stop at nothing in order to get what he wants; Icaza portrays this aspect of the rural priest in *Huasipungo*. There, the Indian Andrés Chilliquinga's wife has died because, driven by hunger, she ate decomposed meat. Desolate, Andrés wants to bury her in a Christian fashion, but he is without money. Taking courage, he decides to ask the priest's permission to bury his wife in the cemetery on credit. Before he can ask such a favor, however, the priest shows him three different sections of the cemetery where Andrés's wife could be buried.

Of the first section, the priest says, "Those who are buried here, in the first row, since they are closer to the altar, to the prayers, and of course, closer to our sacramental Lord . . . are those who go to heaven faster, those who are generally saved." The price to be buried there is 35 sucres. Next, he shows Andrés a section farther from the church, where all those who go to purgatory are buried. You, dear Chilliquinga, adds the priest, "know what the tortures of purgatory are. They are worse than those of hell." The price for this section is 25 sucres. Finally, the priest shows Andrés the farthest spot in the cemetery, covered with bushes and generally unkept, and says, "There . . . those far away, the forgotten ones, the reprobates . . . those of hell!" The price, 5 sucres. After such a tour, the priest adds, "What are thirty-five sucres in comparison with eternal life?"[29] At this moment,

Andrés decides to ask the priest to allow him to bury his wife on credit. The priest angrily refuses and chases Andrés away. The Indian, pushed by his desire to secure eternal life for his wife, steals a bull from the landlord and sells it. He is caught and charged for the cost of the bull, thus augmenting his debt to the landlord, which could make him a slave for life.

The Indian and the Landlord

The landlord in the indigenista novel personifies the Indian's exploiter. He dispossesses the Indian of his land, exploits Indian labor, and rapes Indian women. The relations between landlord and Indian represent the relationship between two cultures and races, the colonizer and the colonized, the conqueror and the conquered. And this relationship is based on violence, which the landlord justifies by his claim to cultural and racial superiority, compounded by his appeal to tradition.

The pervasiveness of violence is symbolized by the landlord's whip, which is paraded before the Indian's eyes from cradle to grave. Icaza gives an example of this in his novel *Hijos del viento*, set in the Ecuadorian highlands. The narrator describes the arrival of a new landlord, who, on his first day, finds a whip lying around the hacienda. "And this?" he asks his mestizo corporal. The mestizo tells him that it was the prior landlord's whip:

> ". . . just as he left it after the last Indian round-up. Now your mercy must handle it. It is yours."
> "My inheritance."
> "With the land, with the mountains, with the Indians, with the animals, with the water, with everything."
> "Without the whip how could you be a great patrón? Who would respect you? Who would obey you? Who . . .?"[30]

The landlord's appeal to cultural superiority is based on the traditional Catholic doctrine in the Andes that sees the landlord as a civilizer, whose duty is to teach the Indians the Christian way to salvation based on obedience and hard work. In some cases, this ideologic justification is voiced by the landlord himself, as in *Ya esta amaneciendo,* where the landlord demands obedience from the Indians by telling them that he represents the culture of those who have made them Christians.[31] In other cases, however, this justification is voiced by representatives of the Catholic Church themselves. In *Los ríos profundos* (1958) by José María Arguedas, for example, a priest who is the director of a Catholic school for members of the Peruvian highland elites placates the Indians by presenting them with a divinely ordered universe, wherein the landlord occupies a superior social position. "We all suffer, brothers. But some more than others. You suffer for your children, for your father and your brother; the *patrón* suffers for all of you; I, for Abancay [the town]; and God, the Father, for the people who suffer in the entire world."[32] From this point of view, any efforts on the Indian's part to change his lot may be construed as a direct offense against the will of God. This Catholic world view also allows the landlord to establish himself as the father of his Indians, whom he may then punish for their errors.

Another justification of the landlord's position is based on racist theories: According to the indigenista writer, the landlord believes that he is a member of a superior race. In *Raza de bronce,* for example, the landlord sees the Indian as lacking "all notion of sentiments and his only superiority over the beasts was that he could translate into words the necessities of his organism."[33] Such racist attitudes are voiced not only by the landlord, but by his ally, the rural priest. In the same novel, the local priest delivers a sermon to the Indians: "The whites, made directly by God, constituted a race of superior men, and they were *patrones*; the Indians, made from other dough and by less perfect hands, carried shortcomings from their origins, and, necessarily, had to be supervised by the whites, always, eternally. . . ."[34]

Finally, all these justifications are compounded by centuries of the Indian's subservience to whites. The landlord sees himself as heir to a long tradition of cultural superiority, and this view is embedded in the very psychology of all Indians. In *Todas las sangres*, for example, a landlord speaking about an Indian leader says, "I have been his master for centuries."[35]

Given all these supporting factors, landlords in indigenista novels see their position as unassailable. How could the Indian challenge the hierarchic view offered to them by the Catholic Church? How could the Indian throw away his belief in his racial inferiority? How could he rebel, having fresh in his mind the repressions resulting from such acts and the whip he feels every day? Under these conditions, according to the indigenista novelist, the landlord regards his position in the highlands as secure. The Indians see the landlord as the incarnation of "all the evil history of the conquerors and priests who tied the Indians and threw them thus into the luminous distances of the future."[36]

Under such circumstances, the Indian is depicted as exhibiting little strength of character in his everyday dealings with the landlord. The utter impotence of the Indian versus the aggressive acts of the landlord is symbolized by the indigenista novelist's treatment of rape, where the rape of Indian women by the landlord is an almost universal topic. But rape is not treated as merely a sexual act; it is an act of domination of one people over another. This view of rape is clearly illustrated by Icaza in *Hijos del viento*, where the landlord justifies raping an Indian girl by saying: "Why not? She is an Indian of my lands. Mine like the cows, like the dogs, like the barracks, like the fences, like the rocks, like the trees, like the river, like the life and the death of the Indians. I can do with her whatever I wish, dammit."[37]

This ultimate act of aggression toward an entire people affects the victims in their very being. Powerless to prevent the crime, many Indians come to see themselves as worthless creatures, their sense of honor and pride having been shattered. In *Todas las sangres*, the Indians show to a sym-

pathetic landlord a girl raped by another landlord and express their contained rage by saying, "They have taken away
her soul."[38] The Indians know who the rapist is; they also
know what should be done, but they are unable to carry out
their expiatory act. Their ancient spirit is stifled by fear of
reprisal from the awesome landlord and all that he represents.

Potentials for Liberation
in the Present

There is a second important difference between socialist
and liberal novels. Liberal writers see the Indian's spirit
constrained by fear of the landlord and his world. The socialist writers, given these awesome constraints on the Indian's
liberation, present factors that, in their view, make such
liberation possible. But, as noted earlier, the Indian's existing oppressive conditions surely did not constitute one of
these factors. After all, these conditions had existed for at
least 400 years, and the Indian had been unsuccessful in
freeing himself from exploitation. What was different now
that caused these writers to maintain their optimism? What
made it possible for the Indian's spirit to surface with enough
impetus to change conditions? The answer is that these writers perceived social processes that were changing Indian
culture, ridding it of detrimental forces that had prevented
the Indian's spirit from surfacing and overcoming the Indian's impotence before injustice.

As noted previously, for all indigenista novelists, the Indian's ancient beliefs in magic were one of the factors responsible for his continued oppression. Socialist writers,
however, thought that these beliefs were finally disintegrating, and in their novels, they often present the Indian as
becoming increasingly aware that his magic has no effect on
the white man. The Indian is shown to be in the process of

realizing that the conquerors can not be defeated with Indian weapons, magic is useless before science, the sorcerer is impotent before the bullet, and the chant is a nullity before the law. Alegría depicts this realization among the Indians in *El mundo es ancho y ajeno*. In this novel, a sorceress is coaxed by the Indians into defending their community, which is about to lose its lands to the landlord. After several unsuccessful attempts, the sorceress admits defeat, "I cannot grasp [the landlord's] soul."[39] In view of her failure, she vanishes from the community without a trace, and the Indians look for other means of accomplishing their goal.

The disintegration of the Indian's culture evidenced by the destruction of its magical aspect is considered by these novelists to take place on other fronts as well. In their treatment of the present, they portray the Indian as undergoing a process of enlightenment. Two of the different ways in which this enlightenment is coming about are considered to be most prominent: the Indian's migration that began during the first decades of this century and the experiences of the Indian as an enlisted soldier. Together, these processes brought about the Indian's increasing awareness of the outside world. Through these experiences, the Indian is thought to be learning alternative world views to those given by landlord and priest in the highlands.

Indian Migratory Movements

Socialist indigenista novelists portray two kinds of Indian migratory movements: on the one hand, migrations that have push factors as their primary cause and those where pull factors operate. The first kind of migration is the more painful process for the Indian, who has little or no choice in the matter. In these novels, Indians are pushed out of their highland enclaves either by such natural disasters as droughts or plagues, by landlords who take their land, or a combination of both. Jorge Icaza depicts this kind of forced migration in his novel *En las calles* (1935). There, the narrator comments that the Indians "followed the escape route; but they did not want to accept that it was an escape. It was an expulsion, placing themselves out of range of the sound of the whip, a prison guarded by the drugs: priest, authority and landlord."[40] The fate of the Indian forced from his lands is depicted as harsh and leading to eventual disaster or death: The Indian migrant is forlorn in an alien world where he enters into economic relations with whites or mestizos always ready to exploit him.

El mundo es ancho y ajeno portrays the fate of Indians forced to migrate from their community due to a combination of natural disasters and their landlord's actions. They scatter throughout the Peruvian territory only to find hardship and death. One family, for example, after much travail ends up in the jungle harvesting coca leaves for a tyrant landlord; the woman is raped by strangers, the husband contracts malaria and eventually dies. Another family is exploited by the landlord of a distant hacienda who makes the Indians plant and harvest a plot of land, then, in the end, buys their crop at his own price, leaving the Indians with barely enough food to stay alive. Another member of the community goes to work in a mine where he is killed by police trying to stop a workers' strike a few days later.

The second type of Indian migration reported in the Andean indigenista novel may be called voluntary migration: The Indian travels down from the mountains to the urban centers on the roads his elders were forced to build. The novelists see this migratory movement starting around the 1920s, when increasing industrialization of the Andes began. In many socialist novels, the Indian sees the roads to the cities as an open invitation to a better life. In *Ya esta amaneciendo*, an Indian contemplates a road built by the landlord with Indian labor and exclaims, "How beautiful! By this road one goes to Riobamba [a large Ecuadorian city]. . . . This is the only good thing made by the *patrones*."[41]

This open invitation to migrate is accentuated when the Indian sees the possibility of going to his nation's capital.

The capital with its gadgets, lights, and aura of urban living constitutes one of the most powerful incentives for the Indian to migrate. According to the writers, knowledge of the metropolis gives the Indian an idea of a different life and, to the one who returns to the highlands, an aura of sophistication that can then be displayed to those who never left. José María Arguedas describes this phenomenon in *Yawar fiesta*: "The [Indians] arrived in Lima when, in all the provinces, there spread, suddenly, like a fever an eagerness to know the capital. To go to Lima and see, even for one day, the capitol, the shops, the automobiles that dash through the streets, the trolleys that shake the ground, and then to return! That was the greatest aspiration of all the [Indians]."[42]

The Indian's desire to return to his community, according to these writers, is crucial to his liberation. Those Indians who return are portrayed as less willing to see the highlands' way of life as an inevitable outcome of their conditions as Indians, and this leads them to question the entire social structure in the highlands. These writers' hopes were partially fulfilled, since many Indians who returned led their communities in liberationist movements and participated in the Bolivian Revolution of 1952 and land repossession in Peru in the early 1960s.

Many of these authors see migration, especially voluntary migration, as a way of correcting the shortcomings inherent in the Indian's culture. Thanks to these processes, they suggest, Indian culture is becoming more flexible, ready to accompany a leap toward the Indian's liberation; such is the message in *El mundo es ancho y ajeno*, for example. Others see the Indian's experience as a mixture of curses and blessings, a position masterfully portrayed by José María Arguedas in his last indigenista novel, *Todas las sangres*. Here, a future Indian leader travels to the coast with the approval of his community. On his departure for Lima, members of the community bid him farewell in their traditional manner. They all accompany him to the road that leads to the city and sing as their last gesture:

You should not forget us, my son,
Never should you forget us.
You go searching for our blood,
You should return to our blood.
Strengthened;
Like a hawk who sees everything
And whose flight no one reaches.[43]

The hope expressed is that the Indian will go to the city to
find the strength necessary to help his people survive. He
must see the city and be enlightened by it; he must learn
how to read and write; he must gain insights into the politics
and philosophy of the metropolis and, thereby, the strengths
of the landlord's world. But, at the same time, he is admon-
ished not to become other, not to be transformed. He must
be "like a hawk who sees everything/and whose flight no one
reaches." The hope of seeing the Indian return unaffected
by his experiences in the outside world is, however, unful-
filled. Arguedas, aware of this problem, portrays the Indian
leader returning very much changed and ready to transform
those who had placed their hopes in him.

The Military Experience

Together with the church, the military in Spanish America has been used to secure highly asymmetric social, economic, and political relations between the ruling classes and
the rest of the population; consequently, relations with the
Indian have been based on violence. Although the Indian
has tried to avoid contact with the armed forces, the military, particularly the army, has always carried out bloody
massacres against the Indian population. Yet, ironically,
Indians have always constituted the bulk of the soldiers in
the Andean armies; even today, they are forced to become
soldiers.

The Indian soldier represents another of the ironies of life
in the Andes: As a soldier, he is used to defend the privileges of non-Indians and repress other Indians who rise to

defend their lands from the landlord. But despite these obvious detrimental effects, indigenista writers note that during the first half of this century the Indian's military experiences were not totally negative but a mixture of good and evil.

The socialist writers are concerned with the Indian's induction into the army: In *El tungsteno*, for example, the subprefect receives orders from his superiors to provide the military with some recruits and, following the tradition, sends several policemen to search for Indians in the countryside. In the middle of the night, the policemen find an Indian sleeping with his family; he is taken away despite the protests of his children, wife, and elderly parents. The Indian is tied to a mule and pulled to the city. During the journey, he tires and refuses to keep running, whereupon he is beaten and forced to keep up with the trotting mule. When the group finally arrives in the city, the Indian dies from exhaustion. The narrator, protesting such treatment of the Indian, asks "What did [the Indians] know of motherland, government, public order or of national security and guarantees?"[44]

Given the practice of forced induction into the army, the Indian soldier, whom the writers see as comprising the majority of recruits from the highlands ("a marching battalion is a battalion of Indians in march," says the Indian leader in *El mundo es ancho y ajeno*), is depicted as an innocent man forced to kill his own people by officers representing the white and mestizo ruling classes. However, in none of these novels is there an outright condemnation of the soldier who carries out violent acts against the Indian.

But these writers also depict the Indian's military experience as an awakening: As a soldier, the Indian learns to speak Spanish, to read and write, and, in addition, he learns new concepts such as nation that allow him to see himself as something other than an Indian. Former Indian soldiers represent yet another spearhead that will eventually enable the Indian to overthrow the landlords' rule in the highlands. Most of the Indian rebellions that these writers set in the twentieth century are led either by former soldiers or by someone connected with them. This is the case even when the Indian leader happens to be a woman, as in *Los Andes vengadores* (1934) by Alfredo Yépez Miranda. In this novel, the Indian leader is a woman whose father had been an "infantry soldier in a regiment stationed in the capital of the republic [Lima] around the year 1919 [who] took part in the coup d'état against President Pardo [Peru, 1915–1919]; there he learned many of the mysteries of politics."[45] Such experiences influenced the Indian, so that he sent his daughter to school, from which she returned determined to change the lot of her people.

The indigenista writers were largely correct in their analysis of the former soldier's military discipline and his knowledge both of weapons and the mentality of military leaders as invaluable assets for Indian liberation. In Bolivia, for example, former Indian soldiers participated effectively in the revolution of 1952. In Peru, in 1963, former Indian conscripts from San Pedro de Cajas in the department of Junin led their community in reappropriating its lands from the American-owned Cerro de Pasco Corporation. Between July 1963 and June 1964, over 200 separate reappropriation measures were effected by communities in the Peruvian highlands.[46] This peasant movement soon developed into a guerrilla struggle when the military was ordered to take back Indian lands. By the end of 1964, the military had largely succeeded in its mission. But what these writers do not note explicitly is that uprooting the Indian from his land for military service also marked the beginning of his cultural death; once having discovered new worlds and beheld new vistas, many Indians were ready to give up their cultural heritage.

In sum, liberal writers regard the Indian's present conditions as stifling his ancient energies and spirit. Socialist writers, while agreeing that the present is oppressive, see other factors operating that will eventually help the Indian in his liberation. Both liberals and socialists view the present as a continuation of the Indian's historic oppression by whites.

Socialists, however, see the present sowing the seeds of a new epoch for the Indian. According to these writers, the Indian for the first time in 400 years is beginning to look beyond the confines of his world toward another of untold possibilities.

The Future

The interpretation of the Indian's culture by all indigenista novelists, as has been pointed out, was in terms of the future. Where is the Indian going in the eyes of these writers? What kind of future do the novelists see in store for the Indian in the Andes? In Andean novels, these questions are answered with a paradox: The Indian is moving at once toward salvation and cultural death. And in this paradox lies the indigenista writers' claim: In order to save the Indian, his culture must be eliminated. In all these novels, the Indian is totally denied a future *as Indian*. Individual authors may disagree on how to eliminate the Indian's culture; but that it must be eliminated is the underlying message of the indigenista novel in the Andes. Thus, Matto's earlier position is fully developed in the twentieth-century novel.

There are two ways in which the Indian is denied a future in the Andean indigenista novels: The first is referred to here as the liberal solution; the second is the socialist solution.

The Liberal Solution

The first of these solutions came about during the initial phase of the indigenista movement and is basically a continuation of Matto's position modified by more developed realism. It is the solution of novelists whose major works were published while liberal influences of such men as González Prada and Juan Montalvo still retained their full impact and socialist ideas had not yet penetrated the cultural milieu of the Andes.

With the notable exception of the Bolivian Alcides Arguedas, whose *Raza de bronce* is one of the finest examples of the indigenista novel, most of these writers were less accomplished than later socialist writers, and their work did not transcend the confines of their own countries. They departed from the romantic tradition, however, in that they depicted the Indian's condition with more clarity and saw him at the center of the white and mestizo world of which he was an exploited member. In some cases, the romantic element still lingers on; but, in contrast to the work of Matto, these writers had already moved decisively toward realism.

Like all indigenista novelists, these liberal men of letters saw the solution to the Indian problem in the abolition of the Indian's culture. They realized, however, that it could not be an easy task to accomplish; after all, the Indian's culture had survived 400 years of oppression. In some cases, therefore, these writers had a dismal view of the Indian's future. The Ecuadorian Cháves is typical of these writers: "Without industry, without charitable hands to remove the blindfold of ignorance, that mass of people walk desolate with their backs turned on civilization. They are thrown, blind and defenseless, into the luminous distances of the future."[47] There is little hope in this portrayal of the Indian's future; however, the way to save the Indian is quite clear: charity, education, and participation on a more equal basis in the political and economic processes of his nation.

These writers realized, however, that opportunities for incorporating the Indian into society were lacking; that those who exploited the Indian would never allow him to educate himself and, therefore, to become a true citizen. They recognized that the landlord needed Indians, not citizens, in order to remain a landlord; that landlord and Indian were inextricably united and would rise and fall together: no Indians, no landlords. Charity clearly did not work in the highlands.

Given their view of the Indian's present conditions, liberal writers did not regard the Indian as a potential revolutionary force. For most of them, the Indian was brutalized, exploited, superstitious, oppressed, and immersed in a soporific existence and, therefore, incapable of changing the socioeconomic structure of Andean societies to any extent. Whenever these writers portrayed bursts of the ancient Indian spirit (rebellions), for example, they treated it as a limited effort, bound to failure, and carrying no further consequences. The solution to the Indian problem had to be found without the help of the Indian himself.

Without the active participation of the Indian in the solution of his problem and given the landlord's reluctance even to allow the Indian to abolish himself through deculturation, the only solution left, in the minds of these writers, was to rely on some force external to the highlands and superior to both landlord and Indian. But such a force was not to be found within the existent socioeconomic and political structures of their societies. Still, these writers considered it in the national interest to eliminate the Indian's culture: Their nations needed a faster pace of industrialization and modernization, which would not be possible without an expanding internal market. The Indian had to be incorporated into the growing national bourgeois economy, especially if that incorporation meant destroying a quasi-feudal system of social relations that were obstacles to the development of modern forms of capitalistic enterprise.

In this sense, these liberal writers embodied the sentiments of the growing middle class that appeared at the turn of the century. In view of all this, such writers were ready to fall back on an old political solution in Spanish America: dictatorship. Since charity was not the solution to the Indian problem, they turned to the paternal policies of a dictator ready to act in the name of national interests.

The need for a dictator is clearly stated by the most accomplished writer of this group, Alcides Arguedas, in *Raza de bronce*. In this novel, an Indian rebellion is described as an attempt on the part of the Indians to remain together and keep alive their ancient spirit. Choquehuanca, the Indian leader, characterizes the rebellious act as an effort to "open between them and us deep abysses of blood and death, so that the hate can live on in the race until it is strong and asserts itself or succumbs to the evils like the herbs of the fields that are weeded out because they are not good for anything."[48] But this future seen by Choquehuanca is too uncertain and too distant; the modernization of the century could not wait so long. The novelist seizes an alternative and offers the dictator as the solution. In defense of the Indian, a liberal member of the landlord's class concludes that "only a dictator can do something worthwhile."[49]

This was the logical conclusion of the position of these writers who, on the one hand, could no longer rely on charity and, on the other hand, felt it imperative for the Indian's culture to disappear. These writers saw the solution to the Indian problem very much as had Matto except that now Matto's choice between charity or death had become a choice between either charity or cultural death through dictatorship. In any event, the Indian had no future to look forward to as an Indian.

The Socialist Solution: Mestizaje

In all indigenista novels, the mestizo is seen sometimes as a scourge of the Indian, sometimes as a helper, but always as an inevitable outcome of social relations existing in the highlands. Mestizaje is regarded as a fact of life there; indeed, in both liberal and socialist novels, it is not seen as the voluntary merging of two races but as the result of a traumatic experience for the Indian, a sign of the Indian's impotence before his master. Consequently, the mestizo is a living testimony of the Indian's defeat and exploitation. Furthermore, in all these novels, white women are never raped or otherwise made pregnant by an Indian, which suggests that the mestizo rises at the expense of the Indian people alone.

Given the unequal social, political, and economic conditions of the two races, it is not surprising that the mestizo, who partakes of both races and cultures, adopts the world view of what he considers to be the superior culture. In all indigenista novels, the mestizo is an ally of the landlord and part of the machinery that exploits the Indian. He is wedged between the landlord and the Indian as *teniente politico*, priest, or corporal, enjoying the spoils of the Indian's exploitation. In his desire to imitate members of the superior culture and be accepted by them, the mestizo often becomes even harsher than the patrón himself in his treatment of the Indians. The more he realizes that he is part Indian, the more he hates them, for such realization always places him beneath those he imitates. Thus, according to these writers, the mestizo in the highlands reproduces on a smaller scale the Spanish American inferiority complex vis-à-vis Europeans.

The rise of the mestizo in the Andes is another point on which liberal and socialist writers differ. It is true that liberal novels also recount the landlords' rape of Indian women, but in these novels there is no powerful and independent mestizo force in the Andes. Although the mestizo is depicted as the Indian's scourge, his position in terms of political consideration is left undefined. As noted, the best liberal novels were written before 1930 (*Raza de bronce*, 1919; *Plata y bronce*, 1926), that is, before the massive acculturation of the Indians into the mestizo world had taken place in the Andes, due in large part to extensive Indian migratory movements. Therefore, liberal writers did not witness the crucial transformation of Andean societies. Equally important for the divergence between the two groups of writers is that liberal writers were still very much under the influence of a cultural milieu that regarded the union of the two races as an impossibility. Indeed, racist theories were still being propagated in the Andes by members of the dying oligarchic groups that held fast to a quasi-feudal mentality, where the distinction between Indian and mestizo was vital.

Alcides Arguedas is convinced of the clear-cut differences between the Indian and white races; the title of his novel, for example, is indicative of this belief: *Raza de bronce* (Race of Bronze) designates a pure Indian race. He sees this division between the races being maintained by a mutual hatred. Cháves also views the union between the races as an impossibility, and the title of his novel is likewise revealing: *Plata y bronce* (Silver and Bronze) designates two unmixed and irreconcilable races. In this novel, a white landowner and an Indian girl die as a result of having tried to unite the races in a bond of love; their unborn child, the product of such a union, dies with them.

By the 1930s and 1940s, the Indian's acculturation accelerated in the Andes. Socialist writers whose major novels were written after 1930 witnessed the full impact of the Indian's transformation, allowing them to see the mestizos as an independent force, a force that they felt augured the eventual disappearance of the Indian. Of the many socialist writers to deal with the Indian's transformation into mestizo, perhaps Icaza gives the most penetrating portrayal in *Hijos del viento*. In this novel, an Indian girl, Manuela, is raped by her landlord. A few weeks later, she is forced to marry an Indian, Pablo Tixi, from a nearby Indian community. The husband soon learns that Manuela is pregnant with a child that is not his. Manuela gives birth to twins, and Tixi reacts with anger and hatred toward them, mistreating the twins to the point of torture. Despite all adversities, however, the twins grow up.

As years pass, the Indian community is threatened by a flood from the nearby river whose waters divide the lands of the community from those of the town. (The town mestizos have managed to divert these waters toward the community in order to take the Indians' lands.) After several attempts to save the community's lands, Tixi, now leader of the community, decides to cross the river to the town in order to find help. As he is about to cross the river, he realizes he needs assistance; looking around, he discovers that he is alone with the twins. Since the waters of the river continue to mount, Tixi sees no alternative but to rely on the help of the two young boys. He ties a rope around his waist and asks the twins to hold onto one end and pull him out if he should lose his balance in the current and be in danger of drowning. When he has reached the middle of the river, Tixi loses his balance; he calls out to the twins for help. The twins, after a brief moment of indecision, let the rope go, killing their stepfather.

Realizing what they have done, the twins try to escape the wrath of members of the Indian community who have seen their action from a distance. They decide to leave the community and find refuge in the town. Realizing that the only means of escape involves crossing the river, they run to a point on the river bank where a god of the community, a tall and ancient tree, stands. They chop down the god in order to make a bridge over the river and escape, leaving their mother on the other side, calling them back.

Here, the trauma that mestizaje represents for the Indian, the hatred that it engenders, and the mestizo's eventual renunciation of his Indian heritage is portrayed. The two cultures are separated by a natural barrier (the river) symbolizing their irreconcilable differences. This barrier is overcome only by the rise of the mestizo, who must kill the Indian's gods, that is, the Indian in him, in order to be incorporated into civilization (the town).

But it is impossible for the mestizo to free himself totally from his Indian heritage; therefore, he will never belong completely in the white world, where he is subject to varying degrees of discrimination. To escape discrimination, he must forge a world holding together two irreconcilable cultures and races. He must straddle both the white and the Indian worlds; for, even if he were to attempt to renounce his Indian heritage, the Indian is in him. Icaza symbolizes this inevitability by the words of Tixi, who, at the moment of drowning, yells to the world, "I remain in them. Indians because of their mother. Indians because of the hut. Indians because of the land. Indians because of the whippings I have given them."[50] In this view of how to eliminate the Indian, the mestizo represents the future wherein both cultures, the white and the Indian, will coexist, blurring the clear differences that have existed up to that period in the Andes; in other words, the mestizo will be the New Man.

The Socialist Solution: Revolution

But socialist writers did not rest in hope that mestizaje and Indian deculturation would eventually eliminate divisions between races and give rise to a more integrated and just society. They saw these processes as either too slow or ineffective in bringing about the Indian's liberation and thus searched for immediate solutions to the Indian problem in the Andes. The Indian's salvation could not wait. Very much like liberal writers, who were impatient with the liberal mechanisms of their nations as a solution to the Indian problem and so fell back on the goodwill of a dictator, socialist indigenista writers saw social revolution as an immediate solution.

These later writers did not view the Indian in a permanent state of slumber; on the contrary, they saw in the Indian a powerful force ready to be guided by leaders who could unleash its revolutionary potential. In fact, in their eyes, the Indian was going to fulfill a messianic role in the Andes: He was a force that by liberating itself would liberate the entire oppressed population in the Andes as well; all the Indian needed was guidance and leadership.

But what kind of leaders would it take to guide the Indian in fulfilling that role? It is clear from these novels that the leaders of the future would not be Indians themselves but mestizos or deculturated Indians who, having learned the ways of the exploiters, were able to guide their people to a better life. Leaders such as Choquehuanca in *Raza de bronce* are gone; new leaders have arisen from a new situation. By the 1940s the mestizo and the deculturated Indian have taken the lead.

Mestizo leadership is portrayed by Alegría in *El mundo es ancho y ajeno*, where the change in leadership is from the Indian's own cultural traditions to a tradition strengthened by knowledge of the white man's world. The first type of leadership is personified by the old Indian mayor Rosendo Maqui; the other by the mestizo Benito Castro.

Castro was born, significantly, as the product of the rape of an Indian woman by a white soldier. After giving signs of independent thinking and initiative, Castro leaves the Indian community to travel throughout Peru, and he eventually reaches Lima, the capital. During the course of his long journey, Castro joins the army, where he becomes a sergeant, learns to read and write, and through contact with socialist workers in Lima becomes acquainted with socialist ideas. When Castro finally returns to the highlands, he finds that the old mayor has died in prison in defense of his community and that the community itself is threatened with total eviction from its land. Castro soon becomes the leader of the community, taking the place of Maqui. Castro, using his knowledge of war tactics learned in the military, organizes the community's armed resistance against the landlord, who asks for military troops. The resistance of the community fails, and Castro is killed in battle; the community is totally dissolved.

The leadership of a deculturated Indian is depicted by another Peruvian, José María Arguedas, in *Todas las sangres*, which portrays the trials and tribulations of a young Indian, Rendón Wilca, who decides to learn from the white man. After showing abilities for leadership, Wilca is sent by the community to the capital of Peru, where he perfects his Spanish, learns to read and write proficiently, and becomes acquainted with socialist ideas. On his return, Wilca leads an Indian resistance against the encroachment of international mining interests that want to expropriate Indian lands. Making use of his knowledge of the white and Indian worlds, Wilca is able to enlist the help of Indians as well as whites in the defense of the Indians' lands. In view of the Indians' determination to defend their land, the mining company requests and receives help from the military. Troops reach the town, killing many Indians on their way, and Wilca is finally eliminated by a firing squad.

According to indigenista novelists, these leaders represent the enlightenment they saw occurring among Indians in the highlands. On his return, for example, Castro begins to destroy Indian culture by attacking their ancient superstitions, myths, and beliefs in magic. At first, he is opposed by some members of the community, but he is finally victorious. Castro uses dynamite to free the waters of an enchanted lake, for example, and convinces the Indians that planting in the newly gained land is not only practical but imperative in order to avoid starvation. The narrator reveals the motives behind Castro's acts: He wanted progress because "only with progress could the Indian develop and liberate himself from slavery."[51]

Wilca's intentions are similar to those of Castro: He wants to abolish the magical aspects of the Indian's culture because he sees them as ills that have plagued the Indian for centuries. The Indian, he thinks, will be "cured" of these ills when he learns that "the mountain is mute, that the snow is water, that the condor [god] dies with a bullet."[52] Only then, when the gods of the Indian are dead and gone, will there be no terror, madness, and bitterness in the Indian's heart.

The Socialist Solution: The Need for Guidance

The fact that the Indian had unsuccessfully rebelled during the first half of this century forced indigenista writers to seek reasons for the failure. Indian rebellions failed, they suggest, because of the local character of the revolts and the lack of an ideological basis.

Such writers depict all Indian rebellions up to the 1950s as local affairs, usually involving single Indian communities. During this period, rebelling Indians were isolated not only from non-Indian sectors of the nations but also from other Indians in the country. This characteristic of Indian rebellions is clearly symbolized by the instrument used for calling the Indian to war—the *pututo*. The limit of the sound of the pututo, it is suggested, is the limit of the scope of the rebellion. Despite the fact that all Indians understand the significance of its sound, the pututo calls only one community to war, not all Indians, and this lack of political unity among Indians in the Andes is clearly portrayed in these novels.

Secondly, Indian rebellions before the 1950s are presented as spontaneous and lacking a clear ideological basis; they are due to hunger, vengeance against particular acts by landlords, or spurred by superstition (as is the case in José María Arguedas's *Los ríos profundos,* where the Indians, dying from a plague, defy the army's bullets in order to hear Mass in the town's church). This lack of an ideological basis for their rebellions is clear in *Ya esta amaneciendo,* where the narrator relates that in a rebellion during the first half of this century, the Indians "showed courage and intelligence, but could not support organized persecutions by the landlords; they had no exact notions of their objectives and they were killed like rabid dogs."[53]

These writers, of course, saw socialism as the appropriate ideology for the Indian's liberation. Some of these writers are quite explicit in their position. Óscar Cerruto, for example, in *Aluvión de fuego* (1935) presents an Indian Revolutionary Manifesto in which the Indians declare that socialism has taught them the way: "And it has lent us more security and faith. Now we know that the oppressed classes, the proletarianized middle class, also accompany us. Our struggle is becoming disciplined and acquiring a revolutionary impulse."[54] Of course, not all socialist writers were as explicit in stating their views, but all did so implicitly. The Indian's future was to be a socialist future wherein the Indian would find and enjoy liberation with all sectors of society.

Not surprisingly, given socialist thought in the Andes, in the eyes of these indigenista writers, such a socialist future constituted a return to the basic elements of the Indian's culture. These writers' concern with Indian communal living, in which they saw the seeds for the future, is clarified in view of this return. If the Indian was to be shown that communal living was, in fact, an important aspect of his future under socialism, would he not follow a socialist path to liberation? The Indian's communal practices became relevant to socialist writers and not to liberals because of their different views of the future. In a dictatorship of the Spanish American kind, there is no room for communal principles. In fact, these communal principles may be viewed as impediments to the nation's development; consequently, liberal writers could not pay attention to such Indian practices. For socialist writers, on the other hand, these principles and the determination with which the Indian clung to them was proof that the Indian was ready for a revolution that would allow him to keep such a custom and expand it to the rest of the society. "Oh, that all work were collective!"[55] summarized this belief.

The socialist solution, with its desire to return to the Indian's past, however, also meant eliminating the Indian as Indian. The socialism these writers sought was not primitive or Indian socialism but a modern form of social organization where the Indian's culture with its magical world was an anachronism or a reactionary force to be eradicated. In this sense, for the Indian, to return also meant to become other.

Some writers thought that the Indian's culture could be incorporated into a socialist world without drastic changes; by eliminating only the negative side of the culture, they suggested, the Indian will continue to exist. Such thinking, however, is faulty: The Indian's culture without its magical aspects is no longer Indian culture, which is held together in the Andes by its magical elements. To destroy these elements would mean destroying the Indian's culture so that whatever remained would not constitute a culture in any real sense, and under such conditions, the Indian's death as an Indian becomes inevitable. In many ways, these indigenista writers saw the solution to the Indian problem in their countries very much as Karl Marx saw the solution to the Jewish question: The Indian will be liberated only when he ceases to be an Indian and participates in society as a man; with such an approach, the Indian's future is closed.

Summary of Liberal and Socialist Viewpoints

The Andean indigenista writers' concern with Indian liberation influenced their treatment of both Indian history and Indian conditions during the first half of this century. Writers selected from the Indian past and presented those elements that were compatible with their solutions to the Indian problem. Liberals felt that any solution to the Indian problem had to come from above, that is, it had to be carried out without affecting the entire social order in which these liberals had much at stake. Ultimately, they fell back on the dictator as the embodiment of national interest that would eliminate the Indian problem without drastically affecting the rest of the social structure.

Since the liberals envisioned the Indian's future liberation as his active participation in a capitalistic economy, it is not surprising that they did not pay too much attention to the value of Indian communal living. Their capitalistic society had no room for collective principles, since it required isolated individuals who would enter an expanding market economy. Also, since the solution to the Indian problem was to be effected without the Indian's active participation, it is not surprising that these writers did not see a potential

for revolution in the present. This is most clearly indicated
by their near neglect of the former Indian soldier as a leader
in the Andes.

On the other hand, socialist writers saw a radical socialist
revolution "around the corner."[56] The Indian's future liberation, socialists suggested, would take place with the onset of
socialism in the Andes. Furthermore, these socialist writers
gave the Indian a most important role to play in this revolution: He was to be the soldier who came down from the
mountain to destroy the unjust society built on his exploitation. It is also not surprising, then, that socialist writers
searched for and found potential for revolution in the most
oppressive conditions of the present; the role of the former
soldier, whom they saw as a potential revolutionary leader,
illustrates this clearly.·

With this vision of the Indian's future liberation, socialist
writers searched for and found in the ancient culture the
vigor and spirit of the race. They saw this spirit embodied in
the Indian's everyday communal life, and this communal element, they suggested, is the source from which the Indian
will seek a final and socialist solution to his problems. It is
not surprising, then, that they chose to stress this aspect of
the Indian's culture.

It is essential to keep in mind that despite their differences in approaching the solution to the Indian problem,
both liberals and socialists demanded the elimination of the
Indian by asking for the elimination of his culture, a culture
that they saw as hosting reactionary forces in terms of the
development of their ideal societies. From either perspective, the Indian had to make room for the mestizo, for the
New Man these writers saw emerging in the near future of
Spanish America.

Chapter Five

The Case
of
Guatemala

One must save oneself in order to lose oneself.
—Donde acaban los caminos

Social Conditions
of the Indians:
An Overview

By the time the Spanish reached Guatemala in the early sixteenth century (1524), the Indian population in the area was estimated at more than three million; by the census of 1810, that number had shrunk to little more than half a million. This demographic collapse of the Indian follows the same pattern as in other parts of Spanish America: It was due to wars of conquest, plagues, and forced labor. But even such a dramatic demographic collapse did not fundamentally change the Indian's numerical superiority over the *ladino*.[1] Mario Rosenthal indicates that on the eve of Guatemala's independence (1829), the population was about 90 percent Indian, 9 percent mestizo, and 1 percent white.[2] These figures should be kept in mind when considering ideas expressed by Guatemalan and Spanish American cultural elites during this period. Indeed, Spanish America was not a place where only the ghosts of Indians walked the land. In Guatemala, the Indian's demographic superiority lasted until at least the 1950s.

Systems of Land Tenure

Among the Mayas and their descendants until the conquest, land tenure was generally based on communal ownership. Although individual families were given portions of communal land for their use and often chose particular tracts of land and passed them along to their descendants, the concept of personal property in relation to land seemed to have been absent in the Indian's culture.[3] To the Indian, land belonged to the community as any other natural resource and could not be either appropriated or alienated according to purely personal interests. In addition, cultivating the family plot was usually carried out both by family members and collectively by the community; in other words, labor, too, was basically a communal activity. Communal labor was particularly used for clearing forests, building homes for new families, and in times of planting and harvesting.[4]

With the arrival of the Spaniards, the Indian's system of land tenure was replaced with a radically different one. To the Spaniards, land was not only a means of subsistence but a primary source of wealth and social prestige. These attitudes toward land form the core of all subsequent relations between Indian and ladino. During the conquest and colonial periods, land was taken by the ladinos as personal property from the Indian who supposedly sold or gave away his land to the conquerors. As the Spaniards advanced into the heart of Guatemala and took possession of large tracts of land, the Indian tried to retreat into the inaccessible forests and highlands. In the highlands, the Indian was able to keep most of the land because access was difficult and the terrain irregular and, more importantly, because to the Spaniards the land in the highlands was poor and not worth taking in view of the rich available lands in the lower regions.[5]

But not all lower lying land in Guatemala was taken by the Spaniards during the first years of the colonial period. In fact, during colonial rule a system of land tenure especially designed for the Indian was established. The system rested on the *ejidos*, which were considerable tracts of land (including forests, pasture, and nonarable land) designated for use by Indian communities. The ejidos were to be inalienable and administered by the Indians themselves;[6] under this colonial institution, Indians in Guatemala enjoyed a modicum of security.

As in other parts of Spanish America, liberals in the nineteenth century carried out an offensive against the communal system of land tenure that had been maintained, with some modifications, throughout the colonial years. These liberals wanted to make every Indian a small proprietor and therefore proceeded to abolish communal ownership altogether. Such misguided efforts, not always the product of ill will, only offered an opportunity for the Indian to be duped or coerced into selling his property to ladinos willing to buy his land at nominal prices.[7] As a consequence of losing more of their land, Indian communities lost their remnants of autonomy; the buffer zone between the Indian and mestizo worlds nearly collapsed, and the very essence of the Indian's culture was threatened. This, of course, was the precise aim of liberals in the nineteenth century who sought to incorporate the Indian into the nation.

A direct consequence of these liberal policies was the slow but unremitting parcelling of the Indian's lands into *micro-fincas*—subsistence plots. To this day, subsistence farming in the highlands of Guatemala takes place at altitudes from 4,500 to 9,000 feet, and land erosion is serious because of intensive tillage even on the slopes.[8] Needless to say, under such conditions, modern methods of cultivation are not to be found; furthermore, the smallness of the plot, the lack of capital, and the Indian's cultural values have prevented such methods from being introduced. Hoes, pointed sticks, and machetes are the most widely used agricultural tools; in sum, the progressive parcelling of the land the Indian was allowed to keep has only perpetuated his poverty.[9] And while the Indian is forced to scratch out a living from small plots of poor land, a handful of white and mestizo landowners control the wealth and the majority of the land in Guatemala. As late as 1964, for example, whereas 88.4 percent of total landholdings comprised only 14.3 percent of the land, 2.1 percent of large landholdings comprised 72.2 percent of the total available land.[10]

Labor Process

Communal labor prevailed in Guatemala before conquest by the Spaniards; to be sure, alongside communal practices there existed slave labor. But this was a limited form of slavery where slaves were "permitted to own property, call some of their time their own, and in which the children of slaves were free."[11] With the arrival of the Spaniards, the Indian in Guatemala was confronted with a new, unlimited slavery that treated him as a commodity sold to mines, sugar mills, and farms and generally used him as an expendable resource.[12]

This form of unlimited slavery was modified somewhat as the Spaniards consolidated their rule. During the colonial period, Indian labor was secured through such legal institutions as the *mandamientos,* which consisted of large squads of forcibly recruited Indians brought from their villages to the coastal plains to take care of such crops for exportation as *añil* and *cochinilla* dyes. The *encomienda* was also based on Indian forced labor not much different from that in the Andes. Indians living in communities within the jurisdiction of an encomienda were heavily taxed and used in the general upkeep of towns. These Indians were often marked and sold as slaves, and the encomendero was free to rent Indians to friends in distant places.[13] This labor relation between landlord and Indian was not significantly altered with the independence of Guatemala from Spain in 1824. Forced to sell his labor to supplement the income he scratched from tiny plots of land, the Indian had to enter into unequal economic relations with white and mestizo landlords.

More than 50 years after independence, in 1877, the law of contract labor (*reglamento de jornaleros*) divided laborers into three groups.[14] *Colonos* were those who contracted to live and work on the ladino plantations. The duration of the contract was four years, during which time the laborer could not leave the plantation or work elsewhere; the contract also meant that the laborer could not leave the patrón until he had paid all debts he owed. *Jornaleros habilitados* were those who had been given advances in cash before going to the coastal region from their communities. They were not bound by a specific time period; instead, they had to remain and work for the *patrón* until all debts had been canceled. *Jornaleros no habilitados* were those who worked for a wage and whose work was usually temporary.

The first two categories, which included most Indian-landlord relations, were similar to debt peonage in the Andes; in fact, a system of debt-peonage had existed since colonial times in Guatemala. The abuses against the Indian under this system were so bad that it was legally abolished by Governor Alvaro de Quiñonez y Osorio (1634–1642). The legal mandate, however, was not sufficient to abolish it in practice. During the republican period, debt-peonage functioned by lending the Indian money just before the local fiestas; such credit was often extended months before the harvest season in the coastal plantations. When the harvest season arrived, the Indian was called to pay the debt. The landlord offered such a meager salary for labor on his plantation that it was impossible for the Indian to earn enough to pay off the debt before the harvest season was over. Thus, the landlord was assured of cheap labor. Further, the Indian's inability to read or write prevented him from keeping a record of payments, giving the landlord the opportunity to stretch out the debt for as long as he needed the labor. If an Indian escaped, he was hunted by the police; if caught, the cost of the pursuit and his return to the plantation could be added to his debt. As in the Andes, too, the debt could be handed down to sons and daughters from generation to generation. When debt-peonage was not enough to provide cheap labor, as was often the case, landowners requested from the government the necessary police or army contingent to round up Indians and bring them to the coastal plantations for work.[15]

More than a 100 years after independence, in 1934, the dictator Jorge Ubico once again abolished the system of debt-peonage. But since the Guatemalan economy still depended on cheap Indian labor, the dictator quickly enacted a law that provided for the Indian's compulsory participation in the labor market. This was the origin of the infamous vagrancy law. Under this law, all people without a trade or profession or who did not cultivate a specified amount of land were forced to work for 100 to 150 days a year for whoever needed their labor. The law was geared to obtain cheap Indian labor, since Indians' plots of land were usually very small. The following year, 1935, this law was made even more specific: By presidential decree, Ubico specified that all people who had no profession or trade and who did not cultivate at least 6.9 acres of land (4 *manzanas*) of coffee, sugar cane, or tobacco had to find additional work. Again, this specification was geared to force Indians to labor for the plantations, since Indians in the highlands did not cultivate commercial crops.[16]

The indispensability of forced Indian labor for maintaining the Guatemalan socioeconomic structure up to the middle of this century was further demonstrated by the fact that even the liberal constitution of 1945 (after the fall of the Ubico government) did not eliminate the vagrancy law. Article 55 of the constitution stated that "labor is an individual right and social obligation. Vagrancy is punishable." In other words, the system of forced labor in Guatemala, as in the Andes, was not the brainchild of dictators but a precondition of the national precapitalist and capitalist system. Cheap Indian labor has been the basis of the Guatemalan economy throughout the nation's history.

The Indian as Soldier

Contrary to the popular myth of Indian passivity in Guatemala, as in the Andes, the Indian has risen time and again against his oppressors. The history of Indian rebellions in

Guatemala goes back as far as the days of conquest, when Pedro de Alvarado executed the Quiché king Tecum Uman and as recently as 1968, when the Indians of Comalapa rebelled against landowners.[17] But all these rebellions have ultimately ended in failure because they were usually haphazard and no match for professional armies led by ladinos. As in the Andes, most of these rebellions have ended in escarmientos. And the irony pointed out in the Andean case repeats itself in Guatemala: To this day, the Guatemalan soldier is an Indian who must act against his own people at the command of his ladino superiors. "To be liable for conscription," writes Richard Newbold Adams, "is a good index to one's lack of power to avoid it."[18] The army reproduces the Guatemalan society on a smaller scale.

Forced labor was also obtained through the military. Indian recruits from all over Guatemala were forced to work as part of their duties in the *compañias de zapadores*, which were instituted by the government in 1930. These companies were in charge of keeping up roads in Guatemala, and many Indians who fled from debt-peonage on the coast ended up working for years in these army batallions. In 1933, Ubico also abolished this system of forced labor only to formalize it under a *vialidad* system. Decree number 147 specified that all individuals were to work for two weeks a year on road construction except those willing to pay one dollar per week. As expected, ultimately only Indians and very poor mestizos worked on these roads.[19]

The Indian and the Church

One of the most important differences between the Indian's situation in the Andes and in Guatemala during the first part of this century is the role of the church and its representatives among the rural population.

During the colonial period, the development of the Catholic Church was similar in both regions: the church accumulated large tracts of land, utilized free Indian labor to construct its temples, and, in general, enjoyed all the privileges of an institution at the service of the conquerors. Differences developed during the republican period. During the administration of Presidents Francisco Barrundia (1829–1831) and Mariano Galvez (1831–1838), a liberal and anticlerical movement attacked the church, depriving it of much of the political and economic power it then enjoyed. After Galvez's presidency, there followed a period of tolerance toward the church that allowed it to build up temporal powers once again. But in 1871, a new wave of anticlerical feelings spread through Guatemala, this time under the presidency of Justo Rufino Barrios, lasting until 1879. To this day, the Catholic Church has not fully recovered from these setbacks; more recently, it has had to rely on massive economic and personnel assistance from Catholic churches in the United States and Europe.[20]

These setbacks had important consequences for the church's relations with Indians in Guatemala during the first half of this century. Unlike the Andes, where mestizo priests were important figures among the Indians, in Guatemala there were few priests in the rural areas during the first half of this century. Most priests, furthermore, were foreigners and remained basically outside the existing sociocultural relations between Indians and landlords in the highlands. Consequently, during the short indigenista period in Guatemalan letters (1945–1953), the Indian did not experience either benevolence or maleficence at the hands of the priest. Thus, while the priest in the Andes was a member of the trinity of terror, in Guatemala he appeared only as an outsider, though very much in defense of the status quo; these differences are reflected in novels from both regions.

The Indian and Politics

In political matters, Indians in Guatemala have always been outsiders. In colonial times, they were under the protection of the kings of Spain and, therefore, without political rights, and this situation did not change with Guatemala's independence from Spain. Furthermore, since the independence was not gained by force, as was the case in the Andes, Indians in Guatemala were not used as either soldiers or symbols in the process. The political event of 1824 was a shift in power from the conservative (royalist) to the liberal (nationalist) wing of the Guatemalan elite; the leaders responsible for this shift were certainly not even romantic revolutionaries.

This long history of Indian nonintervention in national politics seemed about to end with the overthrow of the Ubico dictatorship in 1944. As the left-leaning government of Juan José Arévalo (1945–1951) took control of key sectors of Guatemalan society, the Indian's participation in local and national politics was encouraged. Between 1944 and 1954, there emerged in Guatemala about 345 unions and 300 leagues that represented the peasants, Indians included.[21] Indians, however, heeding the lesson of centuries of mistrust, did not participate in great numbers; furthermore, what little Indian participation in politics took place during this period was drastically halted with the fall of the government of Jacobo Arbenz, Arévalo's successor, in 1954. By 1967, there remained about 93 organizations where Indians could be represented, and most of them had their political leverage drastically undermined.[22] With the overthrow of the Arbenz government, the Indian once again withdrew to the position of an outsider in the political process.

The Writer's Sociocultural Milieu

In 1898, the Spanish American elite was shaken by the war between the United States and Spain. When the United States' forces crushed the Spanish, intellectuals all over Spanish America rallied behind Spanish culture. In an impotent gesture, these intellectuals opposed the military and technological superiority of the United States by claiming superiority of Spanish American culture. A few years later, Rodó's famous distinction between Ariel (the spirit, which represented Spanish America) and Caliban (the material principle, representing the United States) gained many followers across Spanish America. Even the *modernistas*, members of a literary movement that regarded the discussion of social issues as alien to their art, found time to reject the United States' claim to hegemony in the Western hemisphere.

This general reaction by the Spanish American cultural elite to the United States' victory over Spain was particularly strong in Central America, so close to the war theater. From Nicaragua, Rubén Darío (1867–1916), the leading modernista poet, praised the cultural values of *hispanidad*. In Guatemala itself, Maximo Soto-Hall (1871–1944) wrote novels like *El problema* (1899) and *La sombra de la casa blanca* (1927), where he attacked the United States' role in the Americas.

But contrary to some widely shared views, the antinomy presented by Rodó between the forces of materialism and humanism did not bypass the Indian problem in Guatemala. Certainly, for Guatemalan intellectuals and writers, the antinomy was posited between Anglo-America and Ibero-America, but the Indian problem could not possibly be left out. Indeed, the Indian element in Guatemala was a burden, a nuisance, in the eyes of the elite who claimed a humanist tradition. Consequently, such intellectuals tried their best to give the impression that the only culture Guatemala possessed was what mother Spain had bequeathed. In other words, these intellectuals dealt with the Indian problem by omitting the real Indian from their writings; for example, the Indian was depicted in the romantic tradition or historically as a character lurking in the shadows of Guatemalan culture. Herein lies an important factor contributing to the late incorporation of the real Indian into Guatemalan literature.

On top of all this, just after the defeat of Spain, the dictatorship of Estrada Cabrera (1898–1920) ruled Guatemala through one of its darkest periods. This dictator so successfully isolated Guatemala from the rest of the world that the impact of the first two great revolutions in the twentieth century, for example, affected Guatemala minimally. In fact, the Mexican Revolution did not have a sizable impact on Guatemala until Cabrera's overthrow in 1920, and the Russian Revolution did not seriously affect Guatemalan politics until the fall of Ubico in 1944.

Coming just after the Spanish-American War, Cabrera's dictatorship did not leave much time to develop liberal forces, which, together with aristocratic tendencies, gathered around the anti-American movement. Once in power, Cabrera did not allow political or cultural dissent; liberal ideas were drastically suppressed. Officially, for example, the Indian problem did not exist in Guatemala, and voicing a contrary opinion was tantamount to committing political and social suicide.

With the help of university students in Guatemala who followed their counterparts throughout Spanish America, Cabrera was overthrown by popular forces in 1920.[23] Unfortunately, the years that followed the fall of the dictatorship were not conducive to discussing social issues seriously: Twenty-two years of dictatorship had prevented a high degree of political education among the Guatemalan people. In the 11 years that followed between the fall of Cabrera and the rise of another dictator, Ubico, in 1931, Guatemala went through an extremely chaotic period. During this time, six presidents came to power, three of them in a period of three months; all these presidents, it must be added, were either military men or had the support of the armed forces.

For all its shortcomings, this turbulent period in Guatemalan history was regarded by its people as healthy. Spanish American and European cultural influences began slowly to spread through Guatemala; university students who had helped to overthrow Cabrera were organized into federations—the effects of the university reform movement had reached Guatemala. Newspapers spread new ideas on social, political, and economic matters; professional associations came out of hiding. By 1922, Mexican labor organizers had spread throughout Central America, and under their guidance the Confederation of Central American Workers was established; for the first time, Guatemalan workers were able to participate in organizations like these.

With regard to the Indian problem, some efforts were made to discuss it publicly. During this period, Miguel Ángel Asturias, who later became the best known Guatemalan writer, received his law degree with a thesis entitled "The Social Problem of the Indian" (1923). Contrary to the Andean case, however, these discussions of the Indian problem did not lead to a militant indigenista movement, literary or social. Symptomatic of this was the solution offered by Asturias, who took a clearly racist attitude to the problem and recommended eliminating the Indian through planned mestizaje. European migration, Asturias argued, was the solution to Guatemala's problem. In those years, Asturias did not consider the Indian to be a potential revolutionary force; instead, he believed him to constitute a decadent and inferior race whose time on earth had passed.[24]

Promising stability, Ubico came to power in 1931. His dictatorship, which followed in the tradition of Cabrera, pushed Guatemala once again into a dark period. Most of the liberal institutions that had begun to develop during the six prior administrations were effectively neutralized. Organizations that had any semblance of popular support were drastically eliminated; all decisions concerning public policy were personally handled by the dictator. To keep himself informed of all significant events in the nation, the dictator set up an elaborate system of espionage.

Herein lies a second factor contributing to the absence of a militant indigenismo in Guatemala during the 1930s. Writers living inside Guatemala were intimidated by the dictator's display of violence; cut off from direct indigenista influences from other Spanish American countries, they were careful not to offend Guatemala's strong man, for to be against Ubico meant untold hardship and repression. Besides, the Guatemalan intelligentsia had not yet fully developed a coherent critical tradition in the liberal sense. Consequently, during the 1930s and early 1940s, writers continued to depict the Indian in the manner of the nine-teenth-century romantic school, that is, as a historic figure or an exotic and shadowy character.[25]

Ubico's dictatorship lasted 13 years. With his overthrow in 1944, liberal ideas once again permeated Guatemalan po-litical life, this time with some socialist overtones. Intellec-tuals who had spent years in exile returned with hopes of directing Guatemala toward democracy. University students, once again a major force in the fall of a dictator, organized anew; newspapers appeared and liberal and socialist ideas were aired with a feeling of euphoria. The dark hours, it was hoped, had passed at last. In this climate, Mario Monteforte Toledo wrote *Entre la piedra y la cruz* (1945).

The Message of the Guatemalan Indigenista Novel

Treatment of the Indian's Past

Only two novels, both by Monteforte Toledo, can be truly called indigenista; other novels of this period continued to regard the Indian as background to what was essentially a ladino drama.[26] In his treatment of the Indian's mythic past, Monteforte Toledo follows the Andean writers: The Indian hero in *Entre la piedra y la cruz* believes that his race had a past that could never be erased despite present conditions; the Indian race had a "great past, for all times. All its refuge, all its energy, all the reasons for its high dignity were in the past."[27] And as was the case in the Andes, this energy has been repressed with violence since the conquest; these empires, states a landlord in the novel, "were not built without violence and cannot be maintained without violence."[28]

According to Monteforte Toledo, this history of violence has had important psychological consequences for both Indians and ladinos. A young ladino doctor, hero of the second novel, *Donde acaban los caminos* (1953), finds such a legacy of violence introduces a sense of guilt between him and his lover, an Indian girl. Their relationship, he says, "always makes me feel like an executioner, like an accomplice to the conquest."[29] No doubt, here the author echoes other indigenista writers by pointing out the sense of guilt that he believes all white and mestizo Spanish Americans feel when confronted with the Indian problem.

As for the Indian, this history of violence is internalized as a deep fear of the white man and his culture. Monteforte Toledo put forth this view through the experiences of a young child, the hero in *Entre la piedra y la cruz*, who wants to be like any other child among the ladino children in his school but is unable to do so. The child "felt fear in his very bones; an ancestral fear of ladinos, the symbol of the superior for four hundred years."[30]

Given these conditions, what of the Indian's spirit? Monteforte Toledo believes that it has endured but that it is a subterranean force at the edge of collective memory. In his daily existence, the Indian vaguely remembers his heroes who fought slavery from the very beginning.[31] The Indian's energy, repressed by centuries of violence, reaches the present only fleetingly; the Indian's transformation from a passive peon into fearless warrior also comes about in moments of euphoria, especially during fiestas.[32] And here too, as in the Andes, this energy constitutes a potential revolutionary force, at least in the early part of *Entre la piedra y la cruz*, whose Indian hero asks himself, "What would they [ladino rulers in Guatemala] do if one day the whole world would wake up and tell them, like someone spitting: 'Now you work the land, we will no longer defend the system, either as soldiers or as peons. To hell with all of you, cowards. . . .'"[33]

In the novel, this awakening does not take place because of the Indians' total attachment to traditions and particularly to magic: They are so thoroughly immersed in their magical and traditional world view that they completely fail to see beyond it. The writer's negative evaluation of Indian culture is clearly presented in his depiction of an already deculturated hero, who asks himself: "Where could one go in modern times with such [traditional] truths?"[34] The negative evaluation of this aspect of the Indian's past indicates the writer's views of the Indian's future.

Like most indigenista writers, Monteforte Toledo also shows ambivalence toward the Indian's culture. In his two novels there is nostalgia for a life that is close to nature, and, like the Andean writers, Monteforte Toledo sees the white man as alienated from nature, calculating, and lacking mystical feelings. But at the same time, Monteforte Toledo believes that the Indian's closeness to nature is responsible to a high degree for his present wretched condition; after all, where could he go with his truths?

The Present

> *Las Dalias. Monday. June. Tree pruning in*
> *La Piedra, La Joya, and Guayabal. Antonio*
> *Xiquin fled with a debt of two thousand*
> *pesos; he was captured. Pietra the cow has*
> *worms in her right foot. Anastasio Xitamul*
> *died, snake bite. Everything quiet.*"[35]

This telegram from a corporal to a landlord living in the city underscores the Indian's life on plantations in Guatemala; he is no more than a beast of burden. As to how the Indian got to the plantations in the first place, earlier pages describe how Indians were rounded up by police who arrived at night "like the bands of bats that sometimes came down from the caves of the volcano." Then, "the first cries of the community of Tzanjay were heard. The women fought in front of their huts . . . but the soldiers separated them with the butts of their rifles and tied and took away the youths and the fathers of all ages."[36] This is how landlords obtained their labor power and the nation its contingent of road builders.[37]

With these depictions of Indian life, Monteforte Toledo continues the tradition of the writer as witness of injustice and conscience of his own class. The inherited myth of the isolated and exotic Indian is also attacked: "To one side, the natives; to the other side, the ladinos," he writes. "What a beautiful lie—beneath is the temple of the sun; on top, the cathedral; the white man laughs, the Indian works for him; the little town shrinks so that the city or the plantation may expand like the night retreats in the valleys as the sun rises."[38]

And why doesn't the Indian throw down the yoke? Why does he fail when he attempts to do so? Because he is disorganized; because of his attachment to a magically saturated culture. Indeed, the author says, Indians in Guatemala have been soldiers in countless revolutions but always for the ladinos' benefit. And when these revolutions were over, "no one told the government's soldiers that they were Indians and to remember that then they had had guns in their hands."[39] The Indian's love for his village, his deep-rooted localism, prevented him from realizing his common plight and subsequently translating that realization into organized rebellion. For example, the Indian hero in *Entre la piedra y la cruz* enters the army after a disappointing career as a rural teacher; he realizes that in the army "all were young Indians; they came from far away villages and never developed a total trust of one another despite the fact that their race and their living together day and night made them brothers."[40] Thus, Indians in Guatemala, like Indians in the Andes, are depicted as a people without a conscious history and common ideology.

These novels also depict the traumas of deculturation. Pushed by hunger or the landlord's violence, the Indian travels to the coast and the cities on roads he was forced to build; there, he becomes other and must cope with being an outsider. And, as in the Andes, the outcome of the Indian's journey to the cities is a mixture of good and evil: "Some had contracted the abrasive cold of malaria, others had learned to drink; others opened their eyes to the reality of their miserable life and spent long periods of time without refuge in the traditions of their race."[41] These encounters with new worlds point to the beginning of the Indian's massive deculturation and the rise of the mestizo as a potential force in Guatemala.

The Future

The first indigenista novel in Guatemala, Monteforte Toledo's *Entre la piedra y la cruz*, was published in 1945, just after the triumph of the revolution led by Arévalo. At this time, the mood of the country was optimistic, and, for the first time, the Indian problem was given governmental attention. In his second indigenista novel, *Donde acaban los caminos*, published eight years later in 1953, Monteforte Toledo reveals his disillusionment with the results of that revolution. Doubtlessly, the social climate of the times affected the portrayal of the Indian's future in both novels.

Entre la piedra y la cruz is the story of Lu Matza, an Indian born with "a great spirit" to fight "against the strong" and to "believe in that which no one believes."[42] From the very beginning, Lu shows himself to be an independent character: As a young child, he is eager to view the world in ways that differ from those of his people.

After some domestic problems when Lu is still a child, his family is forced to work on the coastal plantations as hired hands. There, Lu experiences the harsh treatment the Indian receives from landlords as well as the first sense of alienation from his people's culture. On the plantation, he learns that other Indians hope to remain on the coast in order to enter the mestizo world. Yet, Lu still feels the pull of his native land. Expressing his childhood dreams, he confides to his sister: "I am going to learn what the ladinos know, and as soon as I grow up, I will return to San Pedro [his village] to teach the Indians and the ladinos. . . . I am going to order a high wall to be made around our village so that no one may come to bother us. . . ."[43]

This fantasy, it turns out, is a premonition of a later trauma in Lu's life, for while still on the plantation he witnesses his sister being raped by the son of a local landlord. Thus, Lu experiences the reality of mestizaje in Guatemala first-hand. As he witnessed the act, Lu felt a regurgitation of "the conscience of all the Indian mothers, mothers by force, mothers by hate, since the conquerors. . . ."[44]

With the help of an old-fashioned, paternal landlord, Lu's father, Antonio, sues the rapist. It is soon discovered, however, that the latter has fled to Europe. After some stalling tactics, the rapist's father offers to pay Antonio for reparations and help him get back some of the land he had lost in his village. Knowing the futility of pursuing the matter, Lu's father accepts the offer. With some of that money, Lu is sent to a school in the city, where he is taken in by a mestizo merchant and his two children, Lucho and Margarita. Margarita, the first ladino girl Lu has ever met, is about his age; he is strongly attracted to her from the very beginning but cannot see her in any other way than as his superior.

When Lu returns to his village two years later, he feels a growing distance from his people. Although he is not fully conscious of it, he has internalized a new world view and no longer fits into his native village; after a brief stay with his family, Lu returns to school. Much like the Indian leader Wilca in *Todas las sangres*, Lu resolves to continue to learn from the ladino in order to return some day "to teach his people the sciences, the metallic truth that was more powerful than the *rajou* [gods] of the air." Lu still feels that he owes something to his people: "Do not forget that you are

Indian, because the people are expecting much from you,"[45] his father had written in a letter, and that debt was to be discharged by Lu's efforts to change his people.

After several years of schooling, Lu graduates and becomes a rural teacher; he begins his labors among the Indians with great expectations. A few months later, however, living in an isolated village with no educational materials, among hungry students, and harrassed by the police for using "revolutionary" teaching materials, Lu becomes totally disillusioned. To forget what he considers his failure, he begins drinking and carries on a love affair with a local ladino woman. Eventually, he abandons his teaching position altogether and becomes a drunkard. During this period of his life, Lu suffers an identity crisis; he compares the Indian's culture to the ladino's

> *almost geometrically, putting opposite values face to face, until he [sees] that without making a sound, his defenseless ideals, the solemn and unfulfilled obligations, his loyalty toward his torpid, ignorant, and ugly race [are] falling apart. [This was] a race without salvation so long as it tried to save itself in its rajou, in its incipient and archaic language, in its primitive manual work of priceless servants.*[46]

The crisis leads Lu to reject his people. He then becomes a soldier, for he believes that only as a soldier can he climb the social ladder.

After carrying out infamous acts against other Indians, Lu becomes a lieutenant in charge of the territory where, years before, his sister had been raped. By now he is arrogant and totally alienated from his people. After some time as the military authority in the region, Lu becomes accidentally involved in a ladino revolution aimed at bringing about social change in Guatemala and is wounded in battle. He is taken to a hospital where he reencounters Margarita, his old, impossible love, who is now a nurse helping the revolutionaries. This time, he feels, the situation is different: The revolution has triumphed and better days await Guatemala, and, for the first time, he sees Margarita as his social equal. Their mutual affection has a promising future. The novel ends with Lu's realization that "in order to redeem his people he was abandoning his father's gods and his father's house."[47]

Clearly, the solution to the Indian problem, the future of the Indian, in this novel is similar to the solution offered in Andean socialist novels. In order for the Indian to be redeemed, he must be culturally eliminated; the writer demands the death of the Indian's culture to make room for the mestizo's. In the end, Lu recognized that "one had to save the Indians and the land, not in the struggle between races, but in the struggle between man and man. The poor of all places: Those were his people."[48] The Indian problem, it turns out, is a class problem after all; the Indian must be saved as a person, not as an Indian.

Monteforte Toledo's second novel, *Donde acaban los caminos*, portrays the impossible love between a ladino medical doctor, Raúl Zamora, and an Indian girl, María Xahil. Raúl comes from the city to begin his practice in a little town in the highlands. There, he falls in love with a 17-year-old Indian girl with whom he lives secretly for little more than a month. The affair lasts long enough, however, for the ladinos in the town to find out about it; shocked, they ostracize and harrass the doctor. When the Indians find out about the affair, they are also shocked; they accuse the girl's father of having sold his daughter to the doctor and see the situation as a bad omen for them.[49] The situation is further complicated when María becomes pregnant. After some vacillation, Raúl decides to ask for María's hand; her father refuses, however. "Your people are separated, separated from my people," he says to Raúl, "and when they get together it is only so that we end up with spit in our faces and bitterness on our tongues. That is how things are."[50]

After a few days of separation and suffering, Raúl must accept the fact that "there no longer [exists] that intermediate territory, totally fictitious, situated between the two races."[51] Unable to stand the separation, Raúl kills himself. In a letter written before his death, Raul had stated that he did not have "the makings of an apostle" and that to him the Indians seemed "an entelechy without redemption."[52]

When Raúl dies, the conflict between the races becomes a fight for the child, which both ladinos and Indians claim as their own. With the help of one of Raúl's friends, María hurries to church to have the child baptized. At the very moment of the baptism, however, Indians appear to demand the child. In a moment of inspiration, the priest threatens them with the wrath of the saints around them. "We don't want quarrels with the saints of the church," reply the Indians, "we only come to take the child; he is our own."[53] The tension is broken when María herself asks the Indians to go away, and they leave.

By asking the Indians to leave, María has done two things: She has opted to raise her son as a mestizo, and, as a consequence, she has made the decision to leave her people forever. Before leaving the church, the sorcerer, in the name of all the Indians, tells María: "Two roads leave town. By one [of these roads], one comes, never to leave again; by the other, one leaves, never to return again. . . ."[54] Not wanted either in the city among the ladinos or in the village among the Indians, María and her son leave because one has to "save oneself in order to lose oneself."[55] After many hours, she reaches a place in the highlands where the roads end; there, she awaits the compassion and justice of humanity.

Donde acaban los caminos is a pessimistic novel: Hope for incorporating the Indian into society is truncated. Even the mestizo is an outcast from both worlds awaiting the understanding of humanity.

A Comparison

Similarities between Andean and Guatemalan indigenista novels are obvious: the depiction of Indians as an oppressed people, the indictment against the oppressors, the attempt to understand the Indians' magical world and its ultimate rejection, the negation of the Indians' future. But, due mainly to national history, Guatemalan novels show differences that are sociologically significant. A discussion of these differences indicates how the Dream of unity and the search for identity has been translated into literature.

I noted earlier that the priest is virtually absent from the Guatemalan novels. Certainly, there is an occasional mention of a Danish priest who has nephews and nieces among the Guatemalans and belongs to those reaping the fruits of the Indian's labor. But the priest is not at all a central character due to the weak presence of the Church in rural Guatemala.

A more significant difference between Andean and Guatemalan novels has to do with their views of the Indian as a revolutionary force. In the Andes, liberals and socialists treated this aspect differently: Liberals, following their conception of salvation, did not portray the Indian as a potential revolutionary force; for the socialists, however, such a potential was of utmost importance. These differences were based essentially on ideologic orientations. But what are the reasons for the absence of the Indian as a revolutionary force in novels of Guatemala? It is clear that the Indians portrayed in these novels are individuals who do not represent all Indians; Lu is exceptional, María is an anomaly in the Indian world. Lu becomes a lieutenant in the ladino army and, contrary to the soldiers of the Andes, does not return to his people to lead them in rebellion; he fights a revolution alongside ladinos, not his own people. In fact, Lu's participation in the revolution was possible because of his total deculturation. Why then wasn't the Indian regarded as a messianic force, especially given Guatemala's geographic proximity to Mexico, where the Indian did participate in a revolution? Clearly, it was not because the Indian's social conditions in Guatemala were different nor because the Indian's energy was weaker than in the Andes nor because ancient customs were less socialistic; in fact, the similarities on all these counts are striking.

The answer to this question lies in the social context in which these novels were written. The more optimistic novel, *Entre la piedra y la cruz*, was written *after* the overthrow of the Ubico dictatorship by the revolution of 1944, but this revolution occurred without the Indian's participation. Of course, after the revolution, Indians were invited to participate, and some ameliorative measures in their favor were instituted. Such government actions, however, were embedded in the long paternalist tradition of Spanish America. In order to remain true to the facts, Monteforte Toledo could not have introduced Indians as central characters in the revolution that takes place at the end of his novel; for this reason, the Indian's energies had to remain locked in the mystical past. In this sense, indigenista novels of Guatemala could be militant only after the fact; a position that proved untenable in the long run and that only led to disillusion as the revolution ran its course.

In light of this, the pessimism of *Donde acaban los caminos* can be explained: Since the Indians had failed to participate in the revolution from the very beginning, the only hope Monteforte Toledo saw for solving the Indian problem was predicated on some action taken from above by sympathetic ladinos. A paternalist solution, however, had to result in disappointment; in fact, when the revolution courted the Indian for its cause, it found him cautious and sometimes apathetic. Despite the revolutionary flavor of their appeals, ladinos in power were unable, as were their counterparts in the Andes, to enlist the Indian's full participation. And this failure eventually led to the failure of the revolution itself. For in Guatemala, in the late 1940s and early 1950s, the majority of the population was still Indian, and without this support, a liberal or socialist government could not possibly survive attacks from conservative forces.

Having recognized that the Indian was reluctant to accept the ladinos' solution to the Indian problem (predicated on the Indian's cultural death), Monteforte Toledo, like some liberal writers in the Andes, partially returns to the prein-digenista mood. His disappointment with the results of the revolution as far as the Indian problem goes is total. Despite his realistic portrayal of the Indian's social conditions in his second novel, he therefore returns to Matto's conclusion: either charity or death. Furthermore, because of the realis-tic portrayal of the Indian's oppressive social conditions and the fact that such conditions had to be presented without solution, the pessimism of the novel takes on even greater weight than in Matto's novel. In María's case, even the coming of the New Man is discarded as a myth; in the impossibility of love between two races, Monteforte Toledo hurls a severe blow at the ideal of a culturally united Span-ish America.

But it is most important to see that the blow issues from disappointment, from a loss of hope, not from a firm belief in cultural pluralism. Thus, precisely in this case, the exis-tence of the Dream of cultural unity is evident. In short, though in a different fashion, Monteforte Toledo follows in the footsteps of the Andean writers. It remains to be seen how the Mexican novelists viewed the Indian problem and its solution in terms of their own sociocultural development.

Chapter Six

Social Factors Affecting the Mexican Indigenista Novel

The misfortune of these people has something of the impersonal, of the inhuman; it repeats itself so uniformly over and over again.
—Oficio de tinieblas

The Land

In ancient Mexico, the *calpulli* system of land tenure resembled the communal ownership of land among Indians in Guatemala and the Andes. The lands of the calpulli were owned by no one in particular but, instead, belonged to the entire community. Each head of a family had the right to use a portion of the communally owned land in accordance with the family's needs and was under the obligation to work on it. If the family could not cultivate the land for two consecutive years, the land automatically reverted to the community for allocation among other members. As in Guatemala, even though the portion of land allocated to a particular family could not be owned by that family, the land did pass from generation to generation within the family, due to claims based on tradition.

With the arrival of the Spaniards, this arrangement of land tenure ceased, and Indian communities began to disappear as viable alternatives to the conquerors' notion of personal property. Shortly after conquest, Indians, driven from their communities by losses of land and water and extremely high taxes (which they had to pay as tribute to the king of Spain for being Indians), began either to retreat to the inaccessible highlands or to enter into individual relationships with the Spaniard: Thus, the hacienda system was born in Mexico; as early as 1540, numerous Indians lived as peons.

The Indian's exodus from his community was beneficial to the Spaniards in two ways: First, such an exodus left the community weaker in terms of manpower and, consequently, easier to annex to the hacienda; secondly, by turning the Indian into a peon, the Spanish obtained the labor force needed to run their highly inefficient but prestigious haciendas. During the 300 years of colonial rule in Mexico, the Indian's lot progressed from bad to worse. Having lost his land, the Indian became a peon and sank to the bottom of the social ladder; from there, he supported the extravagance of the Mexican aristocracy.

The independence movement in the nineteenth century did not affect the colonial system of land tenure to any extent. As in the other countries discussed, the wars of independence, fought largely by mestizos and Indians, benefited these sectors of the society the least. In Mexico, early political efforts by the liberal priests Miguel Hidalgo y Costilla (1753–1811) and José María Morelos (1765–1815) to bring about radical social change did not crystallize. The final steps for Mexico's independence from Spain were carried out precisely by those whom Hidalgo and Morelos had fought against, the wealthy creoles and the landed oligarchy. Thus, Mexican independence meant a change in political power from the Spanish few to the fewer Mexican rich.

From 1821, the year of independence, to 1855, when the liberal reforma movement began its decisive political work, there was no major action taken to change the colonial system of land tenure. The reforma movement itself was basically antifeudal and anticlerical; it translated the resentment of large sectors of Mexican society against conservative powers allied to the Catholic Church, which, as the single most powerful corporation in Mexico, exerted its influence at all levels of society. Led by Benito Juárez, liberal forces attempted to curtail the church's temporal powers and to separate church and state. By 1860, liberal forces had triumphed, and Juárez had decreed the nationalization of the church's property.

Significantly, the liberals abolished the right to communal ownership of land in order to break up the church's corporate power. But the laws enacted for this purpose served another as well: incorporating Indian communities into the world of whites and mestizos. As in the Andes and Guatemala, liberal reforms in nineteenth-century Mexico were aimed at making either a bourgeois or a peon of every Indian. By abolishing the right to communal property ownership across the board, liberals achieved two important objectives: the dissolution of the church's land holdings and the almost total destruction of Indian communities. The first of these objectives advanced liberal interests against conservative sectors of the society; the second provided hacienda owners with much-needed and cheap Indian labor.

In the case of the Indians, the laws required their land to be partitioned into private holdings among the members of the community affected. As in other cases studied, Mexican Indians, having little notion of private ownership, soon lost their land to white and mestizo landowners out of ignorance, deception, or coercion; in many cases, entire communities lost land in one act of aggression. For the most part, these communities had no written titles to their land and were thus easy targets for Mexican and foreign entrepreneurs. The few communities that survived were situated on poor lands that no one wanted or else resisted with organized rebellion against partitioning their land into private holdings. The Yaqui Indians, for example, were very firm in rejecting liberal reforms: "God gave the river to all Yaquis," they argued, "not a piece of it to each one of us."[1] Despite these exceptions, however, Indian communities suffered a severe blow. By enforcing the law in the years between 1821 and 1910, liberals destroyed more Indian communities than had been destroyed during 300 years of conquest and colonization.

As in the Andes and Guatemala, the end of colonial rule meant harsher realities for Mexican Indians. Before the reforma movement, the Indian's community offered some protection from the encroachment of the white world; the Indian had the strength of the group. Besides communal land, in many cases, the Indian could count on the town's ejidos (lands near the town) for his needs; thus, he did not have to work for a wage as a peon, and, consequently, his dealings with landowners were seasonal and carried out with a modicum of independence. With the loss of most of his land, however, the Indian was forced to become a peon permanently.

The Indian
and the Díaz Regime

Dictator Porfirio Díaz (1876–1880; 1884–1911) inherited from the liberals policies for destroying Indian communities and used them fully. Surrounded by a cohort of pseudo-scientists who declared themselves positivists (known as the *científicos*), Díaz employed racial theories to justify usurping the Indian's land and exploiting Indian labor.[2] Like the científicos, Díaz considered the Indian to be inferior, submissive, and incapable of thinking for himself; in contrast, Díaz saw the white man as called on to do the thinking. In practice, this meant that all government action was in the interest of the landowner and to the detriment of the Indian.

During this period, too, as in the Andes, the Mexican "hidalgos" faced an Indian problem. The científicos placed their hopes for its solution on the massive immigration of Europeans, and these hopes served Díaz rather well, justifying many of his policies directed at encouraging foreign settlers on Mexican soil. To facilitate these settlements, the government employed the services of private firms to make an inventory of the land and delineate the geographic location of land available for colonization. In payment for their services, these companies (set up by individuals close to Díaz) were given millions of acres of land. This land, much of it taken from Indian communities, was eventually left uncultivated. As a result of these and similar policies, the accumulation of land by a few individuals at the expense of the Indian and poor mestizo during the Díaz regime increased. By 1910, 8,245 haciendas in Mexico held about 88 million hectares, roughly 40 percent of the total area of the country; these haciendas were, in turn, owned by 834 families, who owned an average of ten haciendas apiece. Most of the labor force on these haciendas, on the other hand, was made up of Indians and poor mestizos who had lost their lands.

Indian Labor

There were several ways for an Indian to enter into socioeconomic relationships with a landlord during the Díaz regime; perhaps the most asymmetric was that of the peon *acasillado*, an individual who resided permanently on the hacienda, received a salary and such benefits as maize, a staple in the peon's diet, which was sold to him at the *tienda de raya* (a store owned by the landlord) as a salary advance. Sometimes the price of maize was lower than at the regular market, but more often it was higher.[3] On haciendas located in the highlands, the peon acasillado was often given a portion of *pulque* (alcoholic beverage) at the end of the day. He had the use of a hut without cost, and, in some cases, especially on haciendas located near governmental posts, the peon acasillado had the benefits of rudimentary education for his children. He was allowed, always subject to the landlord's discretion, a daily credit that could be used to buy clothing, food, and other articles at the tienda de raya. If he was submissive and conformed to the norms established by the landlord, he could receive a cash loan that would enable him to carry out his religious duties.

The peon acasillado was certainly not a free man; his salary, paid mostly in notes, or *fichas*, and not in money, was so low that it hardly kept him and his family alive. In order to pay for clothing and other necessities, he had to ask the landlord for advances or loans against his salary, a situation that made it likely that the peon would constantly be in debt, since he was very seldom able to pay the balance. As was the case in the Andes and Guatemala, the debt contracted by one member of the peon's family was handed down to the next generation, thereby making virtual slaves of the peon and his children.

The second form of socioeconomic relationship between landlord and Indian was the peon *baldillo*, a person who, having lost his land, depended on the patrón for the land necessary for planting crops and feeding his animals. The peon baldillo often lived within the confines of the hacienda, and, in return for the land he was allowed to use, he worked for the patrón without pay. The number of days he was obliged to work varied from case to case but generally depended on the needs of the patrón. During harvest time, the peon baldillo had to tend to the crops of the patrón first, otherwise he stood to lose his borrowed land. Since this type of arrangement included the labor of not only the peon baldillo but all members of his family, wife and children included, his own crop was many times partially or totally ruined for lack of attention.

There were Indians less dependent on the patrón for their livelihood; they were the *aparceros*, individuals who were given a portion of land by the hacienda for a share of their crops. But even the aparceros were not totally free; their dependency on the patrón resulted from the insufficient land available to them. They were, in fact, forced to work for the patrón to stay alive, and, furthermore, in times of drought or other natural disasters, aparceros were forced to ask the patrón for a loan, be it in money, seeds, or food, and thereby became indebted to him in a way that made it difficult to extricate themselves.

During the Díaz regime, Indian labor was also exploited through the system of *contratación*, which began around 1904 and consisted of securing cheap labor for the plantations (mostly foreign-owned) in the lowlands, which, at that time, were expanding. The methods of securing cheap Indian labor for these plantations were similar to those used by Guatemalan landowners: Through coercion or deceit, Mexican Indians were transported by foot for many miles as seasonal workers. They traveled in a state of semi-intoxication, spurred on by a mounted foreman; often, their wives and children accompanied them to pay off debts they had been forced to accept. This form of Indian exploitation was not significantly curtailed until the mid 1930s when President Cárdenas made attempts to stop it.

The Indian, of course, did not accept such relationships without protest, but his efforts to rebel did not pay off. If an indebted acasillado, baldillo, aparcero, or contratado tried to escape, he was hunted down by Díaz's rural police and returned to his masters. In the case of large haciendas, landlords had their own police, passed judgment, and executed sentences; these forces of order punished not only fugitives but all who attempted to break the rules governing their socioeconomic relationship with the landlord. To the peon, writes Frank R. Brandenburg about the Díaz regime, "justice meant the unquestioned word of *hacendado* [hacienda owner], administrator, jailor, and priest."[4] Any attempt at open rebellion could cost the Indian a beating, imprisonment, or the firing squad. Such was the Indian's position during the Díaz regime that even those Indians not under the constraint of forced labor feared the landlord, the state, and its agents.

Indian Rebellions

Indian rebellions against the usurpation of their land, high taxes, and the abuses of governmental authorities were a part of Mexican history ever since the first days of conquest.[5] But, as in the Andes and Guatemala, these rebellions were basically isolated attempts to right particular wrongs and did not stem from an organized effort involving all Indians in Mexico. True, there were attempts to seize power in large territorial units (actions by the Yaquis and Mayas are cases in point), but such attempts ultimately failed because, among other things, they did not include the support of all Indians in Mexico nor of the mestizo sympathizers. This inability to mount a concerted effort allowed government forces to direct their attention to one rebellion at a time and crush it.

The Mexican Indian, like his counterpart in other countries, did not look beyond his community or tribe. Whenever he engaged in a common effort with other communities, he did so on the basis of an ideology not his own, as in the case of the Cristero rebellions, which represented the Catholic Church's reaction to liberal forces marshaled by the revolution of 1910, or trust in a caudillo who transcended local interests, as did Zapata. This lack of political vision is one of many reasons why the Indian was used by competing ideologies during the revolution of 1910, which ultimately pursued the aims of the Mexican middle class.

The Military

As in other parts of Spanish America, the Mexican military has upheld the public order that relegated the Indian to near slavery and dealt harshly with all attempts to stop abuses to which Indians were subjected; indeed, Indian repression is as much a part of Mexican history as Andean and Guatemalan history. Indians taken as prisoners during rebellions were either put in concentration camps (*colónias militares*), deported as slaves to foreign countries, moved around the Mexican territory, or put to death before a firing squad.[6]

The methods and targets of military recruitment for the Mexican army were also similar to those of the Andean and Guatemalan armies; in fact, most of the soldiers who fought against the revolutionary armies in 1910 were obtained through violent induction. The threat of recruitment for those who made trouble was very much a part of the military function, which sought to neutralize opposition to the Díaz regime by eliminating potential troublemakers. Zapata, for example, was conscripted into the army in an effort to stop his political agitation, and other revolutionary leaders had similar experiences.[7]

Due to the increasing impoverishment from the republican period to the end of the Díaz dictatorship, the Indian as well as the poor mestizo of Mexico had little to lose and much to gain from armed revolution. When the time came to vent their repressed anger, these revolutionaries were cruel to their former exploiters and distrustful of all authority. The man who began the revolution in 1910, Francisco Madero, was too naïve to understand, much less control, the forces he was unleashing. The Mexican Revolution stopped, not because its revolutionary measures solved the agrarian problem or the Indian problem, but because of the sheer exhaustion of the masses; because the hatred in the hearts of the majority of the oppressed had somehow been appeased.

The Indian and the Revolution

There was no thunder to warn us that the tempest was coming.

—An Indian Woman[8]

It could be said that Díaz's 34-year dictatorship was responsible for the Mexican Revolution. First, the political stability fostered by Díaz's government made possible, among other things, the modernization of the Mexican economy and the development of the infrastructure of the nation, which encouraged internal commerce, and the education of sizeable sectors of the population. In other words, Díaz fostered the growth of the Mexican bourgeoisie, particularly in the northern part of the nation; this same bourgeoisie eventually found the dictator's methods to be obstacles to its development. Díaz's support of the wealthy oligarchy and foreign companies did not coincide with the aspirations of the Mexican bourgeoisie, which had begun its bid for power at the turn of the century, as in most other Spanish American countries. Second, and as an inevitable consequence, Díaz's dictatorship and the prosperity of the middle classes that it made possible were based on the exploitation of peasants, Indians included, and poor sectors of the population in general. Eventually, these two elements, the rising bourgeoisie from the north and poor peasants from the south, were to converge in Mexico City.

The Mexican Revolution began with the Maderista rebellions in Puebla and Chihuahua on November 20, 1910, but if when the tempest began is more or less certain, when it ended is not at all clear. Some argue that the revolution concluded with the end of its armed phase in 1917, others say that it lasted at least until the death of Venustiano Carranza in 1921. Some maintain that the revolution ended only with the nationalization of Mexican oil by Cárdenas in 1938; still others, though few in number, claim that the revolution is not dead but continues even today. Whatever the merits of these assertions, as far as the bulk of indigenista novels are concerned, the Mexican Revolution covers the period from 1910 until 1940. The plot of the last Mexican indigenista novel, Rosario Castellanos's *Oficio de tinieblas* (1962) is set during the Cárdenas regime, which ended in 1940.

I have already indicated that the Mexican Revolution was not an Indian revolution, but one that advanced the interests of the Mexican bourgeoisie. This is a point that should be examined further because it clarifies the novelistic production and the thesis I support. It seems clear from the record that even if the Indian fought in most of the battles during this social upheaval, he fought for different groups with no clear notion as to where *his* interests lay. With perhaps the exception of Zapata's agrarian movement, the Indian followed caudillos who seldom had an interest in the Indian's cause. In fact, few Indian leaders attained national prominence during the revolution and when they did—as in the case of General Amaro—they did so as subordinates to mestizos or whites.

With the exception of Zapata, most prominent caudillos

during what is generally called the armed phase of the revolution (1910–1917) came from the northern middle- and
lower-middle classes. Alvaro Obregón, for example, had
been a mechanic on a hacienda and a cattle merchant in the
north before becoming involved in politics under the aegis
of Madero. Plutarco Elías Calles was also from the north,
the son of an *arriero* (conductor of a muletrain), who made a
living as a small-scale merchant. He later became a teacher,
a position from which he had to resign due to the pressure
of Díaz's cronies. Francisco Villa, the most famous of the
northern caudillos, was a cattle thief who expanded his activities after his experience in the United States Army. All
of these caudillos formed a group that could hardly be called
peasant or Indian, even though most members had some
Indian blood. Zapata himself was not an Indian but a member of an old mestizo family that had always been involved
in politics. In fact, he did not begin his rebellion with the
help of Indians but as a representative of southern Mexico's
small rancheros and mestizo townspeople who were being
pushed aside by expanding sugar haciendas. It took many
battles before Zapata sought and obtained the support of
peons and large Indian groups.

   If Indians did not lead the revolution against Díaz, they
did form large segments of the revolutionary army, and, as
such, no caudillo could ignore them. To lose the Indians'
support might have meant losing the battle and eventually
the war. It is not surprising, then, that even Madero, who
represented wealthy landowners in the north, reluctantly
included in his program solutions to the Indian problem,
which had been translated into an agrarian problem.[9]

   Madero's overture toward the Indians did not mean that
he was willing to solve the Mexican agrarian problem in the
way it was to be solved later on by other revolutionary
governments. Had Madero consolidated his control over the
revolutionary forces, the Indians would have been only
slightly affected by his government. It took members of the

middle class, whose economic base was the liberal professions, and increasing industrialization—not land itself—
to carry out the agrarian reform that affected the Indians.
Madero's misunderstanding of the conditions that led to the
Mexican Revolution is evident in his naïve remark: "The
people do not ask for bread, they ask for liberty."[10]

The Ejido

The agrarian problem and the Indian problem were too
predominant in Mexico to be bypassed by a revolution of
the proportions of that of 1910. Two years after the initial
days of struggle, in 1912, the revolutionary leader Luís Cabrera gave the first clear indication of one of the directions
the revolution was going to take in agrarian reform. He then
suggested the reconstitution of the old ejidos in the towns.
Three years later, when Carranza, another revolutionary
leader, by decree of January 6, 1915, presented his own
solution to the agrarian problem, the model of the ejido was
already delineated. The final touch to this approach was
given when the ejido, significantly modified by Zapata's in-
sistence on considering his own agrarian platform, as spelled
out in his *Plan de Ayala,* was included in Article 27 of the
constitution signed in Queretaro in 1917. Later laws were to
clarify and support Article 27; its importance in solving the
agrarian problem, however, was secured and the direction
of the solution to the Indian problem given: the communal
ownership of land under the ejido system.[11]

The ejido, which became the cornerstone of agrarian reform in Mexico, is related to an institution created by the
Spaniards in colonial times. At that time, the ejido consisted
of lands situated on the periphery of the town and designated for communal use by the townspeople. This land was
used for a variety of purposes: It was the pound for stray
cattle as well as the public threshing floor and a place where

villagers could winnow their grain in the open air; it sometimes contained the public rubbish heap or the village
slaughter pen. Farmers could unload produce here that was
to be sold in the marketplace, and unoccupied portions of the
ejido could be used as a playground or loafing place; no buildings were constructed on the ejido, nor was it cultivated.

The colonial ejido was obviously not in Cabrera's mind
when he proposed it as the solution to the agrarian problem.
The ejido system that the revolution wanted would not include only lands that were to remain idle or serve essentially
nonagricultural ends. In fact, the ejido system was an attempt on the part of the Mexican government to incorporate
ancient Indian communal practices of labor and land tenure
into a modern economy. The result was basically a mestizo
institution that combined communal and capitalistic elements; the division of the ejido into *parcelas*, for example,
resembled the division of land in the ancient *calpullis*.
However, although the parcelas were not privately owned,
families could enjoy the usufruct from their tracts of land. As
in ancient times, also, there were tracts of land designated
for education; these tracts were to be used for agricultural
demonstrations by the government, and their usufruct was
to cover some of the cost of educating children in the community.

The amount of land affected by laws supporting the modern ejido was the result of a cumulative process of land
redistribution carried out by the Mexican government between 1915 and 1940. This process was by no means straight-
forward but reflected the position of different caudillos toward land reform. Between 1921 and 1924, for example,
about one and a half million hectares were distributed
among 161,788 peasants; from 1935 to 1940, under the presidency of Lázaro Cárdenas, 17,609,131 hectares were distributed among 771,640 peasants. The end of Cárdenas's
administration (1934–1940) marked the decline of agrarian
reform in Mexico. After 30 years, the government was unable or unwilling to end the concentration of land among a

few owners. The overall results of the agrarian reform are nonetheless impressive; for one thing, the reform drastically altered the hacienda system prevalent during the Díaz regime so that few peons were now treated as they had been during the republican period before 1910.

It should be noted here that along with efforts to carry out land reform, leaders of the Mexican Revolution wrought other changes in the lives of the Indian and peasant; the government's efforts to bring education to rural areas were particularly noteworthy. Rural schools and teachers' colleges aimed at incorporating the Indian into national life were built thoughout the country; regional hospitals generally improved health in rural sectors, with a subsequent decline in mortality rates there; the Instituto Nacional Indigenista was created for the express purpose of studying the Indian's sociocultural conditions and making policy recommendations; and, in general, indigenismo as a social cause gained many followers.

The Writer's Sociocultural Milieu

All things considered, the revolution was beneficial to the Mexican Indian. By the 1930s, when the first major indigenista novels appeared in Mexico—*El indio* (1935), *El resplandor* (1936)—the lot of most Indians in Mexico was far better than those in the Andes. But in the Andes and Guatemala, the indigenista novel arose to rescue the Indian from his oppressive conditions; what, then, was the raison d'être of the Mexican novel? In other words, how did the revolution, which ameliorated the Indian's socioeconomic conditions, affect the indigenista novel? Was the rise of the indigenista novel here due perhaps to purely literary influences stemming from the South? The answers to these questions go to the heart of the thesis being developed here, but before answering them, a discussion of the indigenista writers cultural milieu is in order.

If there ever was a period in the history of Spanish America when its literature enjoyed what M. A. Asturias has called abnormal normality, it must have been in Mexico during the Díaz regime. During this period, the government's methods of dealing with dissent were too powerful a deterrent for most writers. Like their counterparts in Guatemala under Cabrera and Ubico, Mexican writers in this period were intimidated or otherwise co-opted into acquiescing to government policies; they had to forego their traditional role of social critic. Many of them took comfortable government posts; others spent their energies writing about the past—preferably about inoffensive periods in Mexican history such as the colonial period; still others explicitly divorced literature from politics. It certainly was no accident that the *modernista* literary movement, which divorced art from politics, developed under Díaz's regime. The movement's hostile attitude toward sociopolitical issues fit hand in glove with the dictator's desire to govern Mexico undisturbed by social concerns of intellectuals.[12]

Given this tendency to turn away from reality, it is not surprising that the Indian was hardly noticed by writers in this period despite the fact that what the cultural elite considered Indian (dark peasants and peons) formed the largest sector of Mexico's population and lived under very harsh conditions. However, a realistic treatment of the Indian in literature during the Díaz regime would have earned the writer the title of rebel and a long jail sentence. Unwilling to suffer the consequences, even writers of the realist school —which had begun in Mexico by the 1860s—left the Indian alone.[13] The works of leading realist writers as Lópes-Portillo stand alongside such escapist works as *Hermana de los ángeles* (1854) by Florencio de Castillo and *Adah, o el amor de un ángel* (1900) by Aurelio Luís Gallardo.

But the intellectual's silence was not total. At the turn of the century, as the Mexican bourgeoisie began to develop, organized resistance by Mexican intellectuals took place. Several newspapers emerged that criticized Díaz's regime, to which the government reacted violently. Some of these publications were closed down by government agents only to reappear days later under a different name. During this period, too, El Ateneo de la Juventud, an organization that pitted itself against Díaz's científicos was founded. Imbued with a notion of vitalism gleaned from the works of Bergson, members of the Ateneo opposed the "materialistic" philosophy of the positivists. Even though its goals were not political but, rather, philosophic and cultural, much like those of the literary circles that were springing up at this time in the Andes, this organization considerably influenced the development of middle-class ideology and eventually the revolution itself. Among its members was José Vasconcelos, who later worked for Villa, became a friend of Zapata, and then was Minister of Education (1921–1924) under the regime of Alvaro Obregón. Vasconcelos had a great deal to do with the growth of the arts in revolutionary Mexico. Another prominent figure in this group of intellectuals was Antonio Caso, an unorthodox thinker who influenced many young intellectuals taking part in the later phase of the revolution.

Guided by their essentially vitalist philosophic position, members of the Ateneo searched for the Mexican essence and *élan vital*. In their search, they plunged into Mexico's history, but their Europhile tendencies stopped them short at the colonial period; that is, following Rodó, they searched for Mexico's essence in its Spanish colonial heritage. Consequently, the Indian element in Mexican history was played down. For all its shortcomings, however, the Ateneo was a major force in the revolution of 1910, which deeply affected the Indian.

The philosophy of the Ateneo marked a clear shift in the Mexican cultural elite. The emergence of spiritualist and vitalist philosophies at this time was an extension of the antipositivist feelings marshalled by Rodó and his Arielista group across Latin America; it was a response to Rodó's call for a return to Spanish humanism. However, while Rodó's ideas were clearly European in outlook, that is, while he called for a return to a Spanish tradition ignoring the Indian element, the Mexican cultural elite, made up of or surrounded by mestizos, could not dismiss the Indian element so readily. Eventually, therefore, the search for the essence of the Mexican became a search for the essence of the mestizo. Without doubt, the Mexican Revolution, which unveiled the Indian problem, was to a large measure responsible for the shift in views of the new cultural elite in Mexico. Ever since then, understanding the mestizo has been the key to understanding the Mexican being.

But this focus on the mestizo as the locus of the Mexican essence required rethinking ethnic and racial theories and labels. During Díaz's regime, científicos identified as Indians all dark and poor peasants and peons who populated the countryside and poor sections of the cities; in other words, the term Indian was synonymous with powerlessness. Now, in the eyes of rising middle-class intellectuals, on the contrary, peons were not Indians at all even if they were genotypically pure Mayan or Aztecan! Antonio Caso, for example, argued that Indians were those who lived in, and felt themselves a part of, a *comunidad* (Indian community), regardless of their biological heritage.[14] Since peons lived on haciendas where they entered into economic relations with the patrón as individuals, it followed that they were not Indians. Aguirre and Pozas used a more technical term, *mestindio*, to refer to this mass of peons living on and around haciendas in Mexico.[15] Biological consideration had given way to cultural considerations in designating one's ethnic group.

This shift of position in the cultural realm was not merely an academic affair; it translated a desire of the Mexican bourgeoisie, which was in control of the revolution, to create an adequate internal market to support its growth. Incorporating the peasantry into a mestizo world became attractive, to say the least. Consequently, the middle class directed the entire governmental apparatus to that end: Education, direct loans to ejidos, and other measures were taken to incorporate the peasant into the Mexican market economy.

This policy of incorporation is best exemplified by the government's concern with the ejido, for, contrary to statements by some government officials to the effect that the ejido was a return to ancient practices, it served precisely the opposite purpose. Through the *ejido*, the government pursued the destruction of traditional (that is, Indian) values among the peasantry to ready them for active participation in an expanding market economy. Aguirre and Pozas have noted, for example, that the government obtained "a high degree of individuation and secularization among the old free pueblos, thus destroying definitively the sacred and communal characteristics that had persisted among them despite brutal attacks by the hacienda; that is to say, it turned the *mestindio* group into mestizo and integrated it into the social and economic life of the nation."[16] If biological mestizaje had been the work of unplanned centuries of white-Indian relations, cultural mestizaje was, in large measure, the result of planned government policies during the first half of the twentieth century.

The revolution was not totally successful in welding a nation, however; Indian groups scattered in the sierras survived the mestizo's encroachment. Although revolutionary leaders enlisted the help of Indian peons and peasants, some isolated Indian communities were largely bypassed by the violence if not the benefits. It was precisely this sector of the Mexican population, the isolated Indian communities, that provided the raison d'être for the Mexican indigenista novel. By depicting the treatment of this ignored sector of society, Mexican indigenista writers attempted to point out what they thought was one of the most serious shortcomings of the Mexican Revolution in general. And this attempt gives Mexican novels their particular flavor and importance within the indigenista movement.

In order to understand the Mexican indigenista novel better, it must first be emphasized that the Mexican Revolution was not based on indigenismo, which, in fact, appeared too late on the Mexican scene to develop into a militant movement. As noted, concern with the Indian and his culture was a result of the revolution and not vice versa.[17] In this sense, Guatemalan and Mexican novels came after a revolutionary phase and, consequently, were deprived of a role in directing the revolution; they were also deprived of the hope of a future revolution.

A second consideration to keep in mind is what may be termed the neutralization of Marxist intellectuals. The Mexican communist party was not founded until 1924, that is, at least seven years after the end of the armed phase of the revolution.[18] In fact, the end of Mexico's armed revolutionary phase coincided with the onset of the Russian October Revolution. The tardy appearance of socialist and communist parties left them without significant influence among the armed peasantry who participated in the revolution. But even after their establishment, these parties were unable to galvanize the support of an organized peasantry or proletariat, the latter at the time being small in number and influenced by anarchist tendencies. Therefore, by the early 1930s, while Marxist tendencies in the Andes had become the backbone of a militant indigenismo by supplanting the peasant with the proletariat, in Mexico, without the support of a strong proletariat or the possibility of a revolutionary peasantry, Marxist thought reverted to academic polemics.

Also, it must be kept in mind that those Indians who fought in the revolution were no longer considered Indian by the new cultural elite. For this reason, indigenista novels are not novels about the Mexican Revolution, and there is no room in them for the description of battles like those found in Azuela's *Los de abajo* (1916), for example. Indeed, according to the cultural leaders, by the time indigenismo became fashionable, there were few Indians left in Mexico; in their eyes, the Indian as a revolutionary potential had been bypassed by events. Thus, when the fight was over, the ground was fertile for creating myths by which the Indian as Indian entered the Mexican Revolution. It was, therefore, the romantic Indian, the Indian of the past, or the exotic Indian who, for the new cultural elite, was at the foreground of the indigenista movement in art and philosophy. Indians scattered in the countryside or crowded in urban centers were either ignored or reclassified.

Given all these considerations, it should not be surprising that Mexican indigenista novels have, for the most part, an anthropologic and historic tendency. Reclassifying the Indian made possible a novel that paid attention to the inner workings of isolated Indian communities where the description of the exotic was commonplace. The settings of these novels are clearly not of Mexico in revolution: "It was a Monday, the ninth of August," recalls a central character in *Nayar* who is mestizo, "when we became travelers in a world totally different from the ordinary."[19] And the novel goes on to describe the Indian's life in remote corners of Mexico; alternatively, these novels are set in the past. In *Donde crecen los tepozanes*, for example, the protagonist wonders about the weight of his past: "Maybe I could not be precise as to what I was or what I did, but I could be sure that I formed part of a people now definitively extinguished."[20]

Chapter Seven

The Message of the Mexican Indigenista Novel

That is why the Indian goes, a ghost to himself, along roads that have no end, certain that the end, the only end possible, the end that frees and allows him to find his lost footprints, is where death awaits.

—Canek

The Mythic and Historic Past

Mexican novels, like those in the Andes and Guatemala, portray the Indian's mythic past, which is an undetermined period. Indians in these novels feel that they belong to one race and culture, but they are not certain how. An old Indian telling the story of his people notes, for example, that "all the customs, similar even in the tribes that speak a different language, show that the trunk was one and that from it many branches sprang."[1] But this theory is posited as a debatable thesis within the novelistic context; it is an assertion against contrary popular opinion. Often, too, the feasibility of communal origins is not introduced by Indian character but by educated whites or mestizos. A teacher, a member of a punitive expedition against the Indian says, for example, that the race "with its traditions, perhaps no longer pure, with its physiognomic features, with its spirit and customs, even though much weakened by exploitative servitude and tutelage, exists and only waits to be redeemed. . . ."[2] In this novel, however, Indians themselves never attempt such a redemption.

Vagueness about the past and the tendency to lump together different people under the term Indian betrays an unwillingness or inability on the part of all Spanish American indigenista writers to examine more deeply the historic record. But this characteristic is most salient in Mexican novels because it forms part of a novel that sees the Indian in isolation and treats him as a historic or anthropologic subject. The least that could be expected from such novels is some effort to dispel the myths surrounding the history of their subjects. Instead, Columbus's mistake of calling all people in the New World Indians without qualification is allowed to continue in Spanish America. Consequently, the Indian's past is depicted in Mexican indigenista novels as the past of a mythic race, vague in terms of both positive qualities and shortcomings.

200

There is another point to be made in connection with the Mexican writer's view of the Indian's mythic past. The vague treatment of the Indian's mythic past in the Andes made possible the view of a golden age in Indian history; the Inca empire, for example, was thought to be an example of Indian creativity and potential. By contrast, in Mexican novels, despite their cultural achievements noted earlier, neither the Aztecan nor the Mayan past are opposed to the present. This clear omission on the part of Mexican novelists shows how political militancy, especially socialist militancy, or lack thereof, affected Spanish American indigenista novels. In the Andes, the Inca's past was held up as an incentive, with the hope that the Indian would elect a socialist future. In Mexico, where the revolution had bypassed the Indian—those whom indigenista writers considered Indians, that is—no such hope is evident. In other words, in Mexican novels, the Indian's past does not have a revolutionary function; it offers no solutions.[3]

Concerning the historic past, Mexican writers are in absolute agreement with all other indigenista writers in Spanish America: The conquest, they argue, made Indians slaves and "after the conquest, they continued being slaves; they ignored the freedom that independence gave them, and when they knew it, its knowledge was useless."[4] As the white men (who came "as if from another world")[5] secured control over the Indian's world, they set themselves up as masters of the land; they imposed their customs, religion, and language on the Indian. The gentle Tzotzil language, Rosario Castellanos tells us, was supplanted by Spanish, and language itself became a "steeled instrument of lordship, arm of conquest, tip of the whip of the law."[6] This is one of the few instances in the indigenista novel where the Spanish language itself is regarded as an instrument of conquest. The Indians suffered the consequences of a conquered people: they lost their lands, their names, and their gods. As the white man advanced, the Indians retreated to inaccessible jungle regions and the highlands; there they remain to this day. Whoever was left behind in this general and desperate retreat became other, a mestizo.

But even in their isolation, Indians are not free from the white man's abuses; in the remotest regions, for example, the white man's genes assail the Indian. There are few pure Indians left in Mexico, for there, too, mestizaje is the product of rape. "Seeing how the two rivers fused into one," an old Indian reminisces, "one of clear and the other of obscured waters, I thought that we were like that: water of two rivers."[7] The fusion the old Indian speaks of is the result of white miners raping Indian women.

Certainly, these acts of aggression were not always passively supported by the Indians; from time to time, they rebelled against their oppressors. But due to the white man's superior technology and organization, the Indians were always defeated. With each defeat, the energy of the race receded into their collective unconscious; slowly, a fatalist attitude enveloped them. With the dawning of Spanish American history, Indians became convinced that "it is useless to rebel."[8] The weight of centuries of dehumanization through harrassment and exploitation has made the isolated Indian world tragic. The Indians, one writer observes, "have forgotten how to sing."[9] Indeed, Indians in these novels do not sing except during religious festivities when singing becomes a life or death affair.

Despite these tremendous odds, the Indian's spirit survives; it survives beneath the Indian's fatalist posture. From beneath its cover, the spirit comes to the surface in moments of daring, danger, or despair. Thus, Mexican novels also bear witness to innumerable Indian rebellions during the nineteenth and twentieth centuries. Such novels as *Canek* (1940), *Cájeme* (1948), and *Oficio de tinieblas* (1962) are built around historic Indian rebellions where the Indian's transformation from peasant to warrior had taken place.

There is a theme in Mexican novels that although present in Andean novels is overshadowed by the writer's belief in the revolutionary potential of the Indian's culture. This is the theme of the psychological mechanism that the Indian has developed over the centuries in order to survive amid oppressive conditions and retain some sense of dignity. According to these writers, most Indians have a dual personality, one that they exhibit among themselves, the other when dealing with their oppressors. Among themselves, Indians in these novels are often brave, proud, affectionate; in their relations with the white man, they are often elusive and appear subservient and stoic. A passage from *El resplandor* exemplifies the Indian's conception of his relationship with his oppressors. An Indian woman advises a young boy:

> *One never says anything to the patrones, understand? Much less what is spoken among the Tlacuaches. They would not understand you, nor you them. One guesses their intentions, one listens and shuts up. The white men have never permitted the Indian to say anything. When they look for us, it is not for our good. "Where are you going?" "Well, I am going there, lord," and on the first hill, turn around and take the opposite direction. "Do you know of this or that?" "Well, no, lord, we Indians don't know anything." "Is it like this or like that?" "As your good mercy wants."[10]*

According to many indigenista novelists, Indian children are often taught survival techniques to employ in their dealings with members of the dominant culture. To be sure, there are novelists who regard the Indian more as a hero or a Sambo than an operator, to use the terminology of recent studies in the survival of oppressed people. However, the best novels of the movement indicate that although the Indian, in fact, possesses a strong personality, he must appear weak and submissive in order to survive in a world where all the odds are against him.[11] In the Andes, this view of the Indian's character only fueled the writer's implicit and explicit hope for revolutionary change; I shall return to these issues in the discussion of the Mexican writer's view of the Indian's future.

The Present

Contrary to Andean novels, where the reader witnesses the appropriation of the Indian's lands by the white man, in Mexican novels, this process is presented as having taken place in the remote past, and the reader is only told how the exploitation took place. There are good reasons for this difference: Since Indians are usually portrayed as living in completely isolated communities in the highlands where the land is extremely poor and inaccessible (the barrenness of the Indian's lands and his reversion to hunting and gathering to insure survival, in fact, constitute a major theme in Mexican novels), it is generally assumed that whatever land they once possessed had already been taken away from them during conquest, colonial, and early republican periods. Furthermore, since some of these novels are historic (set before the revolution of 1910), their account of land usurpation by the landlord is also historic, a long ago occurrence. Consequently, the Mexican novel could not itself constitute a testimony nor the writer a witness to the process by which the Indian's lands were expropriated. For the same reasons, the landlord as representative of the white-mestizo ruling class is also nearly absent from these novels. The reader may be told how he behaved or behaves toward Indians but usually does not witness it. For the most part, the landlord is an absent owner who deals with the Indians only occasionally or through a foreman, as in *El resplandor* and *Balún-canán* (1959), for example.

Another consequence of transporting the Indian's drama to isolated regions is the portrayal of the priest, a representative and ally of the ruling classes in Andean novels, immersed in the sociopolitical affairs of the highlands. In Mexican novels, the priest appears only sporadically, sometimes he is a ghostly figure from the past, a missionary marveling at the backwardness of the heathen—like the priests in *Oficio de tinieblas* and *Fruto de sangre* (1958)—who sees himself as following examples set by conquest and colonial missionaries, a martyr for the faith. At other times, the priest is a representative of conservative interests, but in either case, he is not a central figure. In *El resplandor*, for example, although the priest sides with the landlord against the Indians (it is necessary, he says, "that the peons know that [the landlord's] law is that of their lord, he who gives them to eat."[12]), he is not a central character in the novel. In fact, the novel begins with his departure from the Indian community. In *El indio* (1935), the priest is an enemy of the revolutionary state, education, and progress, but, again, he figures only incidentally in the novel. Whether as a missionary or representative of conservative interests, the priest lacks here the character development he receives in the Andean novel.

Following this general tendency, the government representative is also portrayed as a shadowy figure about whose psychology or position in the Indian world the reader learns little. The judge, too, is hardly present; only in Rogelio Barriga's *La mayordomía* (1952) is the judge actually heard, and even then he is a nebulous figure representing a still more nebulous legal institution situated far away from the Indian's world. There is no equivalent to the Andean subprefect in these novels. The military representative appears and vanishes, leaving bitterness in the lives of the Indians, but his actions take the shape of a natural disaster; he is connected with the *bola*, the endemic revolutionary bands that crossed Mexico in pursuit of glory, revenge, money, and adventure.

Did Mexican writers' portrayal of the Indian do justice to reality? It seems not. Very much as in the case of León Mera's *Cumandá*, the choice of Indian subjects—those living in isolated and self-contained communities—freed Mexican writers from the burden of having to deal with Indians integrated into the sociocultural structure of rural Mexico. During the period in which these novels are set (some in the nineteenth century, all before 1940), isolated Indians were not the only Indians in Mexico. In fact, the incorporation of large numbers of Indians into mestizo Mexico only gained decisive momentum during the Cárdenas regime; but even after 1940, millions of Indians continued to live in rural areas of Mexico under conditions not much different from those existing prior to the Mexican Revolution.

Also, contrary to the Guatemalan case, the influence of the priest in rural Mexico was extensive, despite liberal reforms in the nineteenth and twentieth centuries. In literature, this is realistically portrayed in Augustín Yáñez's *Al filo del agua* (1947), for example, which is about prerevolutionary Mexico. In this nonindigenista work, priests are depicted as controlling the smallest details of daily life in the town, a situation that contributes to the revolutionary movement. Had indigenista writers paid attention to Indians already incorporated into the mestizo world, their portrayal of the priest in rural Mexico would have been different; the same can be said of their treatment of other characters prominent in Andean novels.

It is not surprising that characters central to the Andean novel are absent from the Mexican novel, given the sociocultural differences already noted. This absence can be partially attributed to demographic changes among the Indian population itself. By the 1920s, many Indians had left their towns and even their regions as part of, or following (as in the case of women and children) the revolutionary armies. After the armed phase of the revolution, which caused extensive destruction in rural areas, many Indians migrated to cities in search of food, work, and social benefits. Mexico City experienced a rapid expansion by the 1930s due mainly to this type of immigration, and other large metropolises underwent a similar process. In other words, as in the

Andes, by the 1950s, Indians had become part of mestizo Mexico in large numbers. Their demographic weight was increasingly felt in urban centers, and once in the cities, they were no longer considered Indians but mestizos.

But contrary to the Andean case, Mexican writers were ostensibly concerned with precisely those Indians who stayed behind during the demographic switch. Why, then, did these writers not deal with the Indian who even after the rule of Cárdenas continued to be exploited by landlords in rural areas? For, certainly, the Indian problem in rural Mexico has by no means been solved to this day.

This brings up the second reason why the Mexican writer failed to deal with central figures unlike his Andean counterpart. Mexican cultural leaders tried to incorporate the Indian into their culture by giving him economic assistance for his ejido and reclassifying him as mestindio or mestizo, and, as part of the cultural elite, the Mexican writer translated these efforts into literature. Thus, the writer failed to deal with Indians living under oppressive conditions in rural Mexico because in his eyes these people were either peasants or mestindios or mestizos, but no longer Indian. The only Indians left were those exotic groups who had little or no contact with the mestizo world.

Mexican writers followed other cultural leaders in believing that deculturation was sufficient for a change of skin, that the Indian could actually be transformed both in his own eyes and in the eyes of others by changing his clothing, diet, and so forth. The problems with a purely cultural interpretation of the Indian problem have already been discussed, but it must be reiterated at this point that one does not change social problems by reclassifying them. By the middle of this century, millions of Indians were still living in towns scattered throughout the Mexican countryside, subjected to the authority of landlords and conservative priests and poverty. And about these Indians, the Mexican indigenista novel is largely silent, a situation that led to the theme of the exotic Indian living in isolation.

The Anthropologic Tendency

If the focus on isolated Indians prevented the Mexican writer from depicting important dimensions of the Indian's world so prominent in the Andean novel, it also made it possible for the writer to explore dimensions that had been played down by his Andean counterpart. The importance of the anthropologic side of Indian culture in Mexican novels must be seen in this context; many Mexican novels are, in fact, full of detailed accounts of the Indian's isolated life, his dances, medicine, folklore, and so forth. In Andean novels, Indian customs and culture were an important element, but they were overshadowed by the description of white-Indian relationships based on socioeconomic variables.

Before proceeding, it is important to note that the anthropologic emphasis in Mexican novels does not stem from the writers' anthropologic training. In fact, the reader must always guard against taking reports in these novels as anthropologically correct; they are, above all, impressionistic accounts by white or mestizo writers who lived for only short periods among the Indians. Most of these accounts are woefully superficial and do not compare with such rich views of Indian life as *Juan the Chamula*, recorded by anthropologists.[13] In fact, Indians are presented in these novels through worn-out clichés that reflect centuries of cultural prejudice. In this sense, although not in their romanticism, these writers follow the lead of nineteenth-century romantics, who also presented Indians externally. And not all writers are as honest as the author of *El canto de la grilla* (1952), who actually warns the reader that he does not have anthropologic pretensions and, consequently, is not concerned about being rigorous when presenting the exotic nor worried about polemics.[14]

But despite their shortcomings as anthropologic novels,

such works did make the growing Mexican middle class conscious of the Indian's world as something different, a culture that, though in the process of disappearing, represented a challenge to the mestizo world being created around it. In this sense, too, such novels were an incentive for the social sciences that followed to dispel myths and deal with a disappearing part of Mexico.

Age

Following the general tendency of Spanish American indigenista writers, Mexican writers see positive as well as negative elements in the Indian's culture; the Indian's conception of old age is one of the positive elements. The Indian's culture is integrated by traditions that are often incarnate in the elders, who are believed to possess natural qualities of leadership. The words of the tribe's elders, for example, are to be final and carry the sanctions of the gods. "The submission and obedience to the elders through whose mouths the gods often speak are, among the Huicholes [a nomadic tribe], so definitive that it almost constitutes the basic pillar of all their social structure."[15] A son's disobedience to his father carries the penalty of death among some Indian groups, and what is even more fascinating to these writers, the authority of the elders is seldom questioned or even resented by the young. This is the view expressed in *Los peregrinos inmóviles* (1944): "I only want to be like the old man: to live his experiences in order to govern with justice. . . ."[16]

To these writers, the Indian's respect for his elders is in distinct contrast to the mestizo world where, especially during the revolution, the authority of tradition has begun to decline. Through this cultural trait of the Indian, which goes against the foundation of mestizaje, the authors criticize their own culture, which they regard as highly unstable and an open field for opportunism. But, at the same time, the

Indian's world as a whole does not represent a receding
Arcadia; rather, the positive elements writers find there are
viewed in terms of what they could mean in the modern
world. As in the Andes, these writers wish to extract positive traits from the Indian's culture to benefit the mestizo
world around them; their overall evaluation of the Indian's
culture is, therefore, a negative one.

Man and Nature

A sense of loss is also present in the Mexican writers'
positive evaluation of the Indian's relation to nature, a tendency prevalent in all Spanish American indigenista novels.
Some writers, anticipating later developments in Spanish
American literature, consider this aspect of the Indian's culture to be a possible contribution to Spanish American mestizo culture; a contribution that could prevent, or at least
partially curb, the mestizo's alienation from nature, an alienation that is seen as an inevitable outcome of modernization.
This concept of the Indian's contribution is brought out
explicitly in *Canek*, a novel by Abreu Gómez: "We are the
land," says the Indian leader Canek, "they are the wind. . . .
The Indians . . . live alongside the earth, sleep in peace in
the bosom of the earth; they know the voices of the earth;
and the earth feels the value of their tears. . . . The white
men . . . have forgotten what the earth is. They pass over
her trampling the aches of her being and the grace of her
roses. . . ."[17] Gómez's views echo those of José María Arguedas, discussed earlier, but Gómez goes a step further, for
Canek believes that the union of the white and the Indian is
good. "Look at that boy," says Canek contemplating a mestizo lad, "he has Spanish and Indian blood . . . he is neither
earth nor wind . . . he is where he ought to be."[18] The
Indian's role as the savior of modern man reappears more
clearly in the magicorealist novels discussed in Chapter 8.

Communal Life

Communal life, which in the Andean socialist novels constituted an important and positive element of the Indian's relationship with nature (through communal labor practices), is conspicuously underplayed in Mexican novels. Two related reasons for this can be given: First, the Indian's demographic changes plus his reclassification by cultural leaders prevented Mexican writers from discussing those Indians who still lived in rural Mexico, clinging to ancient practices; many Indians in these novels have either returned or end up returning to hunting and gathering. Secondly, given the isolation and small number of Indians they wrote about, Mexican writers did not see communal life (particularly land tenure systems) as indicative of possible revolutionary potential.

Unlike their Andean counterparts, Mexican writers did not demand a return to ancient communal practices. This would have entailed, for those writing before 1940, calling for a reorientation of the Mexican Revolution itself along indigenista-socialist lines (Andean writers hoped for a revolution of this kind); or, for those writing after 1940, a total misrepresentation of the Mexican Revolution in general. In Mexico, unlike the Andes, a revolution either had run or was running its own course and realistic hopes for a return were now impossible. By the time these writers published, it was clear that the return to the ejido only masked the destruction of the Indian's culture and the advance of a capitalist society. And Mexican writers did not call for another revolution; they had experienced a lengthy and bloody one that had rendered them weary and disappointed. Consequently, Mexican novels are ultimately pessimistic; like the last indigenista novel of Monteforte Toledo, they leave the Indian dangling between a half-forgotten past and an uncertain future.

The Magic Element

Devaluation of the Indian's world in the novel takes many forms, but in all indigenista novels the most fundamental shortcoming of the Indian's culture is considered to be his magical world. There is no need to repeat here in detail this negative evaluation, which parallels almost exactly that of Andean and Guatemalan writers. There are, nonetheless, characteristics that set apart the Mexican novels. In some of the best Andean novels, magic was something that the Indian was ready to throw away in favor of other more rational means of defense. In Mexican novels, the Indian is not seen in that light; he continues to hold on to the magical world. In one of the best indigenista novels of Mexico, *Balún-Canán*, for example, the Indian still considers magic to be an effective weapon against white oppressors; Indian sorcerers symbolically eat the only son of the landlord and thus free their people from continued exploitation by the landlord's family. Without an heir, the landlord abandons the plantation for good, but, tellingly, the Indians have not ultimately solved their socioeconomic problems and continue to live in poverty, which invites further exploitation. Such a view of magic is in total contrast to that expressed in Alegria's *El mundo es ancho y ajeno*, for example; there, the sorceress disappears from the community without a trace when she realizes she cannot grasp the landlord's soul. Her departure leaves room for more effective means of fighting against exploitation. In this sense, Mexican novels reveal affinities with liberal novels in the Andes and those of Monteforte Toledo in Guatemala, where the Indian is seen as retaining his old values and therefore unable to go beyond the present condition.

Religious Syncretism

The Indian's religious views also contribute to the Mexican writers' negative evaluation of the Indian's world. Having been abandoned by the priest, they suggest, the Indian's initial conversion to Christianity has been substantially undermined. The Christian God was never able to rule the Indian's heart; consequently, he dangles between two religious world views. Neither pagan nor Christian, the Indian possesses a syncretic religion where both Christian and pagan beliefs coexist.

One of the most striking examples of this syncretism is found in Castellanos's *Oficio de tinieblas*. Tired of being exploited by the white man, the Indians in this novel decide to rebel; they are afraid, however, of angering the white man's patron saint. As they vacillate in their decision, an Indian sorceress discovers some old Indian idols in a remote cave and interprets this discovery as a sign that the ancient gods will protect the Indian from the power of the white man's saints. A few days later, however, a young priest, full of missionary zeal, finds out about the idols and destroys them. Once again, the Indians feel unprotected. Seeing this, the sorceress makes new idols of clay, but the Indians are not reassured by them and regard these idols as no match for Christian saints.

In a moment of inspiration, the sorceress finds a solution to the problems. The reason for the superiority of the white man's saints, she believes, lies in the fact that they followed a crucified God; consequently, the Indians, too, must have their Christ. She decides that the Indians should crucify a young boy, and they do. "We now also have our Christ . . . [the boy] was not born in vain. Let his birth, his agony, and his death serve to put the Tzotzil, the Chamula, the Indian, level with the white man."[19] Having sacrificed the young boy, the Indians believe themselves to be immune to the white man's bullets. As they march against the town, destroying plantations in their path, many of them die believing in resurrection. At the end of their march, having vented their anger, they retreat, defeated, to the highlands with a dual loss: their lands and their faith in their idols.

This sort of religious syncretism is not something that

surfaces only in moments of anger or transformation. The Indian's everyday life is portrayed as thoroughly infused with a mixture of Christian and pagan beliefs. They punish their saints because they fail to produce miracles; they demand protection from danger regardless of the goal of their actions. In *Donde crecen los tepozanes,* for example, the wife and mother of a man who steals and kills at night pray to the white man's saints that their beloved will not be seen or caught by his victims. Every important event in the Indian's life, according to these writers, forms a long chain of acts based on pagan superstition mixed with other notions borrowed from the Christian faith.

Relations between the Sexes

Another distinguishing characteristic of the Mexican novel is its exploration of sexual relations between Indian men and women. In Andean novels, these relations were of a secondary nature, and women in general were unimportant figures. To be sure, they were present in the depiction of the Indian as victim of the white male, but their victimization was immediately transformed into a problem for the Indian male. Ultimately, it was the Indian male's pride and honor that the white man destroyed; not one of the Andean novels, for example, deals with the problem of rape from the Indian woman's point of view. The subjective dimension of the trauma is objectified into social relations; in other words, male-female relationships in Andean novels were clearly subordinated to the white-Indian relationship. In Mexican novels, on the other hand, male-female relations among Indians often constitutes their very core, for example, *Fruto de sangre, El callado dolor de los tzotziles* (1949), *Guelaguetza* (1947), *El canto de la grilla* (1952); this is not to say that the rape of an Indian woman by a white man becomes unimportant but that the often cruel treatment of the Indian woman by the Indian man is not ignored.

The life of the Indian woman in these novels is tragic, and

if the life of all Indians is hazardous, hers is doubly so. She is the scapegoat for all the frustrations in the Indian man's life; she is a sexual object to be enjoyed by the man at all times, even when intercourse may cost her her life; she is the slave of a slave. In *El callado dolor de los tzotziles*, an Indian woman, María Manuela, remains barren after years of marriage. Resenting her inability to produce offspring, her husband hardly speaks to her during their entire life as husband and wife. She is ostracized within her own home; "María Manuela used to see or hear him eating but did not participate in the feast. More than a wife, she was a slave. . . ."[20] María Manuela could eat only when alone and after her husband had finished. Because of her barrenness, she is finally forced out of her village by the entire tribe. Sick with tuberculosis and dejected, she climbs to the highlands to live alone and hide her shame. But as she resigns herself to living the life of an outcast, she discovers that she is pregnant. Elated, she returns to her village, where she discovers that her husband had been secretly killing sheep, the tribe's sacred animal. Torn between her moral obligation to denounce her husband according to tribal tradition and her duty as a wife to keep her knowledge a secret (to follow her husband "wherever he went"),[21] she finally decides to protect her husband from the anger of the tribe, an anger that would definitely lead to her husband's death. However, her husband is eventually discovered, and she stands alone with her child to face the world.

Drugs

Despite the heavy use of coca leaves by Indians in the Andes—a drug addiction that still poses a serious problem— indigenista writers there hardly ever mentioned drugs. The few passages discussing the use of coca leaves are found in novels written by liberals, who mentioned it only in passing. When socialist writers treated the subject, as in *El mundo es ancho y ajeno*, they did so in connection with the Indian's religious behavior and did not present drugs as a daily habit. The militant posture of the Andean writers, no doubt, had much to do with this omission. Since these writers wanted to show their audiences that the Indian had a potential, they minimized his shortcomings and exalted his virtues. For, if the Indian was portrayed as immersed in a cocaine stupor or if he was strong only because of drugs, how could these authors have made their case for the Indian's potential? Given their militant posture, Andean writers could not present the Indian as having borrowed energies.

This situation changes drastically in the case of Mexico. The Mexican writer, not concerned with revolution or salvation in the same sense as the Andean writer, becomes an observer of the exotic, which results in a naturalistic depiction of daily Indian life in isolation. Many pages in these novels are filled with accounts of native dress, dances, demeanor, and festivities; the consumption of pulque (an intoxicating beverage) or peyote is always introduced at some point in the narrative. In fact, drug-related behavior is often central to the novelist's description of Indian life. By using drugs, "every Huichol believes he acquires such a fabulous lucidity that he almost sees himself as a supernatural being. . . ."[22] Under the influence of drugs, he is able to embark on long treks in search of game or revenge: "May one never lack peyote in the traveling bag!"[23] Without the intoxicating effects of pulque or peyote, these writers claim, Indian life would be unbearable. "Eating it [the Indians] resist everything without feeling anything; it slows down their nerves, renders insensible their muscles. Its effects accustom them to intense and continued suffering: hunger, thirst, long walks, . . . and all the injustices."[24]

To conclude, the anthropologic bent of Mexican novels made it possible to explore traits of the Indian's culture that were played down in the Andean novels. To be sure, most Mexican novels do not attain any depth in understanding the Indian's culture; they give an outsider's description, a tourist's picture of the Indian's world. Nevertheless, as their treatment of male-female relations shows, they do offer some new clues to understanding the Indian's culture. It may be said that Andean and Mexican novels are realistic in a different sense and that by overlapping these two windows on the Indian's world, a more truthful glimpse of a disappearing culture is possible.

The Revolution

In *Los de abajo* (not an indigenista novel), the wife of a revolutionary leader asks:

> "Why do you fight, Demetrio?"
> *Demetrio, with a deep scowl, distractedly takes a pebble and throws it to the bottom of the canyon. He pauses in deep thought— looking at the defile and says:*
> "Look at that pebble, it can no longer stop."[25]

This image translates unpredictability and aimlessness of the revolution that shook Mexico for about 30 years. Following Azuela's lead, indigenista writers argued that the revolution affected the Indian only negatively: there were no conscious and concerted efforts either by the Indian himself or others to better his lot.

Indeed, in these novels, the revolution is compared to a natural disaster, blind to human suffering: Between the bola and the hale, the Indian was left "without a crop and without cattle."[26] The aimless bolas, bands of regular and irregular soldiers, render the countryside chaotic, a place where danger awaits behind any hill, at any moment. As a result of this, the Indians climb the mountains, as in the years of bloody conquest, "to wait for the ball of fire to pass, to roll and pass."[27] But not even in the mountains are they safe; different bolas tax them, take away their animals and crops, violently induct their young into the military, burn their houses, and rape their women. As the bola rolls, the Indians take to even more remote places in the mountains and, together with their gods, become creatures of darkness, inhabiting caves and hoping to escape from "the saviors of one group and redeemers of another."[28]

According to these writers, and contrary to official interpreters, the Indians—those considered as such by the writers, that is—were not saved by the revolution. In fact, between 1910 and 1940, they argued, little had changed for the better in the Indian's world. During those violent times, Indians were only used by self-appointed revolutionary leaders who were after the spoils of civil wars, as depicted in Lópes y Fuentes's *El indio*. There, an Indian learns to read and write, becomes a teacher and later develops political ambitions. He enlists the financial help of other Indians in order to fight for them in the capital. While the Indians scratch out a living from their tiny plots of land, their representative lives comfortably in the capital, drawing on their income and pretending to look after their interests. In other novels (*El resplandor, Fruto de sangre*), political leaders trick Indians with promises and transport them to distant towns to participate in political manifestations on the leaders' behalf. In another novel, several Indians are killed by other Indians while supporting their leaders.

The Catholic Church, too, used the Indian to defend its interests. Threatened by the loss of temporal power due to liberal forces unleashed by the revolution, the church rose up in arms. And who were the soldiers of the famous Cristero Rebellions? The Indians. "Priests with large mustaches [that is, whites] bless the rebellion, hang scapulas over innocent hearts, give indulgences to everyone, and issue passports to glory to all those who die defending God."[29]

According to indigenista writers, the years of revolution were years of calamities for the Indians. Innocent bystanders of the revolution, they watched the fight below their caves and prayed to be left alone. The revolution was not their revolution; it was an affair of mestizos who fought among themselves and used the Indians as cannon fodder.

Therefore it is to be expected that indigenista writers would not recount the Indian's revolutionary activity. The few cases that do follow the Indian into actual combat are historic accounts (*Canek*, *Cájeme*); alternatively, his military facts are narrated, but as secondary to the central plot (*Naufragio de indios*, 1951; *El indio* by Eduardo Luquín, (1923).

Here, there is additional support for the contention that Mexican writers followed the cultural elite's shift in defining Indianness. For these writers, the peons who followed Zapata and other revolutionary leaders were no longer Indians. Distrustful of revolutions and bent on depicting the exotic, such writers fail to depict Indians other than those in remote places of rural Mexico. Not one Mexican indigenista novel follows the military career of an Indian in depth; the novel that approaches these themes most closely, Luquín's *El indio*, for example, is not at all concerned with the Indian's role in the revolution. The revolutionary deeds of the Indian protagonist are totally subordinated to the romantic theme of his impossible love affair with a white girl, daughter of his former patrón. To find a somewhat more realistic portrayal of the Indian's role in the revolution of 1910, the reader must turn to the so-called novels of the revolution, such as Azuela's *Los de abajo*, but even then, it is the nature of such novels to depict the Indian as a secondary character. Those novels are, in fact, generally concerned with leaders of the revolution, who were mostly mestizos or anonymous revolutionary soldiers as part of the masses in movement, or the effects of the revolution on mestizo Mexico. The Indian, under these circumstances, is lost in a plethora of characters.

The Future

In general, all indigenista writers believed that the Indian had no future. In the Andes, liberals demanded the abolition of the Indian by urging that he be integrated into a market economy; socialists did the same when they called for the abolition of racial and class differences and the establishment of a socialist society. In Mexico, given the sociocultural developments of the society, neither solution was possible. From the Mexican writers' point of view, the liberal solution was not possible because the Indian they wrote about represented precisely the failure of the revolution of 1910, a liberal movement to incorporate the Indian into national life; this is clearly indicated by depicting the Indian as a bystander and not a participant in the revolution. Many novels, therefore, used the Indian's predicament to indict the failures of the liberal revolution itself, its ideological vacillations and its leaders' opportunism.

Nor was a socialist solution considered: Those writing before 1940 did not regard socialism as a viable revolutionary stance; their novels reflect the ultimate victory in the revolutionary movement of liberal forces against socialist ones. These early writers correctly saw that due either to exhaustion, demagogy, or genuine commitment liberal ideals governed the masses. Besides, these writers were aware that socialist groups at this time lacked organization and followers among the proletariat and the peasantry, Indians included. As to those writing after the 1940s, they had definitively written off the Indian as a revolutionary potential, whether guided by socialists or liberals. Whatever revolutionary potential existed among Mexico's population, in their view, it now involved preeminently the mestizo.

For these reasons, in the final analysis, Mexican writers view the Indian's participation as an Indian in a new society as negligible. Having neither a liberal nor a socialist hope, Mexican writers project an image of the Indian as an isolated being, suspended in space and time; they see this situation ending only in an undetermined future when the Indian will disappear through mestizaje or violent death. In any case, the Indian's self-immolation is not demanded, as in the Andes; and contrary to the Andean case, there is no messianic role for the Indian in these novels.

The pessimism underlying their view of the Indian problem is further evident in the Mexican writers' treatment of various aspects of Indian life, education, leadership, and mestizaje.

Education

All Mexican writers agree that education is the most promising means of incorporating the Indian into the larger society, but they also agree that this avenue is virtually closed to the Indian. In their novels, education as a means of incorporating the Indian always leads to disillusionment. Some writers portray the Indian as totally unwilling to change his way of life, to become educated in mestizo ways. In one novel, young Indians are hunted down and forcibly brought to the *escuelas rurales* (rural schools) to be taught a trade (*La bruma lo vuelve azul*); in another, they are coaxed into attending schools available in their villages (*El canto de la grilla*). But despite these efforts, their resistance to civilization is adamant. In *Fruto de sangre,* Indians murder several teachers whom they believe to be communists. An irate social reformer tries to make them understand that by killing the teachers they were killing the only ones who could save them from hunger, misery, and slavery.

Some writers see the refusal to be educated as a result of the Indian's poor social conditions; education can only be possible, they argue, if the socioeconomic situation improves. In order to incorporate the Indian into civilization, "something more than schooling" is needed, because "when man does not have what it takes to live, [schooling] is a luxury."[30] And finally, there is the added problem of the methods used in education. In a complaint similar to that found in Monteforte Toledo's work, some Mexican authors note that Indians can hardly be educated in schools where the language spoken is not their own and teachers are inexperienced mestizos.

Whatever the reasons behind the Indian's failure to be educated and the mestizo's failure to educate him, what results from all this is the writer's sense of helplessness to incorporate the Indian into civilization through education. The most liberal position—education as a means to social improvement—is discounted as a feasible way of solving the Indian problem.

Leadership

Mexican indigenista writers see the Indian's political behavior in terms of mass movements where individuals are totally overshadowed; thus, they follow the general trend set by the novels of the revolution so popular during this period in Mexican letters. It is the mass, the *chuzma,* that acts, usually unconsciously, lost in a sea of contradictory demands, and the outcome of this blind movement is often violence and death. The novels' message is clear: Since the Indian can only act as a mass, he needs non-Indian leaders to move him to action; the types of Indian leaders portrayed in these novels, therefore, elucidate the writers' views of the Indian's future.

These leaders are usually deculturated Indians who, having learned the ways of the white man, use the Indian masses to further their own ambitions; there are no leaders resembling José María Arguedas's Rendon Wilca or Alegría's Benito Castro. An extensive quote from *El resplandor* where the narrator describes a mestizo who had been brought up by the Indians contrasts the concept of Indian leadership in Mexican and Andean novels:

> *He was from the lowest class of people, from those who do not have a blanket to die on, and by his fists he had climbed to the high world of politics; sometimes with the help of a general with whom he conspired in a business confabulation, sometimes with the help of a friendly secretary in local government to*

> *whom the mestizo leader was appealing, at other times counting on the backing of a governor without many scruples. He was proud of the Atomi blood that pulsed in his arteries, as if he owed to it his victory in life and his constant and demagogic speeches: We the Indians . . . those who carry indigenous blood . . . sons of the people . . . the underdogs, the brownskinned. . . . However, when he courted and married Matilde Fuentes [daughter of his former patrón], a subterranean longing to be the father of children of another color spoke in his very being. By the time Rafaelito [his son] was 20 years old, he would find himself in possession of a distinguished milieu; he would not have to walk around bragging about a race to which he no longer belonged. . . .[31]*

But even those leaders who, having learned the ways of the mestizo, do return to help their people are either reabsorbed into the Indian world and thereby lose their potential for change (for example, *Oficio de tinieblas*), or they are shadowy figures whose ideology or psychology cannot be fathomed (for example, *Balún-Canán*). Even movements led by Indians themselves (as in *Oficio de tinieblas*) do not lead to salvation but eventually to the continuation of exploitation and misery; in short, all Indian rebellions in these novels end in defeat (*Oficio de tinieblas, Canek, Cájeme*).

In sum, with the elimination of the deculturated leader as a potential source for change, the socialist and liberal hopes that were possible in the Andes had to be abandoned in Mexico. Of course, at the root of this predicament is the assumption that only deculturated Indians can be effective vehicles of socialist and liberal ideals. Given that the Indian needs leaders and that these leaders are not able to bring him to civilization, the Indian's future can only be opaque.

Mestizaje

With no hopes for an indigenista-socialist revolution, disillusioned with liberal efforts based on education, Mexican writers had only one avenue to the solution of the Indian problem: mestizaje. But in Spanish America, mestizaje is the result of violence of one people against another. Consequently, these authors present mestizaje as a solution that neither they nor the Indian wholeheartedly support; they present it, however, as an inevitable solution. In this sense, it can be argued that fatalism was an outgrowth of realism for these writers: In their work, they depict something that was going on despite their protests and the Indian's. In the Andes, too, socialist writers had acknowledged the rape of Indian women and the manipulation of all Indians by their leaders, but these writers had demanded a more immediate and radical solution; they had remained hopeful.

Without hope for a socialist or liberal revolution, without hope for a liberal integration through education, Mexican authors can only foresee the slow disintegration of the Indian's culture through mestizaje. Even the dictator, a solution to which liberals in the Andes were forced to resort, having once lost hope in gradually integrating the Indian into national affairs, is not to be found here. The dictatorship of Díaz and the many short-lived ones following it had shown that in Mexico even this solution was not a viable one.

What mestizaje meant in terms of the Indian's future seemed clear enough: integrating the Indian into national life not as a group but as an individual. The trauma that mestizaje represents is basically personal and can be translated into a group experience only if it is interpreted as an act of aggression against the group. But for Mexican writers to view rape in that fashion required that the group respond by viewing the victim of rape as part of a collectivity with the possibility of redemption. Mestizaje is not liberation but the slow and piecemeal annihilation of a race that is being exploited by another. For these reasons, mestizaje is not something writers exalt or hope for; it is something that assumes the weight of fate; it is a nonsolution. There could be no call for mestizaje.

But despite their belief that all avenues to liberation were closed, these writers did their utmost to see into the future and find justice there. Consequently, their novels portrayed the Indian as still awaiting redemption; but redemption from where? The writers' hope is based on despair in the present and uncertainty of the future. For these writers, despite the revolution and his symbolic and material role in it, the Indian remains as isolated and as wretched as ever. *El indio,* one of the earliest novels of the Mexican indigenista movement, by Gregorio López y Fuentes, ends significantly by describing the Indian's distrust of the outside world. An Indian boy who had been maimed by white adventurers is posted as a sentinel by his people on a protrusion overlooking a road that leads to the mestizo world. He is "distrust itself looking to the highway that is civilization . . . from the craggy, brambled ground."[32] He and his people know that the white man may attack them, that the revolution below is causing havoc, that their leader, a deculturated Indian, "is doing well in the city."[33] But there the sentinel waits, hoping.

Other novels (*Nayar, Oficio de tinieblas*) end with Indians waiting for some solution to their problems while hidden away in caves in the inaccessible highlands. Having cleansed the caves of the evil spirits with incense and flowers, they wrap themselves in a mist of darkness and gather together on "some nights when the desperate coyote howls and when the moon rises pale and bloodless."[34] Even the most optimistic novels end with a demand for someone to fulfill the promises made by the revolution. In *Los hombres verdaderos* (1959), for example, an Indian, having experienced city life and marveled at civilization, returns to his village, where he broods and listens carefully because he believes that those who promised redemption will eventually appear, and he wants to receive them and get to know them.

Contrary to the majority of Andean novels, but similar to the last novel by Monteforte Toledo, in Mexican novels, the Indian has an undetermined future as an Indian; pessimism permeates all these works. It is also important to note that as with Monteforte Toledo whatever future Mexican writers see for the Indian as an Indian is negatively evaluated; therefore, though implicitly in most novels, the demand for the destruction of the Indian's world is no less vehement. Ultimately, to be an Indian, according to these novelists, is to be superstitious, exploited, cruel toward other Indians, barbaric, and without salvation; this negative evaluation of the Indian's world is an expression of their desire for its abolition.

In the final analysis, therefore, the pageantry and exoticism of the Indian's world are overshadowed by the negative aspects of the Indian's culture. To lay claim to an exotic heritage may be interesting, but authors prefer a civilized Indian; here, as in the Andes, authors want to retain the positive side of the Indian's culture while ridding it and Mexico of its negative elements. The Indian, however, cannot survive the cultural split; this dilemma cannot be resolved in any other way than by his death and the destruction of his world.

In short, in these novels, the Indian walks toward death, which is his future. "That is why the Indian goes, a ghost to himself, along roads that have no end, certain that the end, the only end possible, the end that frees and allows him to find his lost footprints, is where death awaits."[35] With these words, I have come full circle to Matto's position and beyond—the prophecies of the ancient teachers have come true:

> Let us die, then
> Let us perish then,
> For our gods are already dead!

Chapter Eight

The Victory of Candanga and the New Man

All is like a dream . . .
no one speaks here of truth. . . .

Destined is my heart to vanish
like the ever withering flowers?

It is true that we leave, truly we part.
We leave the flowers, the songs, and the earth.
It is true that we go; it is true that we part.
                                    —Cantares Mexicanos

The Fall
of the Indigenista Novel

The indigenista novel in the Andes began to decline during the 1950s; the publication of *Todas las sangres* in 1964 by José María Arguedas, the leading indigenista writer, marked the end of the indigenista cycle there. In Guatemala, the indigenista novel rose and fell with the efforts of Monteforte Toledo, whose last indigenista novel was published in 1953; in Mexico, Castellanos published her *Oficio de tinieblas* in 1962. Insofar as the elimination of the Indian's culture lay at the core of its message, the indigenista novel prepared its own dissolution. Without an Indian culture, there can be no Indians in any real sense; and without Indians, the indigenista novel is, by definition, an impossibility. This state of affairs created a paradox for the indigenista writer: The more successful he was in bringing about social change, the less important his task became. At a certain point, the task ceased to be worthwhile.

In fact, the task of the indigenista writer became less and less worthwhile as three closely related factors took their toll: the slow but unremitting demographic collapse of the Indian during 400 years of domination, which culminated in the massive rural-to-urban migration during the 1950s; the general amelioration of the Indian's social condition, an amelioration partly due to writers' efforts; and the growth of the social sciences by the middle of this century.

Migratory Movements

In the first half of this century, but especially in the decades between 1930 and 1960, an accelerated deculturation process of a large number of Indians took place. This

228

process of deculturation, as indigenista novels show, was accomplished mainly by Indians leaving their enclaves in the highlands and traveling to more urbanized regions and centers in their countries.

The extent of rural-to-urban migration among Indians during the first half of this century and particularly after 1930 was staggering. In Bolivia, for example, between 1900 and 1950, the population in urban areas more than doubled that in rural sectors.[1] Even taking into account fertility and mortality differentials for both sectors, the disparities are very high. In the case of Ecuador, Molina Salvador reports that between 1950 and 1960 more than 400 thousand people moved from rural areas to more urbanized coastal regions.[2] Since Ecuador's average population during this period was around four million, the extent of this process can be appreciated. Peru also showed similar demographic drifts: Julio Cotler writes that largely because of increasing rural-to-urban migration, while the urban population (residents of towns of 2,000 inhabitants or more) in 1940 comprised only 25 percent of the Peruvian population, by the 1960s, the proportion was 42 percent.[3] In Guatemala, during the period between 1938 and 1950, Guatemala City grew at an annual rate of 11.9 percent, thus, while Guatemala City had only 77.4 thousand inhabitants in 1938, by 1950, its population had reached 294.3 thousand, quadrupling in 12 years.[4] Mexico also experienced massive Indian migrations. By the 1940s, Indians were pressing against mestizo regions, pushing the mestizo to the urban centers; alternatively, Indians settled on the outskirts of large metropolises.

The principal causes for these massive migratory movements, accurately portrayed in some indigenista novels, were deteriorating conditions in the highlands and the effects of "pull" factors from the urban centers. According to indigenista writers, once the Indian reached the urban centers, he underwent a slow but inevitable transformation from peasant into proletarian and subproletarian (employed as a waiter, maid, and so forth). After a few years' residency in these urban centers, the Indian began to regard his culture as an anachronism and tried to pass for a mestizo.

As a consequence of these migrations and subsequent deculturation, Indians lost their position as a demographic majority in the eyes of the indigenista writer. And, as proportionately fewer Indians remained in the highlands, their prior political importance (potentially, at least) as a group also began to fade. In the case of the Andes, where indigenista writers had regarded the Indian as a messianic force, he lost his revolutionary potential with his position as a majority member. These writers began searching for other groups in their societies to fulfill the revolutionary role, a search that is already present in later indigenista novels where the Indian is led by mestizos and deculturated Indians.

By the 1960s, masses of deculturated Indians surrounded the writers' middle-class environment in the cities, with their shanty towns and regional customs. From then on, the masses in these countries were no longer considered Indians but proletarians and subproletarian mestizos. It is not surprising, therefore, that most novels written in these countries after 1960 deal with the experiences of mestizos and urban dwellers. Their proximity to the writers' environment plus their newly gained political status accentuated the importance of the new masses, assuring them a place in their country's literary production. Such leading indigenista writers as José María Arguedas and Icaza, for example, abandoned the Indian as a central literary subject and began writing novels in which mestizos and deculturated Indians were the main characters. Others abandoned the Indian altogether; Monteforte Toledo experimented with different techniques and wrote psychological novels; Castellanos returned to poetry and stopped writing indigenista novels.

The Amelioration of Social Conditions

Rural-to-urban migrations coincided with political events partly directed at solving the Indian problem. No doubt these efforts were at least partially influenced by the work of indigenista writers.

In 1944, Ecuador underwent a revolution aimed at changing the socioeconomic structure of society. Its thrust was directed against an Ecuadorian oligarchy that had regained control of the nation after a 15-year period of political turmoil from 1925 to 1940. The revolution was led by a popular front organized around the Ecuadorian Democratic Alliance, which included the active participation of students, intellectuals, workers, peasants, and some sectors of the military that wanted to bring progressive government to Ecuador. After a brief armed confrontation with government forces, the Ecuadorian Democratic Alliance triumphed in May 1944.

Once leaders of this popular front had secured control of the nation, they elected former president José María Velasco Ibarra to lead the new government. Velasco Ibarra called for a constituent congress to write a new political constitution, which included a set of guidelines aimed at bringing a more democratic society to Ecuador, including the highlands. Moreover, since socialists and communists had actively contributed in the triumph of the revolution, they were allowed to participate in the new government in its initial days. Shortly after the revolution, however, Velasco Ibarra became increasingly dictatorial and conservative. By the end of 1945, conservative forces had again gained control of the nation, and socialists, communists, and other left-leaning intellectuals found themselves once more in the position of outsiders and critics.

The revolution of 1944 by no means solved the Indian problem in Ecuador, but it did produce legal guidelines aimed at improving the Indian's lot. Ultimately, these measures helped to subdue voices of protests from the generation of writers who rose to defend the Indians during the 1930s and 1940s. In 1957, Jorge Rivadeneyra wrote the last indigenista novel from Ecuador, *Ya esta amaneciendo*, while Icaza, that country's leading indigenista writer, had gone on to write about the experiences of the new majority in Ecuador—the mestizo and the deculturated Indian.

Eight years after the Ecuadorian revolution, in 1952, Bolivia had a more radical revolution, which significantly changed Bolivian society. The Bolivian revolution, too, was led by a coalition; it was composed mainly of such left wing political parties as the Nationalist Leftist Revolutionary Party (PRIN), a party with Stalinist tendencies, the Revolutionary Workers' Party, of Trotskyist orientation, and the National Revolutionary Movement (MNR), a populist nationalist party with a vague socialist orientation. As in the case of Ecuador, this coalition had the support of students, intellectuals, workers, peasants, and sectors of the armed forces.

Despite the strong participation of the socialist and communist parties, the government installed in Bolivia with the triumph of the revolution was controlled by the National Revolutionary Movement, and the party leader, Víctor Paz Estenssoro, assumed the presidency. The MNR remained in power from 1952 to 1964. During this period, especially in the first years after the revolution, the government of Bolivia carried out an extensive agrarian reform that returned to the Indians much of the land in the highlands that prior governments had taken from them. Thus, the power of the landlord in the Bolivian highlands was significantly curtailed.

The revolution of 1952 marked the decline of the indigenista novel in Bolivia as well. Agrarian reform, new laws directed at protecting the rights of Indians, and other acts carried out by the revolution left indigenista writers with fewer reasons to write. Novels written after 1952 no longer dealt with the Indian's conditions in the present, as had been the case before; instead, some novels were set before the revolution, that is, as historic novels. This was the case with Jesús Lara, for example, Bolivia's most prolific indigenista novelist. Alternatively, other novels written after 1952 had the mestizo or deculturated Indian as a central character.

While Bolivia was undergoing a revolutionary process, Peru was under the dictatorship of Manuel A. Odría (1948–1956). The end of Odría's dictatorship in 1956 did not mean a political move to the left, nor did it mean that the Indian's condition was to be seriously altered. It was only seven years later, under President Fernando Belaúnde Terry (1963–1968) and when the Indian himself once again in open rebellion against the landlord demanded change, that ameliorative efforts were made.

Belaúnde had come to power largely because of his pledges to solve the Indian problem in Peru. A major issue in his presidential campaign had been the promise to implement an agrarian reform that would drastically affect the socioeconomic structure of the Peruvian highlands. Once in office, Belaúnde failed to carry out his promise; however, his extensive campaign throughout the Peruvian highlands had aroused the Indians' expectations, who now demanded the return of their lands. Therefore, since Belaúnde would not fulfill his promises, Indians from communities and haciendas began to take over plots of land on their own initiative.

In addition to these direct actions by Indians, guerrilla movements began in the highlands (1963–1966); they were largely led by, and composed of, socialists and other left-wing members of the Peruvian middle classes who desired to enlist the Indian in order to overthrow Belaúnde's government. The call by indigenista writers, it seemed, was about to be answered; these initial steps toward a radical revolution were, however, efficiently repressed by the military. The Indian's unwillingness to mount an all-out revolutionary movement under the guidance of middle-class intellectuals was apparent; his revolutionary zeal was limited to getting and securing a plot of land. Under these conditions, the military easily cornered and eliminated the guerrillas, who lacked widespread support among the rural population.

Belaúnde was able to remain in power until the military overthrew him in 1968 and instituted a revolutionary government. Breaking precedence with Spanish American military history, the new government displayed leftist leanings. Within a few years, the military carried out a much needed agrarian reform in selected parts of the country, particularly where Indian uprisings had taken place; it set up new labor regulations aimed at curtailing the Indian's exploitation and generally improving social conditions for the most oppressed sectors of the society. Significantly, the last indigenista novel from Peru, José María Arguedas's *Todas las sangres,* was published when guerrillas were active in the highlands. The defeat of the guerrillas and later "revolutionary acts" by the military government helped silence the protests of indigenista writers.

In Guatemala, the revolution of 1944 deeply affected the indigenista movement in literature. As in Ecuador after 1944 and in Bolivia after 1952, Guatemalan writers who could have written militant indigenista novels were too busy attempting to influence the policies of the newly established liberal government to dedicate themselves to protest. This was a time to reconstruct Guatemala, not a time for idealism. The leftist position and the rhetoric of the government of Arévalo disarmed writers who may have contemplated protest. After all, for the first time in Guatemalan history, the Indian's voice was coveted; the Indian was regarded as a political force; the even more radical government of Jacabo Arbenz that followed Arévalo's closed the issue. Monteforte Toledo, the only indigenista writer from Guatemala, was himself deeply involved in the political process during this time. Asturias, who had outgrown his racist ideas and developed a magicorealist approach to the Indian theme in literature, aligned himself with the government of his old friend Arévalo and later with that of Arbenz.

For these reasons, Guatemala never had a true gestation period nor a militant period in its indigenista literature; it only had expectations and disillusionment. *Entre la piedra y la cruz,* a novel that shows some militancy, is a historic novel; it ends with the victory of the revolution of 1944. The would-be indigenista writers of Guatemala missed their chance to become as militant as their counterparts in the Andes. Their revolution coincided with Ecuador's, which also marked the decline of the indigenista novel there. Of course, at the fall of the Arbenz government in 1954, it was evident that Guatemala's Indian problem had hardly been ameliorated, but by then, the time for indigenismo had passed. By the early 1960s, the mestizo had developed into a major political force and displaced the Indian. Today, the revolutionary movement growing since the late 1970s is based on a combination of Indian peasant and mestizo forces.

Finally, ameliorative measures carried out in Mexico during this period were significant, notwithstanding the criticism leveled against the successive revolutionary governments by indigenista writers. To be sure, the Indians who had profited the most from the revolution were the so-called mestindios, that is, those who became part of the revolutionary armies. But even on a larger scale, Mexico did embark on a massive and concerted effort to integrate the Indian into national life: An institute of Indian affairs was established for the express purpose of carrying out the "mestization" of the Indian; rural schools were developed for this purpose, as was the ejido. The attack on Indian culture during this period was unprecedented in Mexican history. Even though there was a significant number of Indian peasants who remained basically unaffected by these measures, it cannot be denied that an effort was being made to solve the Indian problem, so that in Mexico, too, as ameliorative measures were carried out in remote villages, the Mexican writer lost part of his raison d'être.

It is important to note that in all these cases Indians were incorporated more fully into a growing market economy without drastically altering their nations' social structure. In the Andes, revolutions were ultimately controlled by the middle classes in order to incorporate the Indian into national life more thoroughly and forestall a possible radical revolution, which would have undermined middle-class interests. Ameliorative measures on the part of the liberal wing of the bourgeoisie neutralized explosive conditions in the Andes that socialist writers had viewed as the promise for a better future. The Indian, indeed, came down from the mountains, but not to destroy bourgeois society; he came to lose himself in it as readily available labor, living on the fringes of the metropolis in shanty towns. In Guatemala, the Indian did not participate significantly in the revolution of 1944, and, in the end, he found himself, like his counterpart in the Andes, searching for a niche in the mestizo world. Finally, as noted, the Mexican middle class enhanced its power by enlarging the internal market where Indian labor and incipient Indian buying power played a part. In sum, the sought-after integration of the Indian into national life did not change his position vis-à-vis other groups; he still remained at the bottom of the social scale.

The Rise of the Social Sciences

Indigenista writers attempted to rewrite the history of their nations as well as portray the Indian's real social conditions. Some of their novels analyzed socioeconomic relations between Indians and mestizos; others presented taxonomies of exotic plants; still others gave vivid descriptions of Indian rites and folk wisdom. In this sense, the indigenista writers were the precursors of social scientists in Spanish America, especially sociologists and anthropologists; for this reason, the growth of the social sciences tended to undermine the aims and foundation of the indigenista novel.

As the social sciences became more firmly established in Spanish America, it became apparent that the indigenista novel could not compete with them; of course, as the novelists Carlos Fuentes and Alberto Moravia have correctly suggested, the social sciences are increasingly competing with novel writing in general. In the case of the indigenista novel, however, the competition was decisive. For one thing, historians, anthropologists, sociologists, and so forth, were more thorough in portraying the Indian's culture than were novelists: Social scientists not only did a better job of depicting the Indian and his world, but their protest carried the weight of scientific findings. The realist tendency that was the basis of the indigenista effort could not be sustained under these circumstances. Novels that appealed to the exotic had even more difficulty in continuing; anthropology had preempted the field. Further, since the exploration of the Indian's psychology, shrouded in magic and myth, was not part of the indigenista effort, these novels could not retreat to the realm of myth. Such a retreat was successfully carried out later by Indian magicorealist novels. Even the future, where wishes are aimed and hopes are stored, was closed to these writers because in their eyes the Indian had no future.

This challenge by the social sciences took place in the novelistic production of all the countries discussed here, but it was in Mexico that it showed its strength. The efforts of Mexican indigenista writers were not seriously undermined by heavy Indian migrations and ameliorative government actions, as in the case of Guatemala and the Andes, precisely because Mexican writers had chosen small and exotic groups of Indians who were bypassed by these processes to begin with. In Mexico, it was the social sciences that challenged the indigenista novel's very foundations. In Spanish America, by the 1950s, anthropologists were studying the exotic, the remote; consequently, anthropologic works from Mexican and foreign universities preempted the exotic Indian as a subject matter. Confronted with this tendency of the social sciences, novelists retreated. As early as the 1940s, some writers had been self-conscious about their limitations and defensive about their portrayal of the Indian; by 1960, they realized they had been outdistanced. In sum, a combination of these factors radically undermined the function of the indigenista novel. In most novels written after 1964 in Spanish America, the Indian as Indian is present either as an historic figure or a secondary character; his most hopeful role, that of a messianic figure in the Andes, is all but forgotten. The Indian who remains in the Andes represents a revolution that miscarried.

Indigenismo,
the Search for Identity,
and the Dream

Indigenismo was a socioliterary movement that was felt throughout Spanish America; it came on the heels of the armed phase of the Mexican Revolution and lasted until about the late 1960s. The expressed aim of the movement was to redeem the Indian, an effort that involved liberating the Indian from present social conditions correctly interpreted as oppressive and rescuing the Indian heritage repressed for centuries under colonial tutelage, romantic fervor, and positivist racism. Taking part in this effort were social scientists (particularly sociologists, anthropologists, and archeologists), artists (including painters, novelists, and poets), and politicos (from Cárdenas to Haya de la Torre).

But to what end was this redemptive effort undertaken? Was it perhaps to restore the Indian and his world to a utopian state? Not at all. Despite all exaltation of the pre-Columbian past, indigenismo was not a movement to restore Indian culture but to sublate it; it was a movement to acknowledge the past, not return to it. For, ultimately, indigenismo was a movement toward self-understanding, and mestizos, not Indians, were members of the movement. And by understanding the Indian's world, the mestizo was attempting to understand himself. In the context of the Spanish American cultural tradition, indigenismo was one more swing in the hate-love pendulum that has moved the mestizo for centuries. At its most militant, indigenismo played down or attacked the Spanish legacy, very much as did caudillos in the nineteenth century. In other words, indigenismo reflected the mestizo's ambivalence vis-à-vis European culture; this time, he seemed inclined to reject the father and exalt the mother.

But, in truth, exalting the mother was only a means of negating her and embracing the child, the product of the clash of two cultures, the product of rape. Thus, indigenismo was an attempt to come to terms with the trauma of birth but not to remain there brooding about it; it was, at the same time, the first step in an attempt to go beyond the trauma to the promised land prefigured in Orozco's vision. Indigenismo was one of the most recent efforts by Spanish Americans in their search for identity.

The basis of the indigenista effort was the deeply held belief that the essence of the Spanish American man was to be found neither in the European legacy (as Rodó and his followers, among others, had claimed) nor in the Indian legacy (as some have argued indigenismo maintained); but, rather, it was to be found in the mestizo. For Spanish Americans to search for their essence in the European world alone, to deny the enslaved mother, indigenismo held, was to labor not toward self-understanding but toward self-deception. Indigenistas argued that it was futile to seek entrance to the European world that denied them; to persist in knocking at European doors would mean continuing to live with a haunted soul, to revolve within the confines of resentimiento. Whatever contribution Spanish America may make to the world's culture and history will not be made by imitating, by aping the old reference group; valuable and lasting contributions will be made only by asserting the uniqueness of the mestizo, by stressing his peculiar situation in the human condition.

Spanish Americans owe the opportunity for coming to terms with the unhealed wounds of conquest and its aftermath to the indigenista movement; they also owe to it the possibility of going beyond those experiences. Through indigenismo, the centuries-old guilt has once again been made visible, palpable, in all its ugliness: a guilt that was often

interposed between human beings and tended to dehuman-
ize both masters and slaves; unspoken guilt that turned
quickly into hatred against the other and ultimately into
self-hatred.

And that is not all Spanish America owes indigenismo: By
searching for its essence in the mestizo, indigenismo enhanced cultural unity across Spanish America. Indeed, the
effort to incorporate the Indian into the mestizo world lay
at the core of the movement. Often, as in Mexico, the indigenista movement allied itself with national governments
to accomplish its purpose; in such cases, eliminating the
Indian's culture was a conscious and planned effort. In other
cases, as seen from the indigenista novels, the call for eliminating the Indian's culture was made indirectly but no less
vehemently. At any rate, successfully incorporating the
Indian into the mestizo world would have meant, at the
same time, neutralizing the Indian's culture as a viable alternative in Spanish America.

Certainly, the indigenista movement's efforts to realize
the Dream of cultural unity and sociocultural identity could
not have been successful had social conditions been different, for no cultural process develops independently of social
processes that fostered it. It was the growth of modern capitalism, generating population migrations and political developments, that made it possible for indigenismo to contribute to Spanish American cultural integration. But if these
social processes affected indigenismo as a cultural movement, indigenismo in turn played on them. This was particularly so in the Andes, where indigenismo developed prior
to the sociopolitical movements just analyzed, for social processes are always affected by cultural movements of the
magnitude of indigenismo.

This dialectic movement between society and culture
made it possible for indigenistas to further the Dream of
cultural unity and forge a Spanish American identity. By
asserting the mestizo as the goal of Spanish American development, the focus of Spanish America's future, indigenista

intellectuals attempted to do away with one of the last bastions militating against mestizo culture. The massive attack on the Indian's culture was all the more effective because it was neither negation nor denigration but exaltation. Across Spanish America, the Indian as Indian was exalted into oblivion. Whether or not the Indian himself sought such exaltation mattered little; after all, the Indian now left in the highlands no longer counted, not even as a silent witness against cultural homogeneity.

The Indigenista Novel and the Dream

Ultimately, the indigenista novel must be judged by the overall effort of the indigenista movement, for the novel was one of the most essential as well as the most militant and visible forms of indigenismo. The efforts of the indigenista writer must also be viewed in this context; in fact, the indigenista movement gives a clear example of the interrelation between literature and writer in the Spanish American tradition.

Given the generally poor socioeconomic conditions of Indians throughout Spanish America and the cultural milieu, who wrote indigenista novels and for whom were they written? As has been implicit in the discussion so far, none of the indigenista writers was Indian. The indigenista literary movement in Spanish America was not a movement within an *indígena* literature but, rather, a literature *about* the Indian written by members of a different class, culture, and ethnic group. All indigenista writers were members of the growing middle class, followed Western European cultural traditions (mediated, of course, by Spanish American realities), and were mestizo. All indigenista novels were written in Spanish and read mostly by the mestizo middle classes. Consequently, although many indigenista writers understood an Indian language or had lived among Indians for some time, in their works (perhaps with the sole exception of José María Arguedas's) the reader senses that the approach to the Indian and his world is an outsider's, however sympathetic that approach may be.

Given these considerations, it was inevitable that the Indian would perceive the indigenista writer as a representative of the ruling class. Social interaction based on equality among Indians and writers was not possible: To the Indian, writers in general were as much patrones as landlords, students, priests, or military officers. And writers, in turn, often acknowledged their conscious effort to write not for the Indians but for members of their own class. They were aware that due to illiteracy and an inadequate knowledge of Western culture in general the Indian seldom, if ever, read their novels.[5] In this sense, indigenista writers continued in the tradition that began with the Indian chroniclers of the early days of conquest, who also wrote *about* their people *for* the Spanish conquerors.

Indigenista novelists continued the Spanish American tradition in other fundamental respects: They were social critics. Many attempted to rewrite Spanish American history, to destroy such myths as the romantic Indian; many, too, assumed the stance of witnesses of the injustices committed against an entire people; and all the while, indigenista writers saw their role as the consciousness of their own class. They attacked feudal social organizations that still lingered in their societies; they criticized the view that the revolutions had solved the Indian problem.

In all this, the quixotic-messianic impulse mentioned earlier in connection with the Spanish American writer can be seen most clearly, for the indigenista writer often saw himself as the redeemer of an entire people as he labored tenaciously to bring about a solution to the Indian problem. He set himself up as a leader, the embodiment of the true hopes, wishes, and yearnings of those whom he wanted to represent. Against all odds, he exerted an effort, and he was willing to pay the price for the chosen role, whether it was ostracism, exile, or imprisonment. He saw his acts as ultimately justified by the vision of a better society for all Spanish America. Even the demand for the Indian's cultural death, the death of those whom he had set out to save, he justified by his vision of that better society in the future. The fact that the Indians themselves did not understand the writer's position, that even if they had understood they may not have agreed with him, was not a deterrent but an incentive.

With this conception of himself at the center of his vision, the indigenista novelist fulfilled an important function within the overall indigenista movement. Through his novels, the indigenista movement, with its hopes and programs, reached middle-class audiences that were seen as crucial to any solution of the Indian problem. For the novel more than any other form of indigenista literature became the political platform, the spearhead, of the indigenista demand for the Indian's cultural death.

This position of the writer within the overall indigenista movement, sustained by the traditional role of literature and the writer in Spanish America, accounts for the virtual absence of first-rate novels in the indigenista movement. In this sense, most indigenista novels show the effects on literature of the Spanish American writer's concerns with socioethical ends. Some novels are political treatises disguised as literary products; others are so simple in plot and structure that they seem to have been written in a week or two; still others are so badly written that they often make for tedious reading.

In view of all this, how effective were these novels as catalysts for action; that is, is it possible that what was lost in aesthetic quality may have been gained in political effectiveness? The answer is not clear-cut. In the Andes, indigenista novels were at least partially successful in initiating social action. Indigenista novels helped to bring the Indian problem in the Andes to the level of consciousness. The revolutions in Bolivia and Ecuador doubtlessly were partly brought about by indigenista writers' efforts. In Peru, Belaúnde's and later governments' ameliorative measures and,

most importantly, military-political efforts by concerned
middle-class groups that had made these measures imperative were also at least partially influenced by the indigenista novel. In Guatemala, however, the situation was different; the indigenista novel was not successful in fostering
significant social change (a failure reflected in the pessimism
of the second indigenista novel) because it came after the
revolution of 1944. In Mexico, the results were mixed; some
novels, no doubt, served as catalysts for subsequent sociopolitical action on the part of social scientists and government
officials with indigenista tendencies; other novels, particularly historic ones (such as *Canek* and *Oficio de tinieblas*)
seem to have been less successful in this regard. In any
case, bringing the Indian problem to the level of consciousness throughout Spanish America was an important contribution of all indigenista novels.

Whether or not the trade-off between art and politics was
worthwhile has no easy answer, but over the years, criticism
of the socioethical concerns embodied in indigenista novels
has been growing. Most of the criticism has come from
younger writers who take the side of aesthetics against politics in literature; literature first, politics second, they argue,
should be the motto of all Spanish American writers. But is
this a viable or desirable position in Spanish America? From
the discussion so far, however, one thing is clear: The indigenista writer was by no means an anomaly in the Spanish
American tradition. To go beyond his efforts in the direction advocated by his detractors would mean overcoming
centuries of tradition; it would mean that the writer would
have to free himself of his milieu. But Spanish America is
changing; the outside world has begun to advocate a movement toward cultural disintegration. Freedom from the
Spanish American writer-critic tradition may, indeed, be
possible.

In sum, as part of the broader indigenista movement,
the novel reflected as well as contributed to the progressive elimination of the Indian as Indian in Spanish America.

A demand for the elimination of the Indian's culture was at the core of the indigenista novel's message; objective social processes were its justification. The writer's assessment of the Indian's position in the broader sociocultural context of society made the demand inevitable, and the writer's cultural bias affected his literary vision. The secret wish of all those writers who set out to save the Indian was to westernize him into oblivion. Ultimately, indigenista writers were unable to see the Indian in any other way than through their own categories and values. Either as subject-object of history or as a potential consumer in a market economy, the Indian was commanded to labor to help bring about a society from which he was, in principle, excluded. And behind the demand for the Indian's self-immolation there lurked the hope that with the Indian's cultural death cultural integration and sociocultural identity for Spanish America might be secured. The ghosts of Manco Capac would have finally been driven out of the world being claimed for the mestizo, the New Man of Spanish America.

The Indian and Magicorealism

Surveying the recent novelistic production in Spanish America, I find the Indian still present in the literary imagination; but, in contrast to the indigenista period, he is only one among many characters that populate these works. Furthermore, the Indianness of the Indian is receding more and more into the background. As an Indian, he is a ghost lurking outside the world of the recently welcomed New Man; the Indian's culture no longer attracts a serious look; it is only seen as it is reflected by the mestizo. The deculturated Indian, thoroughly integrated into the mestizo world, has thereby lost his uniqueness as a literary figure. Such a view of the Indian and his world is to be expected, given the reasons behind the fall of the indigenista novel itself.

But the indigenista novel did not lead directly to the Indian's role in the New Novel of Spanish America. For, if indigenismo as a cultural movement affected the Indian's incorporation into Spanish American culture, the indigenista novel, despite its expressed aim, did not do so in literature. This does not mean that the writer's efforts were not instrumental in bringing about such an integration; rather, it means that indigenista novels served better as incentives for carrying out the task. Why the indigenista novel itself did not affect the Indian's incorporation into the mestizo world lies in the novel's inability to deal thoroughly with the Indian's culture. Most indigenista writers, despite their intentions, could see the Indian only from the outside; they either idealized him, as in the Andes, or saw him through century-old clichés, as in Mexico.

In order to dissolve the Indian in the mestizo world of literature, he had to be viewed from the inside out in all his complexity, as something different, yet that difference had to fit into a larger whole. Because a direct transition from indigenista to the New Novel would have been too abrupt, too superficial, the transition was brought about by what has been called magicorealism—a phase that lingers on in the present, making the Indian's culture very much an element of the Weltanschauung of the mestizo.

The Indian magicorealist novels have as their central characters deculturated Indians or Indians in the process of deculturation living among mestizos. Contrary to nineteenth-century romantic novels and the majority of Mexican indigenista novels, in magicorealist novels, the Indian and his world are not self-contained and isolated in the inaccessible highlands. The Indian is portrayed as thoroughly integrated and exploited, and this is the basis of realism in these novels; in this sense, magicorealist novels follow the direction of Andean indigenista novels. Moreover, the authors attempt to depict the Indian's world from the inside, and their efforts—more or less successful—to elucidate the Indian's psychology permit them to show Indians as veritable and multifaceted human beings. With magicorealism, the naturalist bent in Indian novels is finally overcome. The magicorealist novel is not caught up, as are so many romantic or indigenista novels, with clichés about Indian life that only support the distinction between them and us.

Another important characteristic of these novels is the centrality accorded to the Indian's magical world. Indian legends, myths, and superstitions all seem to come alive in these novels: Indian gods fight their last battles against white and mestizo gods; legendary heroes engage in eternal combat with the Indian's enemies; Indian sacred texts, paraphrased in Spanish, are woven into the novels' texture. And at the interstice between magic and day-to-day living, the Indian's world appears as alluring and enticing as a grandeur that could have been but never really was. Caught in the vertigo of change, in their inevitable movement toward oblivion, Indians in these novels seem to look back through magical windows; back on alternative realities while their struggle for existence continues. Sometimes the window on an alternative reality is a shared treasure uniting the Indian and his fellow man in a bond of hope. The Indian has something to offer the mestizo once again: salvation.

Three works incorporate characteristics of these novels and show the Indian finally incorporated into the mestizo world, thus ending a long project: *El zorro de arriba y el zorro de abajo* (1971) by José María Arguedas, *Hombres de maíz* (1949) and *Mulata de tal* (1963) by Miguel Ángel Asturias. The analysis that follows, I might add, should be considered with reference to the Indian's socioeconomic conditions in the Andes and Guatemala in the first half of this century, as discussed in earlier chapters.

El zorro de arriba y el zorro de abajo

José María Arguedas (1901–1969) began his literary career with a short story about white-Indian relations in a small village in the Andes (*Agua*). As he followed the Indian's

experience in Peru, he expanded his literary vision, dealing
with larger and larger segments of Peruvian society. Eventually, his work reflected Peruvian reality as a whole in
relation to other more industrialized and modern societies.
Arguedas displayed magicorealist tendencies throughout his
novels; however, in *El zorro de arriba y el zorro de abajo*,
his last novel, the magical element is not overshadowed by
political-indigenista militancy and, therefore, comes into its
own.[6] In other words, his magicorealism developed fully only
when a politically militant indigenismo was no longer
possible.

Arguedas never finished writing his last novel; he took his
own life before this was possible. Early in 1969, knowing
that his battle against death was ending, he set down his last
thoughts on sociocultural matters in his personal diary.
Later, realizing that *El zorro* was not to be finished, he
suggested that his publishers publish the novel posthu-
mously and include portions of his diary in the novel. In those
portions included, Arguedas relates, among other things,
how he fought against his suicidal tendencies, his experiences in the highlands of Peru, how *El zorro* was going
to end, and his hopes for a brighter future for Spanish
America.

The entries in Arguedas's diary included in the novel are
an inextricable part of the novel itself; they set the author's
life against the characters' and vice versa. The theme of
Indian deculturation, so central to the novel, is, in significant ways, the story of Arguedas's own life, for he learned
Spanish only at the age of 11 (before that, he saw the world
as a Quechuan Indian) and was never fully incorporated into
Western culture. Like Asto and Caullama in *El zorro*, Arguedas, too, felt the traumas of deculturation because, although mestizo, he was an *Indio sonqo*—an Indian at heart.
His experiences of cultural dislocation affected him deeply;
thus, in *El zorro*, biography and literature are in explicit
counterpoint.

El zorro deals with the collision and interpenetration of two radically distinct worlds. The collision takes place on the coast; that is, after the Indians have come down from the mountains. The novel is set in Chimbote, a northern fishing port in Peru that experienced an economic boom in the 1960s. From Chimbote, echoing the Spanish American Dream of the rise of the New Man, Arguedas envisions the birth of a new Peru; he writes in an entry to his diary: "Bid farewell in me to a time in Peru whose roots will always suck sustenance from the earth to feed those who live in our *patria*, where any man not shackled and brutalized by egoism can live, happily, all *patrias*";[7] where peoples of all races and classes may someday live in harmony.

But what is the cost of realizing this Dream to the Indian? In the highlands, Arguedas says, Indians saw the mestizo "as if from another shore";[8] now, on the coast, he has become part of the noisy process of industrialization. He has become fascinated by industrial machinery, night life, money, and what it can buy. This fascination leads the Indian to undergo rapid deculturation.

The process of deculturation is exemplified in the changing attitudes of Asto, an Indian character, who came down from his mountain village, was taught to swim, and finally became a fisherman. As a fisherman, he earns more money than he ever dreamed possible; he is lured by the night life. On one of his visits to a local brothel, where he is despised by mestizos for being an Indian, Asto buys the affections of a white Argentine prostitute. As he leaves the brothel, he believes himself transformed; after all, he had made love to a white woman: "I . . . *criollo*, dammit; Argentine, dammit. Who is Indian now?" he tells himself in pidgin Spanish.[9] His denial of self is total, and by rejecting his Indianness, Asto has taken the decisive step toward total deculturation. Other Indians in the novel have similar experiences; some no longer want to speak Quechua, their native tongue; others cannot even think in Quechua. For Arguedas, the price Indians must pay for their integration into new Peru is to lose themselves and become other.

As the Indians of this novel become familiar with their new surroundings, they are engulfed by a world ruled by economic interests, the nature and scope of which they often cannot even comprehend. Their new world, they find out, is ruled by impersonal forces; it is a cold world, a rationalized and routine world, in total contrast to the one they had left behind.

This image of the capitalist mestizo world on the coast is present throughout the novel; to give an example, there is a scene where a rooster and some guinea pigs are crushed by a locomotive. A central character in the novel, a crazy mulatto who, from time to time, preaches against the powers-that-be in the streets of the port, tells the people who have gathered in an open market close to the incident: "The rooster is dead, the guinea pigs are dead; the locomotive kills with innocence, my friends. The same the yankees of Talara-Tumbes Limited [American oil interest], Cerro de Pasco Corporation [American mining interest]. No; they are not responsible."[10]

In this rationalized and impersonal world, the owners of the means of production are a small but powerful foreign group who rule over Chimbote and Peru while hidden behind a facade provided by local entrepreneurs. There's no escape, says a messenger for a fishmeal tycoon, "in Peru and in the world only a few of us are in control."[11] And these few men are insatiable: "Their appetites are never quenched," says one character.[12] True, they bring gadgets, cultural artifacts, and technology to poor countries like Peru, but ultimately they grow and prosper because they "eat people."[13]

These economic interests, pushed by an ever growing need for expansion, foster the exploitation of man by man in all its forms. Having used up, or gained control over, most of Peru's natural resources, these interests are now turning their vast momentum toward rendering the native cultures homogeneous. There is an attempt to make every

Peruvian, the Indian included, a member of an international consumer society. Through sophisticated communication systems and other means of propaganda and subversion, the mass culture created and packaged in developed countries is smothering the Peruvian ambiance. But that is not all: Packaging exportable culture is taking place at a rapid pace; "thus one dresses in European, Machu Pichu, Miami Beach style."[14] At the bottom of all this is the attempt to create a worldwide mass culture, to fit everyone into a standardized world, to sacrifice individuality for the efficiency of mass-produced goods and services sold for the benefit of a few.

To Arguedas, the assault on the last remnants of the Indian's culture is formidable, and he sees much of that culture succumbing under the pressure. The homogenization of the Indian is well underway, Arguedas says, as anyone can see by walking through innumerable tourist-oriented galleries in Lima. The Indian's dress, song, art, religious feelings, are all being used for purposes other than fostering cultural individuality. The exploitation of the Indian continues now in a different form, under the facade of pride in the autochthonous; but despite all this, what is deep remains. Arguedas sees the ancient energies still holding their own. Certainly, the mestizo world, where impersonality and rationalization (in the Weberian sense) are the passwords, as he has shown in his indigenista novels, can bury those energies in the deepest recesses of the Indian's spirit; however, they remain there, they endure. But can these energies affect action at all? According to Arguedas, they still do.

In my discussion of Andean indigenista novels, I pointed out that the Indian's ancient energies reached the present through music, dances, songs, and communal practices, particularly communal labor. In *El zorro*, communal labor is no longer an important medium; in the mestizo world, daily life no longer supports the Indian's spirit but, instead, militates against it. Only songs, dances, and music not subverted by the international cultural industry remain now as media through which ancient energies can reach the present. Through these media, the Indian's magical world, clothed in legend and myth, aids him in his peregrinations. Indeed, Arguedas views as a saving element precisely what the indigenista novels evaluated negatively, namely, the Indian's belief in magic. In *El zorro*, magical beliefs offer the Indian an escape from the rationalized world on the coast.

The foxes who watch the Indians and are able to see through the thick veil of rationalization are mythomagical characters. They incarnate themselves in living persons and thus offer respite from the overrationalized and impersonal world. The foxes' magic allows these individuals to defy the laws of time and space so much under rational control: They travel long distances in an instant, transform themselves into larger and more imposing figures, and induce those around them to reveal deep truths usually camouflaged by impassionate arguments, propriety, ideologies, or other means.

Furthermore, continuing here in the indigenista tradition, Arguedas views the Indian's magical world as the basis of their religious and moral values. And these values, retained with the last vestiges of Indianness, prevent some Indians from committing aggressive acts against each other and participating in the degenerate behavior of many mestizos. Caullama, the Indian captain of a fishing boat, represents the deeply moral and religious Indian. At one point in the novel, a fishmeal tycoon organizes the dedication of a statue of Saint Peter, the patron saint of the port. Immediately after the ceremony, the tycoon's cronies bring carloads of prostitutes to fornicate openly in the same place where the religious ceremony had taken place. Caullama does not participate in the orgy because, so the tycoon's men argue, he is an Incan. Later on, when the fishermen learn that they are to pay for the cost of the statue and its dedication, Caullama, speaking for all fishermen, refuses to pay the bill unless the statue is rededicated and cleansed of the blasphemous acts that followed the earlier dedication. Faced with open rebellion, the fishmeal tycoon's men agree. This episode is rem-

iniscent of the plague in *Los ríos profundos*, where the
Indians demand that the highest priest offer a mass and defy
army bullets to get it. In both cases, the Indian's deep mag-
icoreligious feeling is shown to be strong.

The Indian's moral values and religious fervor, which are
ultimately based on magicomythical conceptions of the
world, give him a sense of perspective, affording a respite
from oppressive conditions and serving as a bulwark against
total dehumanization. In all this, Arguedas shows the Indian
to be hanging on to old values tenaciously. In the most
trying moment, amid the most modern labor process, at
least part of his culture is still with him. In a later part of the
novel, Caullama, who is considered a threat to the established order, is threatened with having his ship taken away.
He replies to the messenger who brings this news:

> *The Inca is at my side when we reach the*
> *high seas. Atuahualpa [the last Inca] is not*
> *dead, tell that to Tinocucha or to Teodulo or*
> *anyone who, like a fool but a clever one, a*
> *leach of the capital, has sent you. The Inca is*
> *at my side, more so when in my forehead I*
> *feel the deep sound of the anchovy. There is*
> *the Inca, at my side, serene like a ghost,*
> *huge, colorless. I have been to Cajamarca*
> *where they say they killed him. In the baths*
> *of the Inca, as they say, I've bathed. All over*
> *the Cajamarca valley, the body and soul of*
> *the Inca exists, in the mountain cliff of El*
> *Dorado [in Chimbote], he also chastises the*
> *sea. The capital is going to be defeated, with*
> *time, my poor little dear* paisano. *Get out of*
> *here!*[15]

And the strength of his culture, symbolized by the last Inca
king, accompanies his people like a shadow, "always, until
eternity."[16]

It is this magicomythical moral element, then, that will

save the Indian from corruption by a capitalist system. The increasing rationalization and impersonality of the mestizo world, the iron cage forged around the world by capitalism, find its antidote in this trait of the Indian's culture. Moreover, according to Arguedas, others may learn from the Indian how to fend off the evils that capitalism entails. For example, an American nun, after having lived with some Indians in Chimbote, discovers the irrationality of the capitalist system and returns to California vowing to fight until death in order to make Americans understand that they are brutalizing themselves and walking toward an evil future. This is the new role that the Indian has been called on to play in Spanish America; his messianic function has not been exhausted after all. He might still save the mestizo from alienation in the modern world.

Furthermore, in Arguedas's novel, following the indigenista tradition in the Andes, the messianic role of the Indian continues to be viewed in the context of a transformative political process: a socialist revolution. In one of the entries in his diary included as part of the truncated novel Arguedas writes: "When a socialism like Cuba's reaches here, the trees and *andenes* [agricultural terraces] that are of good earth and paradise will multiply."[17] And it should be emphasized here that the socialism Arguedas has in mind is not one imported from outside Spanish America; it is Cuban socialism that he contemplates and no other. This is undoubtedly based on the view that Spanish America already forms a cultural unity. The Indian participating in that unity contributes his ancestral values and thus aids in creating a new world where the New Man, free from the shackles of egoism, is possible. With this hope, Arguedas bids adieu: "Maybe with me one cycle begins to close and another to open in Peru and what it represents: the cycle of the consoling lark, the whip, the muletrain, the impotent hate, the funereal uprisings, the fear of God, and the superiority of that God and his protégés, his builders, is closing. The [cycle] of the light and the liberating, invincible force of the man of Vietnam; that of the lark of fire, that of the liberating God, that which restores itself is opening."[18] So it was and is hoped. What must not be forgotten is that Arguedas, like many deculturated Indians, could not survive the traumatic experiences of his life.

Hombres de maíz

Asturias (Guatemala, 1899–1974; Nobel Prize, 1967) is perhaps the most accomplished writer in the magicorealist tradition. Unlike his contemporary Monteforte Toledo, Asturias did not write about the Guatemalan Indian in the indigenista manner, nor did he remain on the surface of the Indian world; rather, he explored the Indian's culture through mythology. By working through the Indian's culture, Asturias translated the world view of a people who are disappearing to make room for the mestizo. Like Arguedas, Asturias enriched the Spanish language and folklore by forcing the Spanish to accommodate the Indian's Weltanschauung. Through these efforts, the Indian culture of Guatemala dovetails with the mestizo's becoming part of the Spanish American heritage.

Asturias's earlier novel, *Hombres de maíz,* was published in 1949, four years after Monteforte Toledo's *Entre la piedra y la cruz. Hombres* begins with a powerful description of the telluric forces that affect the Indian in his daily life. Gaspar Ilóm, the Indian hero in the novel, feels these telluric forces in his very being; he feels them as accusations, as demands:

> *"Gaspar Ilóm is letting them steal the sleep from the eyes of the land of Ilóm."*
> *"Gaspar Ilóm is letting them hack away the eyelids of the land of Ilóm with axes. . . ."*
> *"Gaspar Ilóm is letting them scorch the leafy eyelashes of the land of Ilóm with fires that turn the moon the angry brown of an old ant. . . ."[19]*

The telluric forces call on Gaspar to defend his culture and people, whose very being is connected with the land (Guatemalan Indians believed that they were made of maize), both of which are now under attack by mestizos who are cutting down trees and burning them.

To be sure, left to its own course, nature also destroys its creations, but slowly and always to recreate. When the mestizo maize growers destroy, however, things are different: "The *matapalo* is bad, but the maize grower is worse. The matapalo takes years to dry up a tree. The maize grower sets fire to the brush and does in the timber in a matter of hours. And what timber. The most priceless of woods. What guerrillas do to men in time of war, the maize grower does to the trees. Smoke, flames, ashes."[20] And this is not all. The mestizo's concept of land use, his relationship with nature in general, is in total contrast to the Indians'. If he only burned the bushes to plant corn to eat, as Indians do; but, no, he plants corn to sell, and often he even burns for the benefit of others: "Different if it was just to eat. It's to make money. Different, too, if it was on their own account, but they go halves with the boss and sometimes not even halves. The maize impoverishes the earth and makes no one rich. . . . Sown to be eaten, it is the sacred sustenance of the men who were made of maize. Sown to make money, it means famine for the men who were made of maize."[21]

Two cultures confront each other here; two ways of looking at nature, two ways of life. Moreover, one culture retreats as the other burns the countryside, thereby widening its dominion over the land in order to make money. Gaspar sees no other way out of his torment fostered by the demands of ancient values but to go to war. He feels he must go to war; he is "compelled by his blood, his river, the blind knots of his speech."[22] And so he prepares like an ancient warrior summoning his ancestral energies: Look, Piojosa, he says to his wife,

> *The ruckus'll be starting up any day now.*
> *We've got to clear the land of Ilóm of those*

*who knock down the trees with axes, those
who scorch the forest with their fires, those
who dam the waters of the river that sleeps
as it flows and opens its eyes in the pools and
rots for wanting to sleep. . . . The maize
growers, those who've done away with the
shade, for either the earth that falls from the
stars is going to find some place to continue
dreaming its dream in the soil of Ilóm, or
they can send me off to sleep forever.[23]*

And Gaspar prepares for war: He drinks liquor made by
his wife and transforms himself into a fearless warrior; he
drinks ceremoniously—and a good quantity—until he feels
himself ready for war.

*But the liquor didn't burn his face. The
liquor didn't burn his hair. The liquor didn't
decapitate him because it was liquor but because it was water of war. He drank to feel
himself burned, buried, beheaded, which is
how you have to go to war if you want to go
unafraid: no head, no body, no skin.[24]*

Much like the Indians in indigenista novels, Gaspar is
transformed from a passive Indian into a warrior through a
medium, in this case liquor. Thus, he summons his ancestral energies, his inner strength, and off he goes to follow
his calling. As in the indigenista novels, Gaspar's transformation is not accompanied by a plan for action; his energies
are unleashed as a pure force to combat a particular evil.
Gaspar's actions as a warrior, therefore, are desperate attempts to survive as an Indian in a world less and less under
his control.

The lack of an articulated plan of resistance leads Gaspar
to kill and burn mestizo property indiscriminately: "Gaspar
scratched the anthill of his beard with the fingers on his
right hand, took down his shotgun, went down to the river,
and fired from behind a bush on the first maize grower who

passed by."[25] And many more follow; Gaspar's name resonates
around the Guatemalan countryside. The government re-
sponds by sending army troops. At first, Gaspar's knowledge of the terrain and his determination prevent him from
being captured; but, finally, after a long and protracted
guerrilla war, Gaspar and a band of his followers are poisoned by traitors, a mestizo woman and her husband, a
deculturated Indian. Gaspar is able to withstand the poison
and cures himself by almost drinking a river dry; but his
men, caught offguard by the government troops are mas-
sacred. Gaspar comes out of the river only to find his men,
together with their women and children, dead; realizing that
the war has been lost, he throws himself back into the
river and drowns.

These events take place in the first 20 pages of the 328-
page novel; the rest of the novel is woven around Gaspar's
legend and the curse that Indian sorcerers put on all those
who were responsible for his death. Gaspar walks for all
Indians "who have walked, all who walk, and all who will
walk"; and he talks for all Indians "who have talked, and
who talk, and all who will talk."[26] As the novel unfolds, his
rebellion seems to have taken place in long-ago Guatemalan
history, yet his deeds reach the present as part of Guatemalan folklore. And as folklore, Gaspar will remain forever
engrained in the very flesh of the mestizo, for he is part
of him.

Just how far old Indian myths and legends have penetrated mestizo culture to stir emotions and shape approaches
toward life and world is revealed in a passage where an old
woman discusses the creation of legends with a young man
who claims to have invented one. "We often think we've
invented things that other people have forgotten," she tells
the young man. "When you tell a story that no one else
tells anymore, you say: I invented this, it's mine. But what
you're really doing is remembering—you, in your drunken-
ness, remembered what the memory of your forefathers left
in your blood. . . ."[27]

In *Hombres*, there is no hope for a victorious Indian rebellion; the Indian is not viewed as a messianic force. As in the case of Monteforte Toledo's work, too, this is explained by socioeconomic conditions in Guatemala, which had had a revolution in 1944 that the Indian was not part of; and before 1944, the Indian was basically impotent under the rule of Cabrera and Ubico. On the other hand, unlike Monteforte Toledo, Asturias sees the Indian as very much a part of a mestizo world to which he has bequeathed fears, hopes, dreams, and a feeling for the mysterious and magical.

In short, as was Monteforte Toledo's first novel, *Hombres* was affected by the fact that liberal forces had gained power in Guatemala and the Indians were for the first time being courted. The mood in Guatemala was still generally optimistic, and the Indian seemed to be moving toward effective integration into Guatemalan society. In *Hombres*, therefore, the author deals with an Indian who is becoming part and parcel of the mestizo world. To be sure, the Indian's legacy of fears, dreams, and hopes is not all positive; some of this legacy is kept alive to the mestizo's misfortune. For "the gods have disappeared," says a German observer in the novel, "but the legends remain and they, like the gods before them, demand sacrifices."[28] Nonetheless, the mestizo can no longer wish away the Indian.

Mulata de tal

After *Hombres*, Asturias wrote several novels that reflected his concerns with mestizo Guatemala, its liberal government, and the role that United States interests played in the fate of that government (*Viento fuerte*, 1950; *El papa verde*, 1954; *Los ojos de los enterrados*, 1960). It was not until 1963, 14 years after the publication of *Hombres*, that his second Indian magicorealist novel was published; that is, *Mulata de tal* came at a time when the Indian's migration and economic formation had grown in importance in Guatemala. The Indian and his world were now more than ever

threatened by capitalism and the concomitant avalanche of
gadgets, artifacts, and ideas from the west. In *Mulata*, Asturias takes one last glance at a world he sees disappearing;
indeed, this novel reckons thoroughly with the Indian's presence; it is a true effort to acknowledge the past so that the
writer's cherished Dream may then become possible. Thus,
the final confrontation between Indian and mestizo cultures
forms the core of the novel in a confrontation between Cashtoc, the great demon of old who lives by magic, myth, and
legend, and Candanga, "that mestizo demon, a mixture of
Spaniard and Indian in his human incarnation."[29] Candanga is
the demon of the world of clocks, individualism, competition, science, and technology.

The final confrontation between Indian and mestizo cultures takes place in Tierrapaulita, a town the reader approaches as he follows the lives of two ageless Indian lovers.
"In the distance, among abrupt, dry, rocky mountains,
they contemplated a mound of houses surrounded by an
Indian wall that with the centuries had become rock and a
moat, part barren and part planted with dwarf corn, with no
other access to the town than a long and narrow bridge."[30]
There, Cashtoc and his allies have surrounded an old priest
who came to spread the gospel.

Following the old couple's entrance to Tierrapaulita, the
reader finds a town inhabited by mestizos, Indians, and deculturated Indians that is on the brink of disaster. The bat-
tlefield where the struggle between the old and the new is
taking place shows the scars. Tierrapaulita and its inhabitants are crippled, disjointed, distorted; the church is partially in ruins; some people are sexless; there are evil midg-
ets and giants. Where the two worlds meet, it seems, there
is nothing that fits; everything is unnatural and grotesque.

In this town, chaos had been king for centuries; Christian
religions and Indian magical beliefs have intermixed and
fostered alienation and confusion among the people. This indicates that for centuries missionaries and other religious
men have been unable to conquer the Indian's heart; at

most, they have created a fragile religious syncretism. In Tierrapaulita, the church is inhabited by Christian saints and Indian demons; prayers carry dual meanings and intentions; religious gestures are attempts to appease two masters. The local priest admits that priests are scarce and today Indians continue to be "resistant to the true religion, because always, although they come to kneel and to light candles, they bear arms in the legions of Cashtoc, devil of earth, made of this earth, fire of this earth."[31]

But things are to change. The Indian's heart is now demanded by a new god, Candanga, the mestizo, who appears as a rooster announcing the New Man. Cashtoc's powers were sufficient to sustain him while Christian priests propagated their faith with miracles, words of love and brotherhood, guns and holy waters; while these ambassadors of God were all there was to contend with. After all, the Indian was not commanded to give up magic or myth or legend, only to interpret them differently; now, the demand is not to interpret these things anew but to discard them as old rags. And Cashtoc cannot fight on those grounds; he thrives on mysticism, myth, magic. Machines and clocks rob the world of his life-sustaining elements; he must retreat, accept his fate, and wither away with his time. Cashtoc realizes that now he and all other gods of his kind are being abandoned by their creators, long ago metamorphosed into their creatures, their children. But before withering away, he shows his anger in one final act—an act of destruction:

> "Creation was dust and dust remains of the cities we destroy! No more cities! No more men who are nothing but the appearance of beings, like the one made of clay that crumbled by itself and the wooden one, hanging like an ape from the trees! The real men, the ones made of maize, are ceasing to exist in reality and becoming fictitious beings, since they do not live for the community, and that

> is why they should be suppressed. That is
> why I annihilated with my Major Giants, and
> will annihilate as long as they do not mend
> their ways, all those who, forgetting, contra-
> dicting, or denying their condition as kernels
> of corn, parts of an ear, become self-centered,
> egotistical, individualists . . . ha! ha! ha! . . ."
> his laugh turned inwardly, "individualists!
> . . . ha! ha! ha! . . ." he laughed outwardly,
> "until they change into solitary beings, into
> puppets without meaning!"[32]

The city and the countryside, capitalism and communal-
ism, the machine and the myth, the chant and the bullet:
they are now in mortal combat, and one side is losing. The
ancient communal practices are pitted against the newly
born order of market economy—something that was absent
in Monteforte Toledo's work. And these communal practices, with all that the Indian's culture has stored in them,
are being driven from the New Man's world to wither away
in the mountains along with the gods who justified them.

It is clear that Asturias augurs the coming of a New Man
in Spanish America; indeed, parelleling the Popol Vuh, the
Mayan bible, Cashtoc recounts the trial and error process in
creating man. First, the gods made a man of clay, but he
crumbled by himself; then they made a man of wood who
hung from the trees like an ape. But again, this man was not
satisfactory to the gods, who destroyed him. Finally, the
gods made the man of maize, the true man, the Indian of
Middle America; he lasted millennia. And now, this man,
too, is in the process of dissolution; he is being destroyed
for having turned his back on his gods; nothing is left of
Tierrapaulita.

Now that the man of maize is gone, who will take his
place? What kind of man will the gods make next? One
thing is certain, whoever inherits the earth, he will not be a
child of the retreating gods; they are powerless in a world of

machines, clocks, and robots. The New Man will obey the new god Candanga. And what sort of demands will this new god make on his children? Will these demands include a mystic communion between the god and his creatures? Will incense suffice? What sacrifices will have to be made? The demands of the new god are easily met: "generations of men without reason for being, without magic words, unfortunate in the nothingness and the emptiness of their ego."[33] What the Catholic God and his ambassadors could not do in 400 years—eliminate the Indian's culture—will now be accomplished by Candanga, by industrialization, modernization, and rationalization.

But Candanga is none other than Lucifer; the "mathematic archangel," the "guardian of the nebulous and mathematics!" Echoing Max Weber, Asturias says that it was the Christian God who created Candanga after all, and now Candanga is challenging not only Cashtoc but all miracle workers; he tramples not only the Indian but all holy places. And who will oppose Candanga now that Cashtoc is gone? Asturias's concern for the future of Spanish America is clear: Yes, the Indian and Catholic mystic elements are being driven away, and all to make room for Candanga. And to what end? For modernization, industrialization, rationalization? But again, to what end? Is it possible to find meaning for existence in a world more and more forsaken by mystic forces?

Yumi, a central Indian character in the novel wonders: "Can men be real, perhaps? . . . Can things be real, perhaps? Is what we do certain, perhaps?"[34] But maybe it is no longer possible to wonder thus with conviction. Maybe it is necessary to face reality as it is, come what may, but that offers no consolation. Even hopes seem to have vanished from the reality now coming into being; the future seems opaque, uncertain. Asturias is not as optimistic as Arguedas in this respect; for him, the Indian's messianic role was never a possibility. Asturias has captured what was withering away;

he has fixed it in the reader's memory. The Indian is now part of the New Man, and as such, he shares the anguish of things to come.

In sum, it was not the indigenista but the magicorealist novel that succeeded in incorporating the Indian into Spanish America in literature. Magicorealism could do this because, contrary to indigenismo, it presupposed the Indian's actual social incorporation into the mestizo world. For these reasons, too, magicorealism was not concerned with describing the Indian in isolation nor as an outsider but as what he was rapidly becoming: a deculturated individual living among the mestizos and becoming one of them.

At last the Dream of cultural unity and identity in Spanish America could truly be put forth in literature, not as a goal but a fact. Magicorealism found its justification there; it translated broad sociocultural processes that engulfed Spanish America. But as Arguedas and Asturias contemplated the Dream in its realization, they felt anguished because realization of the Dream had come without much drastic change and the dark people were still at the bottom of the social and economic ladder. While Arguedas had hope in the Indian's messianic role, Asturias faced the future empty handed. This anguish of the Indian magicorealist writers is played out in the New Novel.

Chapter Nine

The New Spanish American Novel

> Chain gang of the chingados, linked before and behind, joined to all who have lost and preceded us, to all who will lose and follow us: heir to being chingado by those who stand above you, inheriting the right to chingar those who crawl below you. . . .
>
> —La muerte de Artemio Cruz

> Screw them first before they screw you. There isn't any other way.
>
> —La ciudad y los perros

> He began to decipher the instant he was living, deciphering as he lived it, prophesying himself in the act of deciphering the last page of the parchments. . . . Before reaching the final line, however, he had already understood that he would never leave that room, for it was foreseen that . . . everything written on [the parchments] was unrepeatable since time immemorial and forever more, because lineages condemned to one hundred years of solitude did not have a second opportunity on earth.
>
> —Cien años de soledad

The Demise of the Indian Novel

Having followed the Indian in Spanish American literature from its earliest manifestations to magicorealism, we see that he has been eulogized over the centuries only to reappear with his bundle of promises a moment later. The last eulogy delivered by magicorealism, it seems, will stand; this time, the Indian's demise as a central character in Spanish American literature seems to be definite. The Indian seems destined to play an exotic role in Spanish American letters— either historic or anthropologic—as is already clear in the works of indigenista authors writing after revolutions.

Insofar as authors of Indian novels helped incorporate the Indian into mestizo culture, and thus end a long quest for cultural unity, their work was extremely important for the development of the New Novel. Contemporary writers were freed from having to reckon with the distant past (the trauma of cultural birth) and the existence of alternative cultures in Spanish America, for the New Novel presupposes the realization of the Dream of cultural unity fostered and maintained by the cultural elite. In this dream, the mestizo not only claims the present but attempts to seize the future as well. In this sense, Indian novels are part of the New Novel's foundation; in reality, the New Novel presupposes the end of indigenismo.

The Rise of the Middle Class

The indigenista novel was possible in the transitional phase from a traditional neofeudal society to a more urbanized and modern one. During the nineteenth and early twentieth centuries, neofeudal forces in Spanish America were too strong to allow open and successful dissent among the rising middle class and peasants; thus, a militant indigenista novel would have lacked a social basis. By the 1950s,

266

the acceleration of industrialization and urbanization all but eliminated the Indian's last stronghold of cultural resistance, and without a significant Indian culture, the indigenista novel became increasingly untenable and finally ceased to exist.

As urbanization and industrialization gained momentum in Spanish America, social relations based on exploiting peasants gave way to those based on impersonal market forces. Debt-peonage was large replaced by exploiting proletarians and subproletarians who entered the market as free agents. This fundamental transformation was accompanied by the rapid growth of the Spanish American middle class. As businesses and bureaucracies expanded, the discretionary income of the urban population grew significantly, and literacy levels showed a marked improvement. Around this time, Spanish American urban centers experienced the growth of a consumer society. It was time for professional writers to cater to the needs of a Spanish American culture industry.

The Homogenization of Culture

The consumer society and culture industry that made it possible presupposed the rapid homogenization of Spanish American culture. The growth of literacy levels, sophisticated communication systems, social and geographic mobility, and so on, had fostered by the middle of this century a remarkable Spanish American middle-class culture. Parochial attitudes everywhere were being challenged by an aggressive cosmopolitanism. The same books, dress, and music were found in airports, shops, and plazas in capital cities across the land; at last, it seemed, the Dream of cultural unity was becoming a reality. The mestizo and his culture seemed to have finally reached an unassailable hegemony. The demands for the Indian's cultural death seemed not to have been in vain but, rather, in tune with the movement of history.

But there was a price to be paid for this cultural unity; first of all, industrialization and modernization in general were not an internal development in Spanish America, as was largely the case in Europe and the United States. In fact, this transformation was deeply dependent on the increasing penetration of foreign multinational corporations. Consequently, as Spanish America modernized, it became even more dependent on the international market economy controlled by foreign powers. The growth of the Spanish American middle class, it turned out, was rooted in a form of neocolonialism that undercut its independent development.

Secondly, economic dependency was not all that was involved in this new form of foreign penetration. As Spanish American middle-class culture developed, Spanish Americans became increasingly aware that something was wrong with it. As they looked closer, they realized that their emerging culture was a mass culture no different from what was to be found in Europe or the United States. With increasing frequency, cultural values and products (the New Novel included) were becoming so many items in the international capitalist inventory. The cultural dependency Spanish Americans had been trying to overcome since at least Bolívar was only being reasserted with the advent of the New Man; Candanga was only a front for foreign powers. Economic and cultural dependency showed themselves once more to be two aspects of the same process. For writers and humanists, realization of the Dream was, in fact, becoming a nightmare. They saw it as an irony of history that in its realization the long awaited cultural unity threatened to destroy any truly Spanish American culture altogether. As the Indian had been asked to lose himself for the sake of the mestizo, so now the mestizo was being asked to lose himself for the sake of an international capitalist culture fostered by a pervasive culture industry.

There are nonsociological factors that must be considered in any extensive study of the rise of the New Novel. However, as will be clear presently, the factors noted here are those that form not only the world views of professional writers but the very form and content of their literary production. The appropriation of literary techniques developed in Europe (particularly by the *nouveau roman* school) and the United States (the significant influence of William Faulkner and John Dos Passos, for example) must be seen in this context.

The Professional Writer: An Ideal Type

Absolute distinctions between professional and nonprofessional writers are bound to be misleading. It cannot be said exactly when Spanish American writers as a group took on the characteristics of professionals, namely, earning a living from their work. In fact, speaking in purely economic terms, it could be argued that even today the majority of Spanish American authors continues to be nonprofessional; however, it is not so much these writers' success or failure in the market as the ethos that orients them that is crucial. Since the middle of this century, Spanish American writers have been accustomed to viewing their work as a commodity circulated in the open market to which they would like to devote themselves entirely if they could. Insofar as this ethos predominates, it is proper to speak of professional writers in Spanish America.

There are two questions that seem particularly important in view of the discussion so far: First, what have been the effects of socioeconomic changes experienced in Spanish America on the writer's position within the society at large? Second, how has professionalism affected the traditional self-image of the writer and his conception of literature? Regarding the first question, it is clear that the writer's socioeconomic position has changed markedly in the last 30 years. In contrast to the nonprofessional writer of the past, the professional writer is no longer an ipso-facto member of the ruling classes; he does not mix art and politics as did Sarmiento or Gallegos, who became presidents of their countries. As a writer, he is now part of an intelligentsia that is, in turn, only part of a growing but as yet politically undefined middle class, and his sociopolitical role is less clear and strong than nonprofessional writers'.

Within his own field, too, the professional writer is confronted with problems his nonprofessional counterpart did not have to face with equal urgency. To maintain a reading public—and thus economic solvency, which permits him to continue his chosen career—the professional writer must successfully overcome two challenges: He must compete with the growing proliferation of pulp literature within and outside Spanish America. Sometimes the challenge has been met by producing pulp literature, which meant abandoning the traditional role of writer-critic.

Secondly, and more central to my discussion, the professional writer must compete with great literature from all over the world. This second challenge has led many to try to make inroads into other markets as well; meeting this challenge is one reason for the almost constant innovation in novel-writing techniques in the last 30 years. Indeed, the professional writer seems obsessed with producing literature with an international flavor and status. These considerations plus the long history of cultural dependency discussed earlier make such statements as those by Óscar Collazos— that the New Novel shows the author's inferiority complex vis-à-vis European culture—not only possible but generally understandable.[1]

As for the effects of professionalism on the writer's traditional role and his concept of literature, it seems abundantly clear from even the most cursory reading of writers' statements that most Spanish American professional writers have been not only unable but unwilling to turn totally against their inherited tradition and proclaim themselves apolitical.

To varying degrees, they continue to feel their culture's demand for social critics. But contrary to their nonprofessional counterparts, they want to maintain literature's independence from social concerns. They are torn by the choice between two equal but, in their view, irreconcilable goods, and they have reacted to this conflict in various ways.

Some writers have vehemently protested against cultural demands at every turn; writers, they have argued, have no business advising anyone how to live; they are not priests, *politicos*, or social scientists. Art and politics in particular should not be mixed; professionalism is extolled as a virtue. But even the most forceful exponents of this position have been unable to shake themselves completely loose from the grip of their tradition. Jorge Luís Borges, perhaps the clearest and most emphatic writer against the writer-critic tradition, for example, not only "protests too much" but feels obligated to justify his apolitical stance as writer by pointing out his illustrious Argentine revolutionary ancestors and youthful fight against Perón and Nazism.[2]

A minority of writers have reacted by abandoning literature altogether, convinced that to continue writing great literature in a world in urgent need of social action leads only to living in bad faith. Perhaps the best known writer in this position is Gabriel García Márquez, who temporarily abandoned literature for journalism. Just how many potential writers will never begin a literary career because of this particular resolution of the conflict is hard to know.

The majority of professional writers, however, want to have it both ways; that is, they want to produce great literature while continuing to be social critics. Their position is based on reasons very different from those of nonprofessional writers. To maintain the posture of social critics while producing great literature, professional writers feel they must split their public personalities. As writers, they want to be concerned with only the aesthetic quality of their product; as social critics, they want to record their views through the media or the classroom. And never the twain shall meet. Needless to say, this position has caused confusion about the writer's social role in Spanish America.

What is important to note in all these reactions is the underlying belief (shared by literary critics as well) that writing great literature is incompatible with didacticism. Literature, it is claimed, must be seen not as a means to something else but as an end in itself. Literature written specifically as a means to socioethical ends is explicitly rejected by the professional writer.

The progressive separation of aesthetic consciousness from more general life experiences took place in Europe concomitantly with the growth of middle-class economic power and culture.[3] It began with Descartes's search for self-certainty and reached its clearest expression in Kant's and Schiller's aesthetics in the late eighteenth and early nineteenth centuries. A similar overriding concern with aesthetics is rather recent in Spanish America, not that it was totally absent in the past—*modernismo,* for example, must not be forgotten—but it was generally viewed as an illegitimate concern, given the role of writer and literature and sociocultural constraints in a neofeudal society. As noted, middle-class individualism did not exert itself in Spanish America until roughly the middle of this century, precisely when economic forces finally gained an upper hand against the neofeudal society. Paralleling the European development, it is only then that Spanish American literature sought aesthetic perfection for its own sake and found the search a legitimate one. The current overemphasis on form and aesthetics in general in Spanish America is no accident; it is tied to socioeconomic processes.

The consequences of this sociocultural transformation seem clear enough: As soon as the writer ceases to see art as related to broader social concerns but, instead, as a formal expression of feelings or aesthetic pleasure, he tends to forego the role of social critic. The crucial difference between professional and nonprofessional writers is then clear:

The possibility of consciously separating art and didacticism was not seriously entertained by the nonprofessional, the professional writer takes it as a given. But this assumption, however understandable in view of the professional writer's reaction to the crude social realism that preceded him (and of which indigenismo was a part), is questionable, to say the least. There are no compelling reasons supporting the view that it is possible to write either great or didactic literature but not both. All great art is didactic; indeed, it must be didactic. All great art discloses essential aspects of the human condition as mediated through the world view of the time and thus develops (in the Hegelian sense of Bildung) self- and cultural understanding.[4] In this sense, all great art contains an "ought." In the Western tradition Plato's *Republic*, Dante's *Divine Comedy*, Nietzsche's *Thus Spoke Zarathustra* were all didactic by design; Cervantes's *Don Quixote de la Mancha*, one of the cornerstones of Spanish culture, shaped concepts of life and world even in Spanish America. Works of the best Spanish American writers from Sarmiento through Martí to Vallejo are clearly embedded in this didactic tradition; thus, the important question is not whether the best work of the professional writer is didactic, but, rather, what is the lesson in his work; what is the lesson hidden beneath the aesthetic consciousness.

The Message of the New Novel

The misplaced confidence in separating art from didacticism, plus the real and perceived social injustice surrounding professional writers, led many of them to despair, pessimism, and ultimately to silence before the prospect of the future. In their literature (though not in their other chosen media), many of these writers give the impression that there are no solutions to social problems in Spanish America. As a consequence, the injustices depicted take on the semblance of fateful events; this is clear in García Márquez's *Cien años*

de soledad (1967), for example, where the characters seem
to follow designs preestablished from time immemorial. It is
clear in Carlos Fuentes's *La muerte de Artemio Cruz* (1962),
where Artemio is driven by centuries of cultural traditions
and the traumas of childhood; at the end of the novel, the
reader feels that Artemio is only a vehicle, the temporary ves-
sel of an evil that transcends him and will continue to exist
forever. The same can be said of Vargas Llosa's *La ciudad y
los perros* (1962), where institutional constraints and early
childhood experiences preclude characters' choices and freedom. Human action as a fateful event is clear in Juan Rulfo's
Pedro Páramo (1955), where, by the end of the novel, everyone in Comala is dead and the conversations heard are the
murmurings of a people condemned to eternal suffering.

One way of presenting acts as fateful events in literature is
by depicting the world and human actions according to the
Manichaean concept, which flourished in Spanish American
letters during the first half of this century. There were then
bad landlords and good Indians, bad priests and good wom-
en, bad capitalists and good proletarians, and so on. While
the professional writer strives to avoid such a naïve view of
world and humanity, the Manichaean concept flourishes in
the most widely known New Novels, where central characters are either *chingones* or *chingados*, rapers or the raped.
Characters in many of these novels view life as a constant
struggle to stay on top, and all is ultimately justified by
survival; in this sense, Artemio Cruz's *yo* is prototypic.

Clearly, viewing the world and man's actions as fateful
events shuts the door to the hope for a better future. Why
the pessimism? Certainly not because of the professional
writer's modesty, nor his inability to understand the world
in all its complexity. This would suggest that the nonprofessional writer actually understood his world or was deceived
into believing that he did; either case misses the point. In
the past, whether the writer understood his world or not
was secondary to his role as advisor, and recognizing his
ignorance did not restrain many nonprofessional writers

from advancing their own theories as guides for sociocultural action; this was abundantly clear in the case of the indigenista novel. The reasons for pessimism and the attendant silence before the future lie in two mutually reinforcing factors: the writer's lack of faith in any social agent that would realize positive social action and the structure of the New Novel itself.

Literature and Disillusion

The concept of literature as a means to something else depends on the existence of something that can be transmitted through literary form. For the nonprofessional writer, this something varied according to author and time: there was the faith of the believer, the rage of the moralist, the politics of the socialist, the pride and shame of the indigenista, the Dream that some day Spanish America would be united and free. And in all cases, there was counsel for present action, and more, there was the writers' hope that either the proletariat, the Indian, or members of their own class would be actually moved to action by their work.

The professional writer's pessimism issues from disillusion; for him, there seems to be no divine justice. The proletariat is either easily repressed by the powers that be or easily co-opted via better wages. In any case, many of these writers are either against, or ambivalent toward, a socialist revolution in view of the historic record. Thus, the old elite is rapidly being replaced by a middle class of technocrats, but even the middle class is not considered to be a vehicle for change because, from its inception, it has been allied with markets fostered and controlled by multinational corporations. Even the arrival of the New Man is cause for pessimism, since the realization of the Dream became a nightmare by, ironically, threatening to destroy Spanish American culture altogether. Here, and not on a newly found honesty, lie crucial reasons for the writer's conscious attempt to split art from didacticism. Art became apolitical largely because artists lacked a viable political constituency.

These social factors have led to a state of affairs where there is excellent literature *and* implicit, veiled counseling. The didactic thrust of such novels as Rulfo's *Pedro Páramo* is a clear lesson in pessimism; other novels written by more radical writers show criticism as a god term. Through these novels (such as *Cambio de piel, La muerte de Artemio Cruz, Cien años de soledad, La ciudad y los perros, La casa verde,* and the like), writers criticize everything that is clearly wrong in Spanish America, but they see no alternatives; consequently, their efforts often turn into self- and cultural recrimination. Their criticism of everything is a sign of impotence, which eventually leads to pessimism; their silence before the future is no less conclusive.

The New Novel: Complexity and Isolation

For centuries, Spanish American contributions to world literature were mainly in content rather than form. The hollowness of colonial literature was due mainly to imposing European forms on a different reality. As indicated earlier, an exotic Spanish America was depicted through borrowed forms. Since the nineteenth century, literature has belonged to the polity determining the fate of society; this was most clearly exemplified by militant indigenismo. The professional writer wants to question what he sees as a leftover colonial mentality; he takes issue with the unreflexive adoption of imported forms. He does this because, in his view, whatever is to be delivered through form will not shine forth truthfully unless that form is adequate. This is another reason for constant innovation in literary forms in the last 30 years.

Indeed, over the last 30 years, novels in Spanish America have taken a marked turn toward structural complexity. This dramatic leap accompanied the so-called boom (the very term indicates the market) in Spanish American letters.[5] Such novels as Alejo Carpentier's *Los pasos perdidos* (1953) and Rulfo's *Pedro Páramo* gave impetus to a trend in complexity of structure that reached its peak in Mario Vargas Llosa's *La casa verde* (1965), Cabrera Infante's *Tres tristes tigres* (1967), Julio Cortázar's *62: Modelo para armar* (1968), José Donoso's *El obseno pájaro de la noche* (1970), and Carlos Fuentes's *Terra nostra* (1975).

But this move toward complexity of structure has brought about fundamental changes in the relationship between novel and society—unintended consequences, for the most part, of a genuine desire for self- and cultural clarification. Perhaps the most crucial change has taken place in the interplay between writer, literature, and audience; for instance, the ideal reader demanded by the New Novel is no longer the ideal reader of the nonprofessional writer. The New Novel requires an active reader who is sophisticated and patient enough to become totally involved in the process of creating the work itself; that is, the New Novel requires a reader who is able to piece together assorted and carefully distributed information in order to bring harmony and coherence to the work. One consequence of the new demands placed on readers is that the author no longer tells them how to interpret the actions of characters. Thus, readers of these novels are virtually left on their own, guided perhaps by what Barthes called *plaisir du texte*, assiduously trying to read between the lines or to second guess the author.

This change in demands placed on the audience can be interpreted as a positive outcome of the complexity of structure. It may be argued that by being jolted and shocked at every turn, the reader is not given respite from paying attention to the material at hand and, thus, from being actively involved in constructing the work itself. Further, this creative effort on the readers' part awakens their consciousness. By participating in making the text, readers are educated in other forms of participation as well, such as political or social. (This was Friedrich Schiller's hope—it lies at the base of the defense of modernism.) In this sense, the text would be the social analogue and society, the text analogue.

Indeed, literature would be the medium through which an attack on the passivity of the Spanish American public was mounted. The traditional demands for didacticism on the part of the Spanish American writer would be redeemed; the colonial mentality would be challenged at its roots.

But why hasn't this argument been given more emphasis by Spanish American writers? Why is it that arguments on behalf of modern art, for example, haven't been more widely upheld in Spanish America? Because, theoretical problems aside, there is a catch to all this. The fact remains, and writers recognize it, that the majority in Spanish America are either not well educated enough to understand the technical subtleties involved or are rapidly bored by the complexity and stop at the first chapter.[6] The ideal reader, it turns out, is, for the most part, either a professional writer or someone who makes it a point to understand these works in all their technical aspects and, therefore, acquires esoteric knowledge (such as techniques of literary analysis, structural or hermeneutic). In other words, novel writing has become incestuous, and with this penchant for technical prowess, any hope of tying art to social action and solutions to a viable social agent is virtually abandoned.

But even if there were larger audiences for these works, their very structure counsels readers to learn to live with ambivalence and indecision. Characters in these novels move in a world devoid of criteria for distinguishing between good and evil; in fact, evil is all the more difficult to identify when it seems most palpable. How does one condemn Artemio Cruz or Pedro Páramo, for example, despite their cruel and immoral excesses of power? How does one condemn the actions of a Boa or a Buendía? And where there are no criteria for distinguishing between good and evil, it is not possible to take a final stand. The general feeling is that the negative evaluation of the sociocultural background of these characters is not sufficient to serve as a guide for action; survival is the ultimate and only justification in a Manichaeistic world. In many New Novels, reality appears to be too complex to understand as a whole; indecision, therefore, is the reader's normal response. Thus, lack of faith underlying the author's political position is translated into the very structure of his creation.[7]

The indecision that pervades the New Novel is the result of yet another of its characteristics, namely, its revival of baroque style. This is clear in José Lezama Lima's *Paradiso* (1956) Fuentes's *Terra nostra,* and it is also detectable in the concept of the total novel, particularly in Mario Vargas Llosa's work. It was noted that the realization of the Dream of cultural unity threatened to do away with Spanish American culture altogether; Candanga's actions, for example, obey the half-concealed designs of an international culture industry. It has become clear by now that the triumph of the mestizo over cultural pluralism is not a solution to cultural problems in Spanish America. But if the mestizo is to take a stand against foreign designs that are contributing to cultural disintegration, what defenses could he use? Whence could he draw adequate strength? What would the mestizo require to withstand this new form of cultural dependency? Spanish American cultural leaders, writers included, do not know the answer to these and similar questions; their indecision paralyzes them.

The writers of Indian novels indicated the cultural leaders' options clearly and offered liberal and socialist solutions. Some writers, like Arguedas, even argued that the Indian's magical world offered an antidote to the growing individualism and rationalization of the mestizo world. But the new writers do not believe wholeheartedly in any of these solutions. In their eyes, the Mexican Revolution indicated that liberal revolutions are doomed to failure because class distinctions and social injustices remained untouched. The Cuban Revolution, forced to choose between social justice and freedom, chose social justice, a choice most writers find disquieting, since it goes against their middle-class views of citizens' rights. And in a correct reading of history, they no longer see the Indian as a vehicle for change; the Indian political party in Bolivia, for example, is not taken seriously by most writers. But while skeptical of all possibilities, these writers do not want to reject any of them absolutely; such liberal ideals as freedom of the press and conscience are regarded as permanent contributions of Western culture to mestizo Spanish America. And socialist ideals are the hope for a more just society—even the Indian lurks beneath the mestizo world as if waiting to be summoned once again. This is clear in Fuentes's *La región mas transparente* (1958), where Ixca Cienfuegos roams Mexico City's underground; it is clear in Vargas Llosa's *La ciudad y los perros* in the symbolic presence of the llama, whose enigmatic eyes see corruption, yet he remains untouched by it (recall the Indian's admonition to Rendón Wilca in *Todas las sangres*); it is clear in Rulfo's *Pedro Páramo*, when the rain comes to Comala with the arrival of the Indian merchants.

The result of all this is a fear to shut anything out, for in the baroque style, everything is important, nothing superfluous. Very much like the Indians who fashioned their cathedrals just after the conquest, the new writers want to keep all the options alive. They see their cultural world threatened with disaster, and they want to hold onto it, to record the richness threatened by a homogenized, international culture. Thus, in the New Novel, extensive passages enumerate and catalog cultural products, peoples, lands, words. It is as if Spanish America were a Macondo threatened with the plague of insomnia; often, too, as in *Paradiso*, *Los pasos perdidos*, and *Cien años de soledad*, Spanish America is described as if newly discovered in a flash of recognition before fading from memory. In the total novel of Vargas Llosa, there is an attempt to gather a disparate world in one act of cognition; in *La casa verde*, linear time and space are shattered to bring about the interpenetration of diverse aspects of Peruvian reality. In *La ciudad y los perros*, the military academy becomes a microcosm of the larger Peru, with its diversity of people, cultures, values, classes. All these efforts indicate a sense of urgency paralleled in

Spanish American history only by the sense of urgency Indian leaders experienced just before the destruction of the pre-Columbian world. It is an attempt to hold on to what seems destined to vanish in an aggressive culture industry.

In sum, the best professional writers, like their nonprofessional counterparts, are in the Spanish American tradition; they are bearers of counsel. They write for a nation ransacked by foreign interests and their audience's expectations that they be "leader, judge, legislator, artist."[8] However, without a social agent to redress the wrongs, writers see and support their "engaging" literature, the object of their protest lacks clarity; they speak for no particular group; they seek universality. Without a concrete subject-object of history, some of these writers have tried to abandon their traditional calling, while others have made criticism their god term.

In fact, generally speaking, negation, not affirmation, is the New Novel's strength. Through negation, the writer attempts to transcend his impotence as a catalyst for action while freeing himself from the sociocultural forces built by foreign and native economic powers on a depressing reality. But strength born of criticism is perilous. The writer must engage danger at every turn. If he is not equal to the task, his work turns from a positive statement about reality into a cynical or, what is worse, opportunistic exercise. Negation is positive only when it posits an alternative to what is negated, when it posits a more truthful or just reality. The archimedian point from which to judge must be securely grounded—even if ultimately only in hope or faith.

Perhaps the greatest task for the Spanish American writer may now be self-consciously to fashion a great didactic literature; did not Martí, Vallejo, Neruda point the way? In reacting against the falsification of content due to an inadequacy of form, professional writers have overshot their mark. The emphasis on form brought about by aesthetic considerations violates the very purpose of form, which is to allow content—which must include counsel as the way to truth

—to manifest itself. Hopefully, future developments will reconcile form and content, so that form will be adequate to
content and permit content to shine forth as message, as positive counsel for self- and cultural clarification. Indeed, in
recent novels, writers appear to be willing to draw closer to
their audience, though these indications are yet too weak to
support conclusions. In any event, the attempt to split art
from politics is now the part of Spanish American tradition
that had to fail; as the boom recedes, older voices may again
be heard.

Whither Spanish America?

In this work, I have explored the issues surrounding the
long search for, and reality of, cultural unity in Spanish
America; this work represents an effort to take inventory of
what has been won and what has been lost in the sociocultural transformation accompanying the mestizo's predominance. It now remains to sum up what has been discussed
and to remark on the future of Spanish America.

The search for identity begun by the very first Spanish
Americans has been an arduous task. Over the centuries, it
has taken many forms: Sometimes, it has involved identification with European culture; at other times, a reaction
against it. From the very beginning, too, the search has been
accompanied by utopic desires, guilt, ambivalence, and
often self- and cultural recrimination. Traces of this are evident throughout Spanish American history. The message of
recent professional writers, which ended in pessimism encased in a critical posture toward Spanish America, is not a
radical departure from, but, in fact, consonant with, the
Spanish American tradition. From the midcentury on, the
traditional polar terms of the search—Europe and America
—have been fused in the hope that the mestizo, the New
Spanish American Man, would be the happy historic coda.

But today, the very viability of mestizo culture has once
again been questioned, primarily by a culture industry exo-

genous to Spanish America. The cultural elite know they must resume the search for the path to follow. They now know, however, that there can be no turning back either to indigenismo (or *negrismo*, for that matter) or simply to an exaltation of European values, for it is plain that the long search for identity did not take place in a social vacuum. The miscegenation of the Spanish American population is an overwhelming fact; the mestizo and his happy or dismal cultural trappings now suffuse towns and countryside. The call for a return to European or indigenous cultures would be wishful thinking. The question marks concerning the mestizo revolve around what he might or ought to be, no longer whether or not he can be.

But despite his overwhelming presence, despite his enhanced awareness of his origins and historic importance throughout the land, the mestizo has not gained self-confidence. He continues to measure himself, and be measured, by European standards. Knowledge of what he is has not resulted in a healthy self-love; the mestizo still possesses a haunted soul. Thus, the search for identity has reached a new plateau, but it is clearly not over. The current cultural and political effervescence in Spanish America is both cause and effect of this ongoing search.

How long the search will continue is hard to tell; some have argued that as a Spanish American project the search will become spurious as Spanish America participates more fully in international culture. The search for identity in Spanish America, now carried out consciously, it is argued, is none other than a search for the very meaning of human existence. The Spanish American search is thus seen as part of a broader, deeper, more sublime search common to all men. Spanish Americans will find themselves and the endpoint of their search when they find the basis of all human existence; this is the message in some of Octavio Paz's writings, for example. Given the experiences of indigenismo, and the sacrifices it entailed, however, one wonders if this position only translates another call for cultural suicide. Perhaps it is more correct to say that Spanish Americans will continue to search for their own place under the sun for a long time. The turn to aesthetic consciousness and the universalization of Spanish America's uncertainty by professional writers and other cultural leaders is only a temporary excursus, the product of given historic circumstances.

As to the Dream of unity, it is still present. It has not only withstood political turmoil and setbacks on many fronts during this century, but it has gained momentum in the last years, given the international political realities. Spanish Americans now more than ever seek to speak with one voice, despite the efforts of dictators and ruling groups—the gatekeepers for Candanga's masters—to smother its force. And with the Dream of unity, the desire for justice and happiness, the core of the utopian element in Spanish American political thought, is kindled. The search for identity, the Dream of unity, and the yearning for justice together form a bond of hope. Indeed, the future is not dismal, though it may be difficult to bear in its immediate unfolding. Those who stand against Spanish America's promising movement will be left behind.

To be sure, the suffering incurred by Indian people in the long process of cultural definition cannot be expunged by any present or future act; however, it is important to know that the suffering was not in vain, for Indian people have paid dearly in this process. Through a terrible metamorphosis, "sons of the wind"—the battle cry of old that designated hatred of those white foreigners who came on the wings of the bad wind—now designates remnants of Indian people barely surviving among lingering ancient rocks, jungles, streetlights, and shantytowns. The Indians have been disseminated across Spanish America and beyond on the winds of fate. They truly are sons of the wind; homeless, engulfed by change without hope of respite. In the long process of cultural definition, Spanish Americans have contracted a moral imperative at least to bring to pass what required the suffering of millions.

Notes

Chapter One

1. See Edmundo O'Gorman, "America," *Major Trends of Mexican Philosophy*, ed. Mario de la Cueva, trans. A. Robert Caponigri (Notre Dame: University of Notre Dame Press, 1966).
2. The decree issued in 1519 by Carlos I reads in part: "It is our will and we have promised and swear that they will always be united for their greater perpetuity and strength. We prohibit their alienation, and we decree that never can they be separated from our Royal Crown of Castille, disunited, nor divided in its totality or part neither their towns nor populations for any motive nor in favor of any person. . . ." José Luis Abellán, *La idea de América: Orígen y evolución* (Madrid: Ediciones Istmo, 1972), p. 78. This and all subsequent translations from the original are mine unless otherwise indicated.
3. A contemporary anonymous author has this to say about the *hidalgos* of the New World: "They are arrogant, vain; they act as if they are descended from great nobility and that they are hidalgos of a well-known ancestral dwelling. They are so crazy that those who in Spain were poor officials, as soon as they pass the Arctic Pole to the Antarctic, their thoughts grow and they believe that, due to their lineage, they deserve the company of the best of the earth. . . ." Boleslao Lewin, ed., *Descripción del virreynato del Perú, crónica inédita de comiensos del siglo XVII* (Rosario: Universidad Nacional del Litoral, 1958), p. 68. For further comments on the transformation of Spanish *desorejados* into lords of the New World, see Alberto M. Salas, *Crónica florida del mestizaje de las indias: Siglo XVI*, p. 51.
4. Simón Bolívar, *Documentos*, p. 61.
5. See in this connection José L. Romero, *El pensamiento político de la derecha latinoamericana*; R. A. Humphreys and John Lynch, *The Origins of the Latin American Revolutions: 1808–1826*; Jorge Abelardo Ramos, *Historia de la nación latinoamericana*, vols. 1 and 2; Víctor Alba, *Nationalists Without Nations: The Oligarchy Versus the People in Latin America*.
6. Quoted by Rudolf Rocker, *Nationalism and Culture*, p. 274.
7. Bolívar saw the future of Spanish America at stake in the pull and tug of two forces, anarchy and tyranny. "Legislators! Duty calls on you to resist the clash of two monstrous enemies who combat each other and both attack you in turn. *Tyranny* and *anarchy* form an immense ocean of oppression, which surrounds a small island of freedom perpetually attacked by the violence of waves and hurricanes, which pull it unceasingly to submerge it." Speech to the Bolivian Congress in *Simón Bolívar: Escritos políticos*, p. 128.

Bolívar's desires to build a republic with a president for life put this fear in perspective. Others did not even accept this compromise and opted for outright monarchy. Miranda thought of a Spanish American federation with an Inca with the title of emperor. Similar ideas were part of the political thoughts of Castro Barros, Güemes, Belgrano, and San Martín. Andrés Bello, an educator and one of the most distinguished cultural and political leaders of the period, had this to say about the political picture of Spanish America: "Monarchy (limited of course) is the only convenient government for us, and I see as particularly unfortunate these countries that due to their circumstances cannot think about this type of government. How unfortunate that Venezuela after such a glorious battle, a fight that in virtues and heroism can compete with any one of the more celebrated battles in history and leaves at a great distance behind it that of the fortunate North America!—How unfortunate, I say, that due to the absence of a regular government (for the republican will never be regular among us), it continues to be the theater for civil wars, even after we have nothing to fear from the Spaniards!" Andrés Bello in a letter to Fray Servando Teresa de Mier dated in London 15 November 1821. Fernando Antonio Martinez, "Una carta de don Andrés Bello," *Revista de las indias* 112 (1950): 71–72.

8. It should be noted that in Mexico the fight against the *científicos* was a step toward eventually overthrowing the racist dictatorship of Porfirio Díaz. In other parts of America as in the Andes, positivism influenced such men as Gonzalez Prada, who became the progressive wing of the cultural elite and took the Indian's side against the inept, ruling white minority. Overall, however, racist theories of Ingenieros, Bunge, Sarmiento, Alcides Arguedas, and many others gave positivism a strong hold in Spanish America. For an excellent analysis of the influence of positivism in Spanish America and particularly in Mexico, see Leopoldo Zea, *Positivism in Mexico*, trans. Josephine H. Schulte (Austin: University of Texas Press, 1974) and "Positivism," *Major Trends in Mexican Philosophy*.

9. The idea of progress in positivist thought was seen breaking away from all kinds of constraints, be they religious, economic, or political. Reason, according to these thinkers, tolerated no restrictions. This tendency was summarized by Eugenio María de Hostos when he wrote: "The Christian ideal did not fit in the Catholic unity, and broke away. The social ideal did not fit in the monarchic unity and broke away." "Ayacucho," *Conciencia intelectual de América*, ed. Carlos Ripoll (New York: Eliséo Torres and Sons, 1970), p. 161.

10. José Enrique Rodó published his little book *Ariel* in 1900. Following Renan's (*Caliban*, 1878) rendering of Shakespeare's ideas as presented in *The Tempest*, Rodó posits the antinomy between matter and spirit, materialism and humanism. For Rodó, Ariel stands for a humanism he believed Spain had bequeathed to the New World. Caliban stood for the materialism and pragmatism of the Anglo-Saxons of the north. The Arielistas were intellectuals who, throughout Spanish America, followed Rodó in his exaltation of humanism. It will be clear later to what extent this humanism hid the realities of inhuman treatment.

11. Quoted by José Luis Abellán, *La idea de América: Orígen y evalución*, p. 92.

12. Octavio Paz, *Puertas al campo*, p. 13.
13. Ibid., p. 13.
14. See, for example, Víctor Alba, *Nationalists Without Nations: The Oligarchy versus the People in Latin America*.
15. Zea, "Conciencia de las posibilidades del hombre en América," *La esencia de lo americano*, p. 16.
16. Ibid., p. 45.
17. A. Pareja Diezcanseco, "Tres afirmaciones de conciencia latinoamericana," *Expresión del pensamiento contemporáneo* (Buenos Aires: Editorial Sur, 1965), p. 154.
18. The feeling of inferiority was further accentuated by reading works by their European mentors. Hume, for example, held that there were reasons to believe that the people of all nations situated between the tropics were inferior to the rest of humanity. Echoing Hume, Voltaire wrote that people living in the tropics have always been subjugated to monarchs. Other European intellectuals read and admired by members of the Spanish American elite, such as Buffon, Raynal, Bacon, Demitre, Montesquieu, Bodin, and many others, reinforced these ideas. In more recent years, Antonio Caso in his *Sociología* repeats these arguments. Certainly, the target of this criticism was the Indian, who was considered racially inferior by most Europeans in both the Old and New Worlds. However, it became increasingly more difficult, if not impossible, to distinguish mestizo from European in Spanish America. Such was the state of affairs during the colonial period that when Alexander von Humboldt traveled in the Americas, he wrote: "The most miserable European, without education or cultivated understanding believes himself superior to whites born in the new continent." *Ensayo político sobre la nueva España* (Santiago: Editorial Ercilla, 1942), p. 146. "America knows Europe," wrote the Chilean José Victorino Lastárria (1817–1888), "studies her incessantly, follows her step by step and imitates her as a model; but Europe does not know America, and in fact looks down upon her, or refuses to look at her at all, as if she were a child gone bad, for whom there is no longer hope." José Victorino Lastárria, *La América* (Buenos Aires: Gante, 1867), p. 5.
19. For an analysis of the effects of hegemonic cultures on the development of a revolutionary attitude, see Perry Anderson, "Origins of the Present Crisis," *New Left Review*, 23: 28–53. See also Raymond Williams, *Marxism and Literature*.
20. On the issue of mestizaje, Bolívar had this to say in his famous message of Angostura: "We must bear in mind that our people are neither European nor North American; they are a mixture of Africa and America rather than an emanation of Europe. Even Spain herself has ceased to be European because of her African blood, her institutions, and her character. It is impossible to determine with any degree of accuracy to which human family we belong. The greater portion of the native Indians has been annihilated. Europeans have mixed with Americans and Africans and Africans with Indians and Europeans. While we have all been born of the same mother, our fathers, different in origins and in blood, are foreigners and all differ visibly as to the color of their skin, a dissimilarity that places on

us an obligation of the greatest importance." Quoted by Magnus Mörner, *Race Mixture in the History of Latin America*, p. 86. Further, in one of his letters, Bolívar writes: "We are very far from the wonderful times of Athens and Rome, and we must not compare ourselves in any way to anything European. The origins of our existence are most impure. All that has preceded us is enveloped in the black cloak of crime. We are abominable offsprings of those raging beasts that came to America to waste her blood and to breed with their victims before sacrificing them. Later the fruits of these unions commingled with slaves uprooted from Africa. With such physical mixtures and such elements of morale, can we possibly place laws above heroes and principles above men?" Vicente Lecuna, ed., *Cartas del libertador* (Caracas: Banco de Venezuela, 1967), vol. 6, p. 11.

21. This romantic strain in the wars of liberation had two contradictory tendencies. On the other hand, romanticizing the Indian emphasized the history of the Inca people; that is, the history of the Indian society that had achieved the highest degree of cohesiveness and formed a veritable empire. This translated the yearning for unity on the part of the liberators who believed that a monarchy was the only way to retain cohesion and fend off anarchy. On the other hand, however, this same romantic tendency initiated the first nationalistic feelings among the cultural elites. This was particularly true among exiled Jesuits and men of letters, such as Francisco Javier Clavijero. Their nostalgia for their countries tended to push them to speak of their beloved Mexican, Chilean, or Peruvian soil. See R. A. Humphreys and John Lynch, *The Origins of the Latin American Revolutions: 1808–1926*.

22. This sense of guilt and remorse was present in those who destroyed America. Sensing his own death, Cortés asked himself whether the wars against the Indians were just, "whether Indians can be enslaved on the pretext of teaching them the true faith." He ended his days believing that his acts, far from being holy, were sinful and hoped for expiation and absolution. In his will and testament, he hurls that sense of guilt toward the future. "I charge and direct Martín Cortés, my son and successor, *and all his heirs to my estate*," he wrote, "to make every effort to learn what is appropriate to satisfy my conscience and theirs" (emphasis added). Quoted by Mariano Picón-Salas, *A Cultural History of Spanish America: From Conquest to Independence*, p. 20.

23. "Whoever does not take into account the issue of being," writes H. A. Murena, "should not wait to unravel any of the mysteries of the Latin American haunted soul." "Ser y no ser de la cultura latinoamericana," *Expresión del pensamiento contemporaneo* (Argentina: Editorial Sur, 1965), p. 245.

24. *Mestizaje* refers to the process of miscegenation, especially between the Indian and white races in America. A mestizo is a person who is a product of this process.

25. Antonio Caso, *Sociología*, p. 71.

26. José Vasconcelos, *La raza cósmica*, p. 18.

27. Alfonso Reyes, *Obras completas*, vol. 11, p. 268.

28. José Ingenieros, "La formación de una raza argentina," *Obras completas*, vol. 8, p. 504.

29. San Martín himself was never blind to the role of blacks in the wars of independence. "The best infantry soldiers we have," he wrote, "are the black and the mulatto." Quoted by Emilio Carrilla, *El romanticismo en la América hispánica*, vol. 2, p. 28. Francisco Bilbao also recognized the role of blacks: "The black-African race was a strong and valiant contingent of our armies in the Argentine Republic and in Peru." *El evangelio americano* (Buenos Aires: Editorial Americalee, 1943), p. 114.

30. It is illuminating to listen to the *scherzo* Vasconcelos hears in Spanish America, that "deep and infinite" symphony he sees emerging from the amalgamation of the races:

> Voices that bring the accent of Atlantis; depths contained in the eyes of the red man who knew so much so many years ago and now seems to have forgotten everything. His soul is like the old Mayan *cenote* of green centers, deep, still, in the center of the forest so many centuries ago that now not even the legend remains. And this stillness of the infinite is broken by the drop in our blood that the black man, thirsty for luxuries, contributes. There appears also the Mongoloid with the mystery of his oblique eyes, who sees everything according to a strange angle, who discovers I don't know what nuances and new dimensions. There intervenes also the mind of the white man, clear as his face and dream (*ensueño*).
>
> (*La raza cósmica*, p. 19.)

31. References to this can be found scattered in the letters of Spanish America. Let me note some instances from different periods: Vasconcelos, for example, argued that "In the common language, we now find one of our best instruments of cohesion. . . . Behold the common ties, more vigorous than any treaty or any political charter." *Indología*, p. 94. I sense a resignation here in the face of the real economic and political fragmentation of Spanish America. In this, Vasconcelos accepts José Enrique Rodó's emphasis on the reality of cultural unity in the face of disintegration on other fronts. Mario Sánchez-Barra, a more recent commentator, also argues that despite all fragmentation there is a reality that is clearly evident: "The profound unity that in so many things makes Spanish America a community," and supporting this unity is the Spanish language. *Dialectica contemporánea de Hispanoamérica*, p. 47. See also Raphael Lapesa, "América y la unidad de la lengua española," *Revista de occidente* 4, no. 38 (1966): 300–310.

32. Reyes, *Obras completas*.

33. Eric Wolf pointed out in 1959 that at the present rate Indian language in Meso-America will disappear within a hundred years or so. See *Sons of the Shaking Earth*.

34. Juan Bautista Alberdi, *Bases y puntos de partida para la organización de la confederación argentina*, p. 59.

35. Perhaps the clearest exponent of the desire to develop a new language for Spanish America was Juan María Gutiérrez: "Then, Spanish science and literature being null, we should divorce ourselves completely from them and emancipate ourselves in this respect from the traditions of the peninsula, as we did in politics when we proclaimed ourselves free. We are still

bound by the strong and narrow bond of language, but this should be loosened day by day as we enter the intellectual movement of the developed countries of Europe. To that end, it is necessary that we familiarize ourselves with foreign languages and constantly study the way to acclimatize our country to all the good, the interesting, and the beautiful that is produced in those [European] countries." Juan María Gutiérrez, "Fisonomía del saber español cual deba ser entre nosotros," *Dogma socialista*, ed. Esteban Echevarría (La Plata: Universidad Nacional de la Plata, 1940), pp. 257–258.

This possibility plus the de facto utilization of neologisms and local grammatical constructions led Andrés Bello to warn that such developments may lead to a "multitude of irregular and barbarous dialects, embryos of future languages that over a long elaboration will reproduce in America what was the case in Europe in the dark period of the corruption of Latin." Andrés Bello, *Gramática de la lengua castellana destinada al uso de los americanos*, p. viii. If this comes about, argues Bello, "ten nations will lose one of their strongest bonds of brotherhood, one of their most precious instruments of communication and commerce." Andrés Bello, "Discurso," *Obras completas*, vol. 8, p. 315.

36. About the nature of modern Spanish in Spanish America José Lezama Lima says: "El occidental, amaestrado en la gota alquitarada, añade el refino de la esencia del cafe, traido por la magia de las culturas orientales. . . . Era esa escencia, como un segundo punto al dulzor de la crema, un lujo occidental que ampliaba con esa gota oriental las metafísicas variantes del gusto." *La expresión americana* (Santiago: Editorial Universitaria, 1969), pp. 84–85.

37. The writer who came closer than anyone to the Indian's world and who now and then attempted to write in the Indian's language was José María Arguedas. But even he, under the pressure of other eminent cultural leaders, reserved his greatest energy for writing in Spanish; although, in all fairness, he attempted to mold Spanish to fit the Indian's world view and not the other way around.

38. Antonio Caso, *Sociología*, p. 147.

39. For a penetrating treatment of the holocaust that Spanish conquerors brought to the Indians, see Alejandro Lipschütz, *El indoamericanismo y el problem racial en las Américas*; Alberto M. Salas, *Crónica florida del mestizaje de las indias*; Miguel León-Portilla, ed., *The Broken Spears: The Aztec Account of the Conquest of Mexico*; Magnus Mörner, *Race Mixture in the History of Latin America*; Nathan Wachtel, *The Vision of the Vanquished: The Spanish Conquest of Peru Through Indian Eyes 1530–1570*.

40. In a way, writes Mörner, "the Spanish conquest of the Americas was a conquest of women. . . . However the Spaniard and the Portuguese of the early sixteenth century had obtained them, by force, purchase, or gift, he lived surrounded by Indian women." *Race Mixture*, pp. 22, 24. The governor of Tucuman Francisco de Aguirre, an old conquistador, confessed at the Inquisition that he had declared that "the service rendered to God in producing mestizos is greater than the sin committed by the same act." José Toribio Medina, *Historia del tribunal del santo oficio de la inquisición en Chile* (Santiago: Fondo Historico y Bibliografico, 1952), p. 85, quoted by Mörner, *Race Mixture*, p. 25.

41. See, for example, Caso, *Sociología*.
42. See Georg Lukacs, *The Theory of the Novel: A Historico-Philosophical Essay on the Forms of Great Epic Literature*, trans. Anna Bostock (Boston: M.I.T. Press, 1971).
43. For an interesting analysis of the sense of charity in Latin American culture in general, see Sergio Buarque de Holanda, *Raices del Brasil* (México: Fondo de Cultura Económica, 1945).
44. See Gustavo Gutiérrez, *A Theology of Liberation*; also Louis M. Colonnese, ed., *Conscientization for Liberation* (Washington, D.C.: United States Catholic Conference, 1971).
45. See Manuel Maldonado-Denis, "Ideologies and Attitudes Among the Spanish-Speaking Intelligentsia in the Carribean," *Social Research* 33, no. 4 (1966); and Fred P. Ellison, "The Writer," *Continuity and Change in Latin America*, ed. John J. Johnson (Stanford: Stanford University Press, 1964).
46. Walter Benjamin, *Illuminations* (New York: Schoken, 1977); Miguel León-Portilla, *Aztec Thought and Culture*.
47. For an overall view of the image and deeds of men of letters during this period see Carl L. Becker, *The Heavenly City of the Eighteenth-Century Philosophers*; César Graña, *Bohemian Versus Bourgeois: French Society and French Men of Letters in the Nineteenth Century*; Emilio Carrilla, *El romanticismo en la América hispanica*, vols. 1 and 2.
48. Describing the calling of the Spanish American writer, H. A. Murena characterizes a writer who examines his calling on a starry night under the pressures of incomprehension and terrible odds. The writer asks himself why "he doesn't succumb to the temptation of abandonment, of giving himself to a placid vegetation. But he knows that these are vain questions. He knows he carries within himself something more obstinate and resistant than any catastrophe, than any dark age. He knows that what he carries is a substance—indifferent to triumph or failure—that has made possible the resurrection of *homo pintor* across millennia despite terrible enemies. He knows that it is that substance that tomorrow—be he willing or not—will make him bend anew over those pages of destiny ever more uncertain. . . ." "Ser y no ser de la cultura latinoamericana," *Expressión del pensamiento contemporaneo* (Buenos Aires: Editorial Sur, 1965), p. 261.
49. The role of the writer as social critic has been characterized in different ways throughout the history of republican Spanish America. Manuel González Prada does it most graphically: "Arduous is the task of the national writer; called to counter the pernicious influx of public men, his work has to be propaganda and attack. Maybe we do not live under conditions so that we can attempt collective action, only individual and solitary effort; maybe the book is not so required as the pamphlet, the newspaper, and the leaflet. One must show the people the horror of their corruption and misery; never was an excellent autopsy possible without cutting up the body nor was a society ever known without bearing it to the bones. . . ." "Propaganda y ataque," *Horas de lucha* (Paris: Biblioteca de Cultura Peruana, no. 9, 1938), p. 330. Even Darío, the leader of *modernismo*, found time to write "O-Jambo" and "Ode to Roosevelt."
50. Faustino Sarmiento's *Facundo*, Juan Vicente González's *Biografía de José Felix Ribas*, Mansilla's *Una excursión a los indios ranqueles*, Juan Montal-

vo's *Siete tratados,* José María de Hostos's *Moral social,* the works of José Martí (the ideal and typical writer-critic) and numerous others form part of this tradition.
51. The theme of *civilización o barbarie* has been the concern of Spanish American intellectuals ever since Faustino Sarmiento's formulation in the nineteenth century. Carlos Fuentes has recently argued that Spanish American writers have increasingly taken the side of the barbarians. See Fuentes, *La novela hispanoamericana* (Mexico: Cuadernos de Joaquin Mortiz, 1969).
52. In the highlands, *patrón* usually refers to a landlord or an individual of high social position who acts as protector, master, host, or boss of a person of inferior social standing. The term usually suggests feudal social relations between two individuals of unequal social position. The situation in which the Spanish American writer sees himself comes close to what Jean-Paul Sartre has called blood guilt. See Fredric Jameson, *Marxism and Form: Twentieth-Century Dialectical Theories of Literature.*
53. See Jean Franco, *The Modern Culture of Latin America: Society and the Artist.* Poets and short-story writers have a better chance of descending to the people. Many of Neruda's poems, for example, have become part of Chile's folklore; Baldelomar's and Palma's short stories have done the same in Peru.
54. A note of clarification: I argue that during this period Spanish American literature was a means to socioethical ends and that the writer's role was that of social critic. But, some may ask, is not the long tradition that now culminates in Borges an indication that literature has not always been critical? A partial answer to this requires examining what is meant by *critique.* When I maintain that the writer is a social critic, I do not necessarily mean that he is a leftist. Criticism of the taken-for-granted can be made from a variety of perspectives. In principle, as a social critic, the Spanish American writer could be either conservative or radical. In the case of Rodó and his followers, for example, there are discernible aristocratic tendencies. However, such aristocratic tendencies made possible their criticism of the growing penetration of foreign culture and economic interests in Latin America. A more conclusive answer would have to include considerations of both the leftist position of the majority of the twentieth-century writers and the apolitical stand of their counterparts; this will be taken up in the last chapter. What is important to note here is that the writer in Spanish America has been conservative or radical but seldom democratic; that is, the writer has seen himself as a leader and seldom on the same level with the people (such writers as José María Arguedas are exceptions to the rule). This was not necessarily due to the writer's wishes but to the reality that has relentlessly denied him closer ties with the "barbarians," or "the people." Coupling art and politics has been a matter of course in Spanish America.
55. Lukacs, *The Theory of the Novel,* p. 88.
56. Michel Zeraffa, *Roman et société.*
57. Such works as *Los sirgueros de la virgen* by Francisco Baramón, *Sucesos de Fernando* by Antonio de Ochoa, *Los infortunios de Alonso* by Sugüenza y Congora, *El cautiverio feliz* by Francisco Nuñez de Pineda y Bascunan,

Fabiano y Aurelia by José González de Sáncha, and the like, are no more than anticipations, truncated efforts of a novelistic tendency. See in this connection Carrilla, *El Romanticismo*; and Pedro Henríquez Ureña, "Apuntaciones sobre la novela en América," *Humanidades* 15 (1927): 138–40.

58. Octavio Paz, *El arco y la lira*, pp. 224–225.
59. John E. Englekirk, "The 'Discovery' of Los de Abajo," *Hispania* 18 (1935): 410–445.
60. The reasons for dealing with only *indigenista* novels written during this period will be presented later when sociocultural processes underlying their production are discussed. Suffice at this point to note that by the mid 1960s the Indian had ceased to be a significant character in the novelistic production of Spanish America. Novels written after this period must be classified as magicorealist (as in the case of Miguel Ángel Asturias's *Mulata de tal* and *Hombres de maíz* and José María Arguedas's *El zorro de arriba y el zorro de abajo*) or neoindigenista novels, which, in very important respects, partake of the New Novel's techniques (as in Manuel Scorza's *Redobles por Rancas*, for example), or they are historical in a way that departs from the indigenista position.

Chapter Two

1. Magnus Mörner, *Race Mixture in the History of Latin America*, p. 31.
2. George E. Simpson, "Ethnic Groups, Social Mobility, and Power in Latin America," *Social Structure, Stratification, and Mobility* (Washington, D. C.: Pan American Union, Studies Monograph 8, 1967).
3. See José Carlos Mariátegui, *Seven Interpretive Essays on Peruvian Reality*; Octavio Ianni, "Race and Class," *Social Structure, Stratification, and Mobility* (Washington, D.C.: Pan American Union, Studies Monograph 8, 1967); Alejandro Lipschütz, *El indoamericanismo y el problema racial en las Américas*.
4. See Julian Pitts-Rivers, "Race in Latin America: The Concept of 'Raza'," *Archives européennes de sociologie* 14 (1973).
5. For a concise treatment of pre-Columbian Indian cultures see Benjamin Keen and Mark Wasserman, *A Short History of Latin America*.
6. For a detailed discussion of Incan literature, see Jesús Lara, *La poesía quéchua: Ensayo y antología*; Garcilaso de la Vega, *Los comentarios reales de los incas*. For an analysis of Nahuatl literature see Garibay K. Ángel, *Epica nahuátl* (Mexico: Universidad Nacional de Mexico, 1945); *Historia de la literatura nahuátl*, vols. 1 and 2 (Mexico: Editorial Porrua, 1953–1954); Miguel León-Portilla, "Pre-Hispanic Thought," *Major Trends in Mexican Philosophy*, trans. A. Robert Caponigri (Notre Dame: Notre Dame University Press, 1966). For a more complete bibliography on Mexican preconquest literature, see León-Portilla, ed., *The Broken Spears: The Aztec Account of the Conquest of Mexico*.
7. Léon-Portilla, "Pre-Hispanic Thought," p. 18.
8. Ibid., p. 30.
9. Ibid., pp. 33–34.

10. Other efforts to record the literature and history of pre-Columbian America were made by those who survived the conquest and wanted to preserve some of their tradition. Fernando de Alvarado Tezozomoc (ca. 1520–1600) and Fernando de Alva Ixtlilxóchitl (1568–1648) wrote extensively about their Indian heritage. In the Andes, Inca Garcilaso de la Vega, Felipe Gusmán Poma de Ayala (ca. 1526–1613), and Juan de Santa Cruz Pachacuti Yanqui Salcamaywa (ca. 1540–?) wrote down some of their ancestors' literature and gave a portrait of Incan culture.
11. See, for example, Octavio Paz, "Los hijos de la Malinche," *El laberinto de la soledad* (Mexico: Fondo de Cultura Económica, 1963).
12. Miguel León-Portilla, *Visión de los vencidos: Relaciones indígenas de la conquista* (Mexico: Universidad Nacional Autonoma, 1958), p. 99. I am using here the Spanish text. A somewhat different translation is found in León-Portilla, *The Broken Spears*, p. 68.
13. *El libro de los libros de Chilam Balam*, trans. Alfredo Barrera Vásquez and Silvia Rendón, (Mexico: Fondo de Cultura Económica, 1969), pp. 50, 72.
14. Ibid., pp. 27–28.
15. Ibid., p. 27.
16. *Anales de los cakchiqueles*, trans. Adrian Recinos (Mexico: Fondo de Cultura Económica, 1950), annotation April 1598, p. 207.
17. For an excellent analysis of the Indian's presence in Spanish American poetry during the conquest and colonization, see Aida Cometta Manzoni, *El indio en la poesía de América española*.
18. Concha Meléndes, *La novela indianista en Hispanoamérica: 1832–1889* (Buenos Aires: Joaquin Torres, 1939), p. 22.
19. For an analysis of the utopian element in the work of Inca Garcilaso de la Vega, see Juan Guillermo Durand, *Literatura y utopía en Hispanoamérica* (Ithaca: Latin American Studies Program, Dissertation Series, Cornell University, no. 53, 1972).
20. Bartolomé de Las Casas wrote extensively; his most influential works include *Brevísima relación de la destrucción de las indias*, written in 1552, and *Historia de las indias*, written between 1552 and 1561.
21. Andrés Bello, *Obras completas*, vol. 1, p. 50.
22. Simón Bolívar said before the newly constituted Congress of Lima in 1825: "The kind hand of the liberating army has healed the wounds that the nation suffered in her heart, it has broken the chains that Pizarro had put on the sons of Manco Capac, founder of the Empire of the Sun, and has placed Peru under the sacred regime of her ancient rights." Quoted by Concha Meléndes, *La novela indianista*, p. 66.
23. The movement toward the legal dissolution of Indian communities that had protected Indian lands for centuries, for example, began as early as 1824, when Simón Bolívar decreed that lands in Indian communities could be divided according to statute amongst all Indians who did not have other kinds of land. See Mario Cástro Arenas, *La novela peruana y la evolución social*, p. 54.
24. Insofar as Echeverría not only wrote the first truly romantic literature (*Elvira o la novia del Plata*, 1834) but also organized the first romantic cénacles in Spanish America (Salón Literario, 1837, and Asociación do Mayo,

1838), I can properly speak of his work as the starting point for a Spanish American romantic literary movement. See Emilio Carrilla, *El romanticismo en la América hispánica*, vols. I and II.

25. In Cometta Manzoni's *El indio en la poesía de América española* (Buenos Aires: Joaquin Torres, 1939), p. 167.

26. In Augusto Tamayo Vargas, *Literatura en Hispano América*, vol. 1, p. 172.

27. In the tradition of Spanish American research, the nineteenth century romantic novel is called *indianista* to differentiate it from the realist novel of the twentieth century, which is called indigenista.

28. Juan León Mera, *Cumandá, o un drama entre salvajes*, pp. 21–22.

29. For the thoroughly romantic writer of Spanish America in general, there were only two ways to treat the Indian: He could see him, as did León Mera, in the exotic setting of the jungle, isolated and savage; or he could see him in an equally exotic past where courage and pride were part of his world. In either case, he bypassed the real Indian.

30. León Mera, *Cumandá*, p. 117.

31. Ibid., p. 196.

32. About the Indian problem, León Mera said: "You are not to blame [for your condition as savage]; it is the fault of the civilized society whose egoism does not allow it to take a kind look upon your regions." Ibid., p. 51.

33. Commenting on her husband's and Manuel's efforts to save an Indian unjustly jailed for the assault on her house, Lucía exclaims, "Oh! Poor Indians! Poor race! If we could only liberate the whole race as we are going to liberate Isidro. . . ." Clorinda Matto de Turner, *Aves sin nido*, p. 176.

34. Ibid., p. 206.

35. Ibid., p. 199.

36. The case of Mexico, which constitutes a slight departure from this basic position, will be analyzed later. I should also note here that indigenismo follows more or less the same development of realism in general in Spanish America.

Chapter Three

1. On this and related subjects see the works of Beate R. Salz, *The Human Element in Industrialization: A Hypothetical Case Study of Ecuadorian Indians*; Julio Cotler, "La mecánica de la dominación interna y del cambio social en el Perú," *Perú actual: Sociedad y política* (Mexico: Universidad de Mexico, 1970); Thomas M. Davis, Jr., *Indian Integration in Peru: A Half Century of Experience 1900–1948*; Amado Canelas O., *Mito y realidad de la reforma agraria*.

2. Carlos A. Astiz, *Pressure Groups and Power Elites in Peruvian Politics*, p. 85.

3. See Henry F. Dobyns, *The Social Matrix of Peruvian Indigenous Communities*.

4. See, for example, Cotler, "La mecánica de la dominación interna."

5. Dobyns, *Social Matrix*, p. 48.

6. For a more detailed account of these liberationist movements, see Mary

Callaghan (Sister Mary Consuela), "Indianismo in Peru 1883–1939" (Ph.D. diss., University of Pennsylvania, 1951).

7. For a detailed account of the life and work of Tupac Amaru II, see Boleslao Lewin, *La insurrección de Túpac Amaru* (Buenos Aires: Editorial Universitaria de Buenos Aires, 1967).

8. For a historian's account of the period see Callaghan, *Indianismo in Peru.*

9. Luis Carranza, *Colección de artículos publicados* (Lima: 1888).

10. See Alfredo Yépez Miranda, *Peruanidad literaria y revolución* (Cuzco: H. G. Rozas Sucesores, 1934).

11. The student movement in the Andes was part of a wider movement that reflected similar societal processes throughout Spanish America. The most important aspects of the movement took shape in 1918 with student rebellions in Cordoba, Argentina. From there, student protest spread as a university-reform movement throughout Spanish America.

12. See Manuel González Prada, *Horas de lucha.*

13. An excellent account of the differences and similarities between Víctor Raúl Haya de la Torre and José Carlos Mariátegui is found in Eugenio Chang-Rodriguez, *La literatura política de González Prada, Mariátegui y Haya de la Torre* (Mexico: Ediciones de Andrea, 1957).

Chapter Four

1. César Vallejo, *El tungsteno*, p. 51.

2. Ciro Alegría, *El mundo es ancho y ajeno* (Santiago: Ediciones Ercilla, 1941), p. 17.

3. Alcides Arguedas, *Raza de bronce*, p. 225.

4. Fernando Cháves, *Plata y bronce*, p. 26.

5. Indigenista writers were taking issue here with racist theories that circulated in the Andes during the early part of this century.

6. José María Arguedas, *Los ríos profundos*, p. 90.

7. Alcides Arguedas, *Raza de bronce*, p. 250.

8. Jorge Icaza, *Hijos del viento (Huairapamushcas)*, p. 81.

9. Alegría, *El mundo es ancho y ajeno*, p. 139.

10. Jorge Rivadeneyra, *Ya esta amaneciendo*, pp. 78–79.

11. Ibid., p. 80.

12. José María Arguedas, *Yawar fiesta*, p. 36.

13. Alcides Arguedas, *Raza de bronce*, pp. 113–114.

14. José María Arguedas, *Yawar fiesta*, p. 24.

15. Ibid., p. 24.

16. Alcides Arguedas, *Raza de bronce*, p. 93.

17. José María Arguedas, *Todas las sangres*, p. 35.

18. Alcides Arguedas, *Raza de bronce*, p. 261.

19. José María Arguedas, *Yawar fiesta*, p. 26.

20. Jorge Icaza, *Huasipungo*, p. 43.

21. Alcides Arguedas, *Raza de bronce*, p. 93.

22. Rivadeneyra, *Ya esta amaneciendo*, p. 21.

23. For a sociological treatment of the accounts that follow see: Alejandro Lipschütz, *El indoamericanismo y el problema racial en las Américas; Conditions of Life and Work of Indigenous Populations of Latin American Countries* (Geneva: International Labor Office, 1949); Thomas M. Davis, Jr., *Indian Integration in Peru: A Half Century of Experience 1900–1948*; Moisés Saenz, *Sobre el indio ecuatoriano y su incorporación al medio nacional*; Luis E. Antezama, *El feudalsimo de Melgarejo y la reforma agraria: Proceso de la propiedad territorial y de la política de Bolivia* and his *Estudios de la realidad campesina: Cooperación y cambio de informes materiales de campo recogidos en Venezuela, Ecuador, y Colombia* (Geneva: Instituto de Investigaciones de las Naciones Unidas para el Desarrollo Social, 1970); Carlos A. Astiz, *Pressure Groups and Power Elites in Peruvian Politics.*

24. Raúl Botelho Gosálvez, *Altiplano*, p. 121.

25. José María Arguedas, *Yawar fiesta*, p. 27.

26. Ibid., p. 56.

27. Roberto Leytón, *Los eternos vagabundos* (Bolivia: Editorial Potosi, 1939), p. 140.

28. Jesús Lara, *Yawarninchij*, p. 75.

29. Icaza, *Huasipungo*, p. 151–152.

30. Icaza, *Hijos del viento*, p. 21.

31. Rivadeneyra, *Ya esta amaneciendo*, p. 43.

32. José María Arguedas, *Los ríos profundos*, p. 157.

33. Alcides Arguedas, *Raza de bronce*, p. 94.

34. Ibid., p. 192.

35. José María Arguedas, *Todas las sangres*, p. 77.

36. Cháves, *Plata y bronce*, p. 60.

37. Icaza, *Hijos del viento*, p. 32.

38. José María Arguedas, *Todas las sangres*, p. 278.

39. Alegría, *El mundo es ancho y ajeno*, p. 194.

40. Jorge Icaza, *En las calles*, p. 51.

41. Rivadeneyra, *Ya esta amaneciendo*, p. 105.

42. José María Arguedas, *Yawar Fiesta*, p. 63.

43. José María Arguedas, *Todas las sangres*, p. 64.

44. Vallejo, *El tungsteno*, p. 110.

45. Alfredo Yépez Miranda, *Los Andes vengadores*, p. 9.

46. See Henry F. Dobyns and Paul L. Doughty, *Peru: A Cultural History* (New York: Oxford University Press, 1976), pp. 235–236.

47. Cháves, *Plata y bronce*, p. 87.

48. Alcides Arguedas, *Raza de bronce*, p. 263.

49. Ibid., p. 204.

50. Icaza, *Hijos del viento*, p. 182.

51. Alegría, *El mundo es ancho y ajeno*, p. 495.

52. José María Arguedas, *Todas las sangres*, p. 407.

53. Rivadeneyra, *Ya esta amaneciendo*, p. 70.

54. Óscar Cerruto, *Aluvión de fuego*, p. 100.

55. Rivadeneyra, *Ya esta amaneciendo*, p. 80.

56. See Antonio Cornejo Polar, *Los universos narrativos de José María Arguedas*, p. 27.

Chapter Five

1. In Guatemala, ladino refers to the non-Indian population, usually white or mestizo.
2. Mario Rosenthal, *The Story of an Emergent Latin American Democracy*, p. 73. Other estimates vary. George Arias B., for example, gives the following figures for four different census periods: 1823—64.7 percent; 1921—64.8 percent; 1940—55.7 percent; 1950—53.6 percent. "Aspectos demográficos de la población indígena de Guatemala," *Guatemala indígena* 1, no. 2 (1961): 5–39.
3. See Robert A. Naylor, "Guatemala: Indian Attitudes toward Land Tenure," *Journal of Inter-American Studies* (Oct. 1967): 622.
4. Charles Wagley, *Santiago Chimaltenango: Estudio antropológico-social de una comunidad indígena de Huehuetenango*, pp. 59–76.
5. See Thomas and Marjorie Melville, *Guatemala: The Politics of Land Ownership*; Wagley, *Santiago Chimaltenango*.
6. See Melville and Melville, *Guatemala*; Wagley, *Santiago Chimaltenango*.
7. See Benjamin N. Colby and Pierre L. Van den Berghe, *Ixil Country: A Plural Society in Highland Guatemala*.
8. See Nathan L. Whetten, *Guatemala: The Land and the People*.
9. See John R. Hildebrand, "Latin American Economic Development, Land Reform, and U.S.A. Aid with Special Reference to Guatemala," *Journal of Inter-American Studies* 4 (1962): 356.
10. In 1944, the Ubico dictatorship was toppled by liberal and socialist forces supporting Juan José Arévalo; later, these same forces supported the more radical government of Jacobo Arbenz. In the ten years that this liberal and socialist combination of forces held power (1944–1954), some efforts were made to carry out land reform. With the overthrow of Arbenz's government in 1954, however, these efforts ceased. By 1964, most of the land affected by reform had been repossessed by landlords, as Guatemala reverted to its pre-1944 pattern of land tenure. The leading indigenista writer of Guatemala, Mario Monteforte Toledo, reported that 90 percent of the land affected by reform had been repossessed. Richard Newbold Adams, *Crucifixion by Power: Essays on Guatemalan National Social Structure 1944–1966*, pp. 397, 400.
11. Eric Wolf, *Sons of the Shaking Earth*, p. 189.
12. Ibid.
13. On this and related matters see Melville and Melville, *Guatemala*; Comité Interamericano de Desarrollo Agrícola, *Tenencia de la tierra y desarrollo socio-económico del sector agrícola: Guatemala* (Washington, D.C.: Pan American Union, 1965); Valentín F. Solórzano, *Evolución económica de Guatemala*.
14. See Jorge Skinner-Klee, *Recopilación de legislación indigenista de Guatemala*.
15. For an overview of Indian labor in Guatemala see Skinner-Klee, *Recopila-*

ción; Melville and Melville, *Guatemala;* Whetten, *Guatemala;* Vera Kelsey and Lilly de Tongh Osborne, *Four Keys to Guatemala.*

16. The vagrancy law was vigorously enforced by the Ubico government. The peasant had to carry his *libreto* identification with him at all times and was subject to detention and questioning. All those who did not comply with the law were arrested for vagrancy. Moreover, "since the only proof a laborer had that he had fulfilled the required work was an annotation [in his *libreto*] by his patrón and the corresponding record that the patrón was required to keep in his own books, it was common for a patrón to keep a laborer on simply by refusing to sign the books." Richard Newbold Adams, *Crucifixion by Power: Essays on Guatemalan National Social Structure 1944–1966,* pp. 178–179.

17. These spasmodic rebellions, however, have been more and more local, resembling a pattern also found in the Andes. With the destruction of the old Indian's elites, there was also the destruction of a central force that could unite Indians in an overreaching, common effort. Nevertheless, sporadic and spontaneous rebellions have threatened ladino rule in Guatemala. In 1817, for example, Anastasio Tzul, a member of the ancient royal families declared himself king of the Quiché and unsuccessfully rebelled against ladinos in Totonicapan. In 1889, another uprising, this time by the K'Anjobal in San Juan Ixcoy, resulted in the death of all ladinos in the area. This rebellion was also a failure since Indians in San Juan were no match for government troops. They had risen to demand the return of their lands stolen during many years of ladino rule and to stop abuses against them on the part of their conquerors. At the end of the fight, they had lost more land and suffered another bloody repression. In 1922, other Indian communities rose up; these uprisings took place in five departments: San Pedro in Jalapa, San Vicente Pacaya and the town of Escuintla in Escuintla, San Agustin Acasaguastlan in El Progreso, Ciudad Vieja and Antigua, Sacate Pequez, and San José del Golfo and Palencia in Guatemala. In 1931, there were four serious uprisings in Suchitepequez alone. In 1943, Indians in Patzicia began a revolt, again to recover their stolen lands; Ubico was able to suppress the uprising before it spread.

18. Adams, *Crucifixion by Power,* p. 247.

19. To enforce the law, the government issued *boletos de vialidad* on which the labor contribution of the people was recorded. The local government representative was responsible for carrying out periodic censuses in order to enforce the law. The boletos de vialidad, like the libretos, were under ladino control.

20. See Bruce Johnson Calder, *Crecimiento y cambio de la iglésia católica Guatemalteca: 1944–1966,* p. 24; Elizabeth E. Hoyt, "The Indian Laborer on Guatemala Coffe Fincas, *Inter-American Economic Affairs* 9, no. 1 (summer 1955): 301.

21. Interestingly, organizers from all parts of Central America and Mexico began to set up these organizations. Here, there is further evidence that for labor, too, the Spanish American nation is a living idea.

22. Adams, *Crucifixion by Power,* p. 452, gives the following figures:

Campesino Organizations with Juridic Personality (1920–1967)

	Unions	Leagues	Total
Prerevolution		5[a]	5[a]
Revolution	345	320	665
Postrevolution	66	27	93

[a]These are estimates.

23. A thorough analysis of the student movement in Guatemala is not possible here. Suffice it to say that the movement had characteristics similar to those in other Spanish American countries in the same period. That is, it translated middle-class aspirations, and it grew radical as it was frustrated in accomplishing its goals.

24. About the Indian's biological inferiority Asturias said: "The Indians have exhausted themselves. Their blood has done nothing throughout countless generations except to revolve in a circle, in this case, a small one. . . . New blood is lacking—reviving currents that could relieve the fatigue of their systems, life that would spring strong and harmonious. . . . *New blood*, this is our motto to save the Indian from his present state. We must counter his functional deficiencies, his moral vices, and his biological exhaustion." Miguel Ángel Asturias, *El problema social del indio y otros textos*, p. 106.

25. Carlos Wyld Ospena's story, *La tierra de los nahuayacas* (Guatemala: Tipografía Nacional, 1933), was but a timid step toward indigenista literature from Guatemala. This attempt was soon abandoned: In 1936, the same author wrote *La gringa: novela criolla* (Guatemala: Tipografía Nacional), a novel where the Indian was not at all central.

26. For an overview of the image of the Indian in the Guatemalan narrative, see Adelaide Lorand de Olazagasti, *El indio en la narrative guatemalteca*. Lorand uses indigenismo in a broader sense than mine, so that some of the works she lists as belonging to the indigenista movement are not considered here to be in that category.

27. Mario Monteforte Toledo, *Entre la piedra y la cruz*, p. 260.

28. Ibid., p. 109.

29. Mario Monteforte Toledo, *Donde acaban los caminos*, p. 94.

30. Ibid., p. 168.

31. The narrator characterizes the hero in *Entre la piedra y la cruz* as a representative of a "powerful line of the Zutuhil people, the one capable of prolonging the fecundity of the seed and defending the hearth at the door, like the ancient men of the legend." How much of this the Indians of the novel themselves were conscious of is not at all clear, the narrator intervenes for a reason. Monteforte Toledo, p. 42.

32. In *Entre la piedra y la cruz*, for example, after a long season of work, plantation owners allow the Indians to have a feast. During this feast, an Indian speaks loudly in order to be heard by the ladinos: "I am pure Indian, pure Indian and need no one. I am a little drunk, but it is with my own

money and it's no one's goddam business. I'm not afraid of the patrón or anyone else, because I'm pure man. . . ." Monteforte Toledo, p. 84.

33. Ibid., p. 210.
34. Ibid., p. 185.
35. Ibid., p. 73.
36. Ibid., p. 32.
37. On road construction Monteforte Toledo says: "Always Indians, disfigured by fatigue and by the contraction of their muscles in impotent and terrified anger. Always Indians of the *vialidad*, constructing roads for vehicles to pass that the poor never traveled, so that once a year the presidential party may go there to perpetuate the progress of the country with cameras and speeches by disgusting journalists." *Entre la piedra y la cruz*, p. 201.

Before the law, too, Indians are portrayed as defenseless; Indian lands are stolen or taken away with trickery in the courts where Spanish is the language. The priest, who, contrary to his counterpart in the Andes, had little to do with the Indians, is nonetheless portrayed as supporting the status quo and in alliance with landlord and state. In *Donde acaban los caminos*, for example, the priest, a Danish man who had left blue-eyed nephews in other parts of Guatemala, represents the church that is comprised of "men of claws, quick in thinking and acting, usually foreign, who seemed more interested in local politics than in the lofty regions of their ministry." All these men worked together and surreptitiously with "influential ladies" and men who "employed all means to take control of the republic." Monteforte Toledo, p. 60.

38. Monteforte Toledo, *Entre la piedra y la cruz*, p. 117.
39. Ibid., p. 40.
40. Ibid., p. 244.
41. Ibid., p. 98.
42. Ibid., p. 13.
43. Ibid., p. 114.
44. Ibid., p. 117.
45. Ibid., p. 193.
46. Ibid., p. 252.
47. Ibid., p. 302.
48. Ibid., p. 301.
49. Monteforte Toledo, *Donde acaban los caminos*, p. 86.
50. Ibid., p. 120.
51. Ibid., p. 111.
52. Ibid., p. 173.
53. Ibid., p. 189.
54. Ibid., p. 190.
55. Ibid., p. 199.

Chapter Six

1. See Moisés Gonzáles Navarro, "Instituciones indígenas en México actual," *Memorias del instituto nacional indigenista: Métodos y resultados de la polí-*

tica indigenista en México, vol. 6 (Mexico: Institutio Nacional Indigenista, 1954), p. 162.

2. During the Díaz regime, writes Jésus Silva Herzog, "there was a relation between decency and wealth, between decency and skin color: an articulated racial discrimination, a legacy of past centuries." Silva Herzog, *Breve historia de la revolución mexicana*, vol. 1, p. 40.

3. The tienda de raya was as old as the hacienda itself. It consisted of a general store owned and operated by the owner of the hacienda where the peons could find most of the items needed for their daily life. Often, the peon was paid with goods dispensed by the tienda de raya, and money was not used in his socioeconomic relations with the landlord.

4. Frank R. Brandenburg, "Causes of the Revolution," *Revolution in Mexico: Years of Upheaval 1910–1940*, ed. James W. Wilkie and Albert L. Michaels (New York: Alfred Knopf, 1969), p. 19.

5. For a detailed discussion of Indian rebellions in Mexico during its republican period see González Navarro, "Instituciones indígenas," pp. 143–194.

6. See González Navarro, "Instituciones indígenas."

7. To what extent these military policies fostered the development of peasant militancy is not clear. Some leaders of the peasant movement seem to have been directly affected by that type of experience. Besides Zapata, for example, his cousin and revolutionary leader Amador Salazar was also forced to spend some time in the army as a recruit; so did Lorenzo Vásquez, another leader of the armed phase of the revolution. To what extent Andean indigenista writers were aware of these experiences of the Mexican peasant leaders and to what extent such awareness fostered their hope of Indian militancy in the way I have described, I do not know.

8. Fernando Horcásitas, *De Porfirio Díaz a Zapata: Memorias nahuátl de Milpa Alta*.

9. Part of the Plan de San Luís Potosí reads: "It being just to restore to their rightful owners lands of which they have been dispossessed in such an arbitrary way, it is hereby declared that all such dispositions and findings are subject to revision and it will be demanded of all those who acquired these lands in such an immoral manner, or of their heirs, that they restore [these lands] to their rightful owners, to whom they will also pay an indemnity for damages suffered." The text also promises "the protection of the indigenous races who, educated and dignified, could contribute powerfully to the strengthening of our nationality." See Silva Herzog, *Breve historia de la revolución*, pp. 138, 93.

10. Ibid., p. 125.

11. As Rodolfo Stavenhagen points out, the Mexican agrarian reform had from the very beginning two opposed currents of thought about the social functions of land ownership. One of these tendencies favored communal land tenure, of which the ejido was a central fixture; the other tendency favored private property. I shall only touch on the first tendency since it affected the Indians more directly. See Stavenhagen, "Social Aspects of Agrarian Structure in Mexico," *Agrarian Problems and Peasant Movements in Latin America*, ed. Rodolfo Stavenhagen.

12. During this period, M. Gutiérrez Nájera founded *Revista azul* (*Blue Maga-*

zine) and Amado Nervo, with his fellow modernista Jesús Valenzuela, published *Revista moderna* (*Modern Magazine*). Not an inkling of the general discontent that was to erupt in the revolution of 1910 can be found in these publications so attentive to exploring art for art's sake.

13. Not all writers were intimidated all of the time by· Díaz's police. Heriberto Frías was a courageous writer during this period and his ¡*Temochic!* *Episodios de la campaña de Chihuahua, 1892* (Rio Grande City, Texas: Impr. de J. T. Recio, 1894) is an example of intellectual honesty. ¡*Temochic!*, mild in comparison to the militant indigenista novels, earned Frías the hatred of government officials, who arrested him on charges of disclosing government secrets. For a detailed treatment of literary realism under Díaz, see Joaquina Navarro, *La novela realista mexicana*.

14. See Gonzalo Aguirre Beltran and Ricardo Pozas A., "Instituciones indígenas en el México actual," *Memorias del instituto nacional indigenista: Métodos y resultados de la política indigenista en México*, vol. 6 (Mexico: Instituto Nacional Indigenista, 1954).

15. Ibid.

16. Ibid., 207.

17. In Mexico as in the Andes, there were societies concerned with the Indian problem as early as 1910. But the goals of these societies, again as in the Andes, were avowedly apolitical; they were theoretical and moral. The direction of these organizations was set in 1911 when the Junta Permanente of the Sociedad Indianista Mexicana (founded in 1910) stated that the aims of the society were "purely scientific, social and not political." See Juan Comas, "Algunos datos para la historia del indianismo en México," *Ensayos sobre indigenismo*, p. 79.

18. For an analysis of the role of the communist party in the Mexican Revolution and its effects on literary production, see Adalbert Dessau, *La novela de la revolución mexicana*.

19. Miguel Ángel Menéndez, *Nayar*, p. 93.

20. Miguel Lira, *Donde crecen los tepozanes*, p. 235.

Chapter Seven

1. Gregorio López y Fuentes, *Los peregrinos inmóviles*, pp. 129–130.

2. Gregorio López y Fuentes, *El indio*, p. 55.

3. To be sure, the view of the past as a source of revolutionary potential was further discounted by archeological and historic knowledge of Aztecan society, which showed that no utopia had existed in Mexico. But scientific research of this nature did not become widely known and accepted by Mexican writers until at least the 1940s. However, novels written before this period also do not use the past as it was used in the Andes. Besides, knowledge of the Incan past, which showed that it, too, had not been utopian, had not deterred Andean writers from presenting the Incan period as a golden age.

4. Eduardo Luquín, *El indio*, p. 21.

5. Rosario Castellanos, *Oficio de tinieblas*, p. 9.

6. Ibid., p. 9.
7. López y Fuentes, *Los peregrinos inmóviles*, p 180.
8. Mauricio Magdaleno, *El resplandor*, p. 18.
9. Miguel Ángel Menéndez, *Nayar*, p. 194.
10. Magdaleno, *El resplandor*, p. 144.
11. See Ricardo Pozas, *Juan the Chamula: An Ethnological Recreation of the Life of a Mexican Indian*, trans. L. Kemp (Berkeley: University of California Press, 1962).
12. Magdaleno, *El resplandor*, p. 113.
13. Pozas, *Juan the Chamula*, p. 11.
14. Ramón Rubín, *El canto de la grilla*, p. 194.
15. Ramón Rubín, *La bruma lo vuelve azul*, p. 13.
16. López y Fuentes, *Los peregrinos inmóviles*, p. 59.
17. E. Abreu Gómez, *Canek*, pp. 47, 49.
18. Ibid., p. 48.
19. Castellanos, *Oficio de tinieblas*, p. 324.
20. Ramón Rubín, *El callado dolor de los tzotziles* (Mexico: Libro Mex, 1957).
21. Ibid., p. 169.
22. Rubín, *La bruma lo vuelve azul*, p. 21.
23. Menéndez, *Nayar*, p. 124.
24. Ibid., p. 124.
25. Mariano Azuela, *Los de abajo: Novela de la revolución mexicana*, p. 66.
26. Menéndez, *Nayar*, p. 193.
27. Ibid., p. 164.
28. Ibid., p. 164.
29. Ibid., p. 160.
30. López y Fuentes, *El indio*, p. 170.
31. Magdaleno, *El resplandor*, p. 214.
32. López y Fuentes, *El indio*, p. 83.
33. Ibid., p. 83.
34. Castellanos, *Oficio de tinieblas*, p. 363.
35. Gómez, *Canek*, p. 46.

Chapter Eight

1. Herbert K. Klein, "Prelude to Revolution," *Beyond the Revolution: Bolivia Since 1952*, ed. James M. Malloy and Richard S. Thorn (Pittsburgh: University of Pittsburgh Press, 1971), p. 41.
2. Juan Molina Salvador, *Las migraciones internas en el Ecuador* (Quito: Editorial Universitaria, 1965), p. 86.
3. Julio Cotler, "La mecánica de la dominación interna y el cambio social en el Perú," *Perú actual: Sociedad y polítia* (Mexico: Instituto de Investigaciones Sociales, Universidad de Mexico, 1970).
4. *Población de la Ciudad de Guatemala, Resultado de tabulación y muestreo* (Guatemala: Ministerio de Economía, Dirección General de Estadística, 1964).
5. In a footnote to *El pueblo sin Dios* (Madrid: Historia Nueva, 1928) César

Falcón writes: "I saw it all. One of my words, after the chains were fastened, would have been of no use to you, unfortunate one. You yourself, at that moment, would not have been able to hear it; and now, for being illiterate, neither will you be able to read it."

6. The best treatment of José María Arguedas's overall work is Cornejo Polar, *Los universos narrativos de José María Arguedas* (Buenos Aires: Editorial Losada, 1973). Although I disagree with some of the particulars, I believe Cornejo's work deals with Arguedas's literature in a thorough and sympathetic manner.
7. José María Arguedas, *El zorro de arriba y el zorro de abajo*, p. 271.
8. Ibid., p. 102.
9. Ibid., p. 46.
10. Ibid., p. 67–68.
11. Ibid., p. 111.
12. Ibid., p. 34.
13. Ibid.
14. Ibid., p. 96.
15. Ibid., p. 211.
16. Ibid., p. 213.
17. Ibid., p. 13.
18. Ibid., p. 270.
19. Miguel Ángel Asturias, *Hombres de maíz*, p. 9.
20. Ibid., p. 12.
21. Ibid., p. 12.
22. Ibid., p. 10.
23. Ibid., p. 12.
24. Ibid., p. 11.
25. Ibid., p. 12.
26. Ibid., p. 13.
27. Ibid., p. 180.
28. Ibid., p. 175.
29. Miguel Ángel Asturias, *Mulata de tal*, p. 188.
30. Ibid., p. 96.
31. Ibid., p. 144.
32. Ibid., p. 172.
33. Ibid., p. 174.
34. Ibid., p. 214.

Chapter Nine

1. See Óscar Collazos, Julio Cortázar, Mario Vargas Llosa, *Literatura en la revolución y revolución en la literatura* (Mexico: Siglo Veintiuno, 1970).
2. See María Esther Vazquez, *Borges: Imágines, memórias, diálogos* (Caracas: Monte Avila Editores, 1977); and Richard Burgin, *Conversaciones con Jorge Luis Borges* (Madrid: Taurus, 1974).
3. Hans-Georg Gadamer, *Truth and Method*.
4. See Gadamer, *Truth and Method*; Lucien Goldmann, *Pour une sociologie*

du roman (Paris: Gallimard, 1965); Jameson, *Marxism and Form*; and Lukacs, *The Theory of the Novel*.

5. For an interesting, though partial, account of the boom in Spanish American letters, especially in the sixties, see José Donoso, *Historia personal del "boom"* (Barcelona: Editorial Anagrama, 1972).

6. This was the reason José María Arguedas himself gave for not having read many of Cortázar's works, for example (see *El zorro de arriba y el zorro de abajo*). How many readers have actually finished Fuentes's *Terra nostra* or have bothered to read the French newspaper clippings included in Cortázar's *Libro de Manuel*? When novels in Spanish America are written with the ideal bilingual reader in mind, the intended audience is not the general population.

7. This view of life and man often leads to fictional worlds devoid of humor or even irony. Gabriel García Márquez's *Cien años de soledad* is a case in point. The reader finds a depressing world inhabited by selfish characters, suffused with whimsical violence. In Vargas Llosa's *Pantaleón y las visitadoras* (1973), too, the author does not succeed in provoking an ironic smile; ultimately, the reader is unable to escape the oppressive atmosphere of the work. See Luis Alberto Sánchez, *La literatura peruana* (Lima: P. L. Villanueva, 1975), pp. 1605–1606.

   To the extent that these and similar works end in pessimism, and are critical of all that is wrong in Spanish America while offering no positive counsel, they are not just to Spanish Americans. Despite all clichés to the contrary, it cannot be denied that there are men and women in Spanish America who are working toward solving their problems—and making progress. By their one-sided portrayal of Spanish America, these writers only fuel the traditional image of Spanish America abroad—an exotic land condemned to eternal hardship, violence, and impotence. These writers have closed the circle too soon, not all Spanish Americans are like the characters of Macondo, Comala, Leoncio Prado or resemble Artemio Cruz. All sincere and idealistic people are not crushed by evil forces; all people in Spanish America are not egotists, blinded by pride, incapable of loving and being loved. This is only part of Spanish America.

8. Carlos Fuentes, in an interview by Christopher Davis, *The Pennsylvania Gazette* 76, no. 7 (May 1978).

Selected
Bibliography

Abellán, José Luis. *La idea de América: Orígen y evolución*. Madrid: Ediciones Istmo, 1972.

Adams, Richard Newbold. *Crucifixion by Power: Essays on Guatemalan National Social Structure 1944–1966*. Austin and London: University of Texas Press, 1970.

Alba, Víctor. *Nationalists Without Nations: The Oligarchy versus the People in Latin America*. New York: Praeger, 1968.

Alberdi, Juan Bautista. *Bases y puntos de partida para la organización de la confederación argentina*. Buenos Aires: Francisco Cruz Editorial, 1914.

Alegría, Ciro. *El mundo es ancho y ajeno*. Santiago: Ediciones Ercilla, 1941.

Antezama, Luis E. *El feudalismo de Melgarejo y la reforma agraria: Proceso de la propiedad territorial y la política de Boliva*. La Paz: 1970.

Arguedas, Alcides. *Raza de bronce*. Buenos Aires: Losada, 1972.

Arguedas, José María. *Los rios profundos*. Havana: Casa de las Américas, 1965.

———. *Todas las sangres*. Buenos Aires: Editorial Losada, 1964.

———. *Yawar fiesta*. Chile: Editorial Universitaria, 1968.

———. *El zorro de arriba y el zorro de abajo*. Buenos Aires: Editorial Losada, 1971.

Arias, Augusto. *Panorama de la literatura ecuatoriana*. Quito: Editorial de la Cultura Ecuatoriana, 1971.

Arias Campoamor, J. F. *Novelistas de México: Esquema de la historia de la novela mexicana*. Mexico: Editorial Cultura Hispánica, 1952.

Astiz, Carlos A. *Pressure Groups and Power Elites in Peruvian Politics*. Ithaca: Cornell University Press, 1969.

Asturias, Miguel Ángel. *Latinoamérica y otros ensayos*. Madrid: Publicaciones Guardiana, 1970.

———. *Hombres de maíz*. Buenos Aires: Editorial Losada, 1966.

———. *Mulata de tal*. Buenos Aires: Editorial Losada, 1963.

———. *El problema social del indio y otros textos*. Paris: Centre de Recherches de l'Institut d'Etudes Hispaniques, 1971.

Azuela, Mariano. *Los de abajo: Novela de la revolución mexicana*. Mexico: Fondo de Cultura Económica, 1966.

Barrera Vásquez, Alfredo, and Rendón, Silvia, trans. *El libro de los libros de Chilam Balam*. Mexico: Fondo de Cultura Económica, 1969.

Basadre, Jorge, *Literatura inca*. Paris: Biblioteca de Cultura Peruana, Desclee de Brouwer, 1938.

Becker, Carl L. *The Heavenly City of the Eighteenth-Century Philosophers*. New Haven: Yale University Press, 1978.

Bello, Andrés. *Gramática de la lengua castellana destinada al uso de los americanos*. Paris: Roger Y. F. Chernoviz Ed., 1918.

———. *Obras completas*. Vol. 8. Santiago, 1885.

———. *Obras completas*. Vol. 1. Caracas: Ministerio de Éducación, 1952.

Bilbao, Francisco. *El evangelio americano*. Buenos Aires: Editorial Americalee, 1943.

Bolívar, Simón. *Documentos*. Havana: Casa de las Américas, 1964.

———. *Simón Bolívar: Escritos políticos*. Madrid: Alianza Editorial, 1969.

Botelho Gosálvez, Raúl. *Altiplano*. Buenos Aires: Editorial Ayacucho, 1945.

Brushwood, John S. *Mexico in its Novel: A Nation's Search for Identity*. Austin: University of Texas Press, 1966.

Calder, Bruce Johnson. *Crecimiento y cambio de la iglésia católica Guatemalteca: 1944–1966*. Guatemala: Ministerio de Educación Pública, 1970.

Canelas, Amado O., *Mito y realidad de la reforma agraria*. La Paz: Editorial de los Amigos del Libro, 1966.

Carrilla, Emilio. *El romanticismo en la América hispánica*. Madrid: Editorial Gredos, 1967.

Caso, Antonio. *Sociología*. Mexico: Editorial Polis, 1939.

Castellanos, Rosario. *Balún-Canán*. Mexico: Fondo de Cultura Económica, 1968.

————. *Oficio de tinieblas*. Mexico: Editorial Joaquin Mortiz: 1962.

Cástro Arenas, Mario. *La novela peruana y la evolución social*. Lima: Ediciones Cultura y Libertad, 1964.

Cerruto, Óscar. *Aluvión de fuego*. Santiago: Ediciones Ercilla, 1935.

Cháves, Fernando. *Plata y bronce*. Quito: Editorial Casa de la Cultura Ecuatoriana, 1954.

Colby, Benjamin N., and Van den Berghe, Pierre L. *Ixil Country: A Plural Society in Highland Guatemala*. Berkeley: University of California Press, 1969.

Comas, Juan. *Ensayos sobre indigenismo*. Mexico: Instituto Indigenista Interamericano, 1953.

Cometta Manzoni, Aida. *El indio en la poesía de América española*. Buenos Aires: Joaquin Torres, 1939.

Cornejo Polar, Antonio. *Los universos narrativos de José María Arguedas*. Buenos Aires: Editorial Losada, 1974.

Cueva, Mario de la. *Major Trends in Mexican Philosophy*. Edited and translated by A. Robert Caponigri. Notre Dame, Ind.: University of Notre Dame Press, 1966.

Davis, Thomas M., Jr. *Indian Integration in Peru: A Half a Century of Experience 1900–1948*. Lincoln: University of Nebraska Press, 1974.

Dessau, Adalbert. *La novela de la revolución mexicana*. Translated by Juan J. Utrilla. Mexico: Fondo de Cultura Económica, 1972.

Dobyns, Henry F. *The Social Matrix of Peruvian Indigenous Communities*. Ithaca, N.Y.: Cornell University Press, 1964.

Echeverría, Esteban. *Dogma socialista*. La Plata: Universidad Nacional de la Plata, 1940.

Expressión del pensamiento contemporáneo. Buenos Aires: Editorial Sur, 1965.

Franco, Jean. *The Modern Culture of Latin America: Society and the Artist*. London: Pall Mall Press, 1967.

Fuentes, Carlos. *La muerte de Artemio Cruz*. Mexico: Fondo de Cultura Económica, 1970.

Gadamer, Hans-Georg. *Truth and Method*. Translation edited by Garrett Barden and John Cumming. New York: Seabury Press, 1975.

García Márquez, Gabriel. *Cien años de soledad*. Buenos Aires: Editorial Sudamericana, 1969.

Garibay, Ángel F. *Epica nahuátl*. Mexico: Universidad Nacional, 1945.

———. *Historia de la literatura nahuátl*. Mexico: Editorial Porrúa, 1953–1954.

Gómez, E. Abreu. *Canek*. Mexico: Ediciones Canek, 1940.

González Prada, Manuel. *Horas de lucha*. Paris: Biblioteca de Cultura Peruana, No. 9, 1938.

Graña, César. *Bohemian versus Bourgeois: French Society and French Men of Letters in the Nineteenth Century*. New York: Basic Books, 1964.

Grossman, Rudolf. *Historia y problemas de la literatura latinoamericana*. Madrid: Ediciones de la Revista de Occidente, 1972.

Gutiérrez, Gustavo. *A Theology of Liberation*. Edited and translated by Sister Caridad Inda and John Eagleson. New York: Orbis Books, 1973.

Guzmán, Augusto. *Historia de Bolivia*. La Paz: Editorial Los Amigos del Libro, 1973.

Henriques Ureña, Pedro. *Las corrientes literarias en la América hispánica*. Mexico: Fondo de Cultura Económica, 1949.

Holleran, Mary P. *Church and State in Guatemala*. New York: Columbia University Press, 1949.

Horcásitas, Fernando. *De Porifirio Díaz a Zapata: Memorias nahuátl de Milpa Alta*. Mexico: Instituto de Investigaciones Historicas, 1968.

Hubard de Bravo, Eliane. *Roman et société en Equateur: 1939–1949*. Cuernavaca: Centro Intercultural de Documentación, 1970.

Humbolt, Alexander von. *Ensayo político sobre la nueva España*. Santiago: Editorial Ercilla, 1942.

Humphreys, R. A., and Lynch, John. *The Origins of the Latin American Revolutions: 1808–1826*. New York: Alfred A. Knopf, 1966.

Icaza, Jorge. *En las calles*. Buenos Aires: Losada, 1954.

———. *Hijos del viento (Huairapamushcas)*. Barcelona: Plaza y Janes, 1973.

———. *Huasipungo*. Buenos Aires: Editorial Losada, 1961.

Ingenieros, José. *Obras completas*. Edited by Anibal Ponce. Buenos Aires: Ediciones L. J. Rosso, 1918.

Jameson, Fredric. *Marxism and Form: Twentieth-Century Dialectical Theories of Literature*. Princeton, N.J.: Princeton University Press, 1971.

Jaramillo Alvarado, Pio. *El indio ecuatoriano*. Quito: Casa de la Cultura Ecuatoriana, 1954.

Jones, Willis Knapp. *Behind Spanish American Footlights*. Austin: University of Texas Press, 1966.

Keen, Benjamin, and Wasserman, Mark. *A Short History of Latin America*. Palo Alto, Cal.: Houghton Mifflin, 1980.

Kelsey, Vera, and Osborne, Lilly de Tongh. *Four Keys to Guatemala*. New York: Funk and Wagnalls, 1939.

Lara, Jesús. *La poesía quéchua: Ensayo y antología*. Cochabamba, Bolivia: Universidad Mayor de San Simón, 1974.

———. *Yawarninchij*. Buenos Aires: Editorial Platina, 1959.

Lastarria, José Victorino. *La América*. 2d ed. Buenos Aires: Gante, 1867.

Leytón, Roberto. *Los eternos vagabundos*. Bolivia: Editorial Potosí, 1939.

Leon Hill, Eladia. *Miguel Ángel Asturias: Lo ancestral en su obra literaria*. New York: Eliséo Torres and Sons, 1972.

León Mera, Juan. *Cumandá, o un drama entre salvajes*. Quito: Talleres Gráficos Nacionales, 195–.

León-Portilla, Miguel. *Aztec Thought and Culture: A Study of the Ancient Nahuatl Mind*. Translated by Jack Emory Davis. Norman: University of Oklahoma Press, 1963.

———, ed. *The Broken Spears: The Aztec Account of the Conquest of Mexico*. Translated by Lysander Kemp. Boston: Beacon Press, 1962.

Lipschütz, Alejandro. *El indoamericanismo y el problema racial en las Américas*. Santiago: Editorial Andrés Bello, 1967.

Lira, Miguel. *Donde crecen los tepozanes*. Mexico: E.D.I.A., 1947.

López y Fuentes, Gregorio. *Los peregrinos inmóviles*. Mexico: Ediciones Botas, 1944.

———. *El indio*. Mexico: Editorial Navaro, 1956.

Lorand de Olazagasti, Adelaide. *El indio en la narrativa guatemalteca*. San Juan, P.R.: Editorial Universitaria, 1968.

Luquín, Eduardo. *El indio*. Mexico: Herrero Hermanos, 1923.

Magdaleno, Mauricio. *El resplandor*. Mexico: Ediciones Botas, 1937.

Malloy, James, M., and Thorn, Richard S., eds. *Beyond the Revolution: Bolivia Since 1952*. Pittsburgh: University of Pittsburgh Press, 1965.

Mariátegui, José Carlos. *Seven Interpretive Essays on Peruvian Reality*. Translated by Marjory Urquidi. Austin: University of Texas Press, 1971.

Matto de Turner, Clorinda. *Aves sin nido*. Buenos Aires: Solar-Hachette, 1968.

Meléndes, Concha. *La novela indianista en Hispanoamérica: 1832–1889*. Río Piedras: Ediciones de la Universidad de Puerto Rico, 1961.

Melville, Thomas, and Melville, Marjorie. *Guatemala: The Politics of Land Ownership*. New York: Free Press, 1971.

Memorias del instituto nacional indigenista: Métodos y resultados de la política indigenista en México. Mexico: Instituto Nacional Indigenista, 1954.

Menéndez, Miguel Ángel. *Nayar*. Mexico: La Prensa, 1965.

Meyer, Jean A. *La christiade: l'Eglise, l'état, et le peuple dans la révolution mexicaine*. Paris: Payot, 1975.

Monteforte Toledo, Mario. *Donde acaban los caminos*. Santiago: Empresa Editorial Zig-Zag, 1966.

———. *Entre la piedra y la cruz*. Guatemala: Editorial "El Libro de Guatemala," 1948.

Mörner, Magnus. *Race Mixture in the History of Latin America*. Boston: Little, Brown and Company, 1967.

Navarro, Joaquina. *La novela realista mexicana*. Mexico: Compañía General de Ediciones, 1955.

Paz, Octavio. *El arco y la lira*. Mexico: Fondo de Cultura Económica, 1956.

———. *El laberinto de la soledad*. Mexico: Fondo de Cultura Económica, 1963.

———. *Puertas al campo*. Mexico: Universidad Nacional Autónoma de Mexico, 1966.

Picón-Salas, Mariano. *A Cultural History of Spanish America: from Conquest to Independence*. Translated by Irving A. Leonard. Berkeley: University of California Press, 1966.

Ramos, Jorge Abelardo. *Historia de la nación latinoamericana*. Vols. 1 and 2. Buenos Aires: A. Peña Lillo, 1958.

Recinos, Adrian, trans. *Anales de los cakchiqueles*. Mexico: Fondo de Cultura Económica, 1950.

Reyes, Alfonso. *Obras completas*. Vol. 11. Mexico: Fondo de Cultura Económica, 1959.

Ripoll, Carlos, ed. *Conciencia intelectual de América*. New York: Eliséo Torres and Sons, 1970.

Rivadeneyra, Jorge. *Ya esta amaneciendo*. Quito: Ediciones Minerva, 1957.

Rocker, Rudolf. *Nationalism and Culture*. Translated by Roy E. Chase. Los Angeles: Procker Publications Committees, 1937.

Rojas, Ángel. *La novela ecuatoriana*. Mexico: Fondo de Cultura Económica, 1948.

Rojas, Ricardo. *Obras de Ricardo Rojas*. Buenos Aires: Librería, La Facultad, n.d.

Romero, José L. *El pensamiento político de la derecha latinoamericana*. Buenos Aires: Editorial Paidos, 1970.

Rosenthal, Mario. *The Story of an Emergent Latin American Democracy*. New York: Twayne Publishers, 1962.

Rubín, Ramón. *La bruma lo vuelve azul*. Mexico: Fondo de Cultura Económica, 1954.

————. *El callado dolor de los tszotziles*. Mexico: Libro Mex, 1957.

————. *El canto de la grilla*. Mexico: Ediciones Altiplano, 1952.

Rulfo, Juan. *Pedro Páramo*. Translated by Lysander Kemp. New York: Grove Press, 1959.

Rutherford, John. *Mexican Society During the Revolution: A Literary Approach*. Oxford: Clarendon Press, 1971.

Saenz, Moisés. *Sobre el indio ecuatoriano y su incorporación al medio nacional*. Mexico: Publicaciones de la Secretaría de Educación Pública, 1933.

Salas, Alberto M. *Crónica florida del mestizaje de las indias: Siglo XVI*. Buenos Aires: Editorial Losada, 1960.

Salz, Beate R. *The Human Element in Industrialization: A Hypothetical Case Study of Ecuadorian Indians*. Chicago: The University of Chicago Research Center in Economic Development and Cultural Change, Vol. 1, no. 1, part 2, 1955.

Sánchez-Barra, Mario. *Dialectica contemporánea de Hispanoamérica*. Madrid: Ediciones Porrua Turanzas, 1973.

Siles Salinas, Jorge. *La literatura boliviana de la guerra del Chaco*. La Paz: Ediciones de la Universidad Católica Boliviana, 1969.

Silva Herzog, Jesús. *Breve historia de la revolución mexicana*. Vols. 1 and 2. Mexico: Fondo de Cultura Económica, 1960.

Skinner-Klee, Jorge. *Recopilación de la legislación indigenista de Guatemala.* Mexico: Ediciones Especiales del Instituto Indigenista Inter-Americano, 1954.

Solórzano F., Valentín. *Evolución económica de Guatemala.* Guatemala: Ministerio de Educación Pública, 1963.

Stavenhagen, Rodolfo, ed. *Agrarian Problems and Peasant Movements in Latin America.* New York: Anchor Books, 1970.

Tamayo Vargas, Augusto. *Literatura en Hispano América.* Vol. 1. Lima: Ediciones Peisa, 1973.

Vallejo, César. *Poemas Humanos: Human Poems.* Bilingual edition translated by Clayton Eshleman. New York: Grove Press, 1968.

―――. *El tungsteno.* Lima: Ediciones Peisa, 1973.

Vargas Llosa, Mario. *La cuidad y los perros.* Buenos Aires: Editorial Sudamericana, 1969.

Vargas Llosa, and García Márquez, Gabriel. *Diálogo: La novela en América Latina.* Buenos Aires: Ediciones Latinoamericanas, 1972.

Vasconcelos, José. *Indología.* Barcelona: Agencia Mundial de Librería, 19–.

―――. *La raza cósmica.* Barcelona: Agencia Mundial de Librería, 192–.

Vega, Garcilaso de la. *Los comentarios reales de los Incas.* Madrid: Biblioteca de Autores Españoles, Ediciones Atlas, 1957.

Wachtel, Nathan. *The Vision of the Vanquished: The Spanish Conquest of Peru Through Indian Eyes 1530–1570.* Translated by Ben and Sian Reynolds. New York: Harper and Row, 1977.

Wagley, Charles. *Santiago Chimaltenango: Estudio antropológico-social de una comunidad indígena de Huehuetenango.* Guatemala: Seminario de Integración Social Guatemalteca, 1957.

Whetten, Nathan L. *Guatemala: The Land and the People.* New Haven, Ct.: Yale University Press, 1961.

Wilkie, James W., and Michaels, Albert L. *Revolution in Mexico: Years of Upheaval 1910–1940.* New York: Alfred Knopf, 1969.

Williams, Raymond. *Marxism and Literature.* London: Oxford University Press, 1977.

Wolf, Eric. *Sons of the Shaking Earth.* Chicago: University of Chicago Press, 1962.

Yépez Miranda, Alfredo. *Los Andes vengadores*. Cuzco: H. G. Rozas Sucesores, 1934.

Zea, Leopoldo. *La esencia de lo americano*. Buenos Aires: Editorial Pleamar, 1971.

————. *The Latin American Mind*. Translated by James H. Abbott and Lowell Dunham. Norman: University of Oklahoma Press, 1963.

Zeraffa, Michel. *Roman et société*. Paris: Presses Universitaires de France, 1971.

Indian
Novels
Cited

Bolivia

Arguedas, Alcides
  Raza de bronce (Race of Bronze), 1919
Botelho Gosálvez Raúl
  Altiplano (Highlands), 1945
Cerruto, Óscar
  Aluvión de fuego (Flood of Fire), 1935
Lara, Jesús
  Yawarninchij, 1959
Leytón, Roberto
  Los eternos vagabundos (The Eternal Vagabonds), 1939

Ecuador

Cháves, Fernando
  Plata y bronce (Silver and Bronze), 1927
Icaza, Jorge
  Huasipungo, 1934
  En las calles (In the Streets), 1935
  Hijos del viento (Sons of the Wind), 1948
León Mera, Juan
  Cumandá, o un drama entre salvajes (Cumandá, or a Drama among Savages), 1879

Rivadeneyra, Jorge
  Ya esta amaneciendo (Dawn is Breaking), 1957

Guatemala

Asturias, Miguel Ángel
  Hombres de maíz (Men of Maize), 1949
  Mulata de tal (Mulatta), 1963
Monteforte Toledo, Mario
  Entre la piedra y la cruz (Between the Stone and the Cross), 1948
  Donde acaban los caminos (Where the Roads End), 1953

Mexico

Azuela, Mariano
  Los de abajo (The Underdogs), 1915
Barriga Rivas, Rogelio
  Guelaguetza, 1947
  La mayordomía (The Stewardship), 1952
Castaño, Rosa de
  Fruto de sangre (Fruit of Blood), 1958
Castellanos, Rosario
  Balún-canán, 1957
  Oficio de tinieblas (Craft of Darkness), 1962
Cástro, Carlos Antonio
  Los hombres verdaderos (True Men), 1959
Chávez Camacho, Armando
  Cájeme, novela de indios (Cajeme, An Indian Novel), 1948
Gómez, E. Abreu
  Canek, 1940
  Naufragio de indios (Indian Calamity), 1951
Lira, Miguel
  Donde crecen los tepozanes (Where the Tepozanes Grow), 1947
López y Fuentes, Gregorio
  El indio (The Indian), 1935
  Los peregrinos inmóviles (The Immobile Pilgrims), 1944

Luquín, Eduardo
  El indio (The Indian), 1923
Magdaleno, Mauricio
  El resplandor (The Glittering), 1937
Menéndez, Miguel Ángel
  Nayar, 1941
Rubín, Ramón
  El callado dolor de los tszotziles (The Silent Pain of the Tsot-
  zils), 1949
  El canto de la grilla (The Song of the Cricket), 1952
  La bruma lo vuelve azul (The Mist Turns it Blue), 1954

Peru

Alegría, Ciro
  El mundo es ancho y ajeno (Broad and Alien is the World), 1941
Arguedas, José María.
  Yawar fiesta (Feast of Blood), 1941
  Los rios profundos (Deep Rivers), 1958
  Todas las sangres (All Bloods), 1964
  El zorro de arriba y el zorro de abajo (The Fox from the
  Highlands and the Fox from the Coast), 1970
Del Mar, Serafín
  La tierra es el hombre (Man is the Earth), 1943
Falcón, César
  El pueblo sin Dios (The Town without God), 1928
Matto de Turner, Clorinda
  Aves sin nido (Birds without Nest), 1889
Vallejo, César
  El tungsteno (Tungsten), 1931
Yépez Miranda, Alfredo
  Los Andes vengadores (The Avenging Andes), 1934

Index

Guevara, Ché, 7–8, 19
Gutiérrez, Juan María, 291n35

Haya de la Torre, Víctor Raúl, 7, 12, 35, 93–96
hidalgos, 2, 8, 24, 181, 287n3
Hidalgo y Costilla, Miguel, 179
Humboldt, Alexander von, 289n18

Icaza, Jorge, 73, 108–109, 118–120, 126–129, 131–132, 142–143, 230
Incas, 2, 10, 42–45, 47, 76
indianismo, 83–87
Indians: and Church, 158–159; communities of, 79–81; definition of, 34–37; and labor process, 76–79, 155–157, 182–184; land tenure of, 44–45, 152–154, 178–180; language of, 14–15; migration of, 206–207, 228–230; military experience of, 157–158, 185–186; and politics, 159–160; rebellions of, 81–82, 157–158, 184–185, 233, 301n17
indigenismo, 30; and didacticism, 243–244; and the Dream, 238, 241
Ingenieros, José, 13–14

Juárez, Benito, 179

Kant, Immanuel, 272

landlord, in indigenista novel, 127–130, 166–167, 204–205
language: Indian (see Indians); Spanish, 14–16
Lara, Jesús, 125, 232
Las Casas, Fray Bartolomé de, 57–58, 104
Lastárria, José Victorino, 289n18
law, in indigenista novel, 120–122, 205
leadership, in indigenista novel, 144–149, 222–223
León Mera, Juan, 60–65, 205
Leytón, Roberto, 123

liberalism, in indigenista novel, 137–140. See also andinismo and indianismo
literature: and baroque style, 272–282; colonial, 55–57; of Conquest, 54–55; and didacticism, 25–26, 273, 275–276, 281 (see also indigenismo); indigenista (see novel); pre-Columbian, 46–54; realist (see realism); romantic (see romanticism)
López y Fuentes, Gregorio, 218, 225
Lukacs, George, 27

Madero, Francisco, 187–188
magic, in indigenista novel, 111–113, 131, 146, 166. See also magicorealism
magicorealism, and Indian, 245–264
Malinche, Marina, 2, 10
Mariátegui, José Carlos, 12, 86, 96–98
Martí, José, 11–12, 19, 25, 95, 281
Marxism, 72–73, 90–93, 97–98
Matto de Turner, Clorinda, 66–71, 86, 137–138, 140, 175
Maya, 41–42, 46–47
mestizo, as basis of unity, 10–14
Mexican Revolution, in indigenista novel, 211, 217–219. See revolution
middle class, rise of, 266–267
migration, in indigenista novel, 131–134, 168. See Indians
military, in indigenista novel, 134–137, 167, 170–171
modernism, 271, 276–278
modernismo, 192, 304n12
Montalvo, Juan, 62
Monteforte Toledo, Mario, 164–175, 212, 230, 259
Morelos, José María, 179
mythical past, in indigenista novel, 104–114, 164–166, 200–201

New Man, 6, 11–18, 94, 150, 245, 254, 262–264, 275, 282
Nezahualcoyotl, 49–50